CLASSIC HOLLYWOOD

CLASSIC HOLLYWOOD

Lifestyles and Film Styles of American Cinema, 1930–1960

VERONICA PRAVADELLI

Translated by
MICHAEL THEODORE MEADOWS

UNIVERSITY OF ILLINOIS PRESS
Urbana, Chicago, and Springfield

Originally published as *La grande Hollywood. Stili di vita e di regia nel cinema classico americano* © 2007 by Marsilio Editori s.p.a. in Venezia. Revised and updated.

Manufactured in the United States of America
1 2 3 4 5 C P 5 4 3 2 1
∞ This book is printed on acid-free paper.

Library of Congress Cataloging-in-Publication Data
Pravadelli, Veronica
[Grande Hollywood. English]
Classic Hollywood: lifestyles and film styles of American cinema, 1930–1960 / Veronica Pravadelli ; translated by Michael Theodore Meadows.
pages cm
Includes bibliographical references and index.
ISBN 978-0-252-03877-8 (cloth : alk. paper)
ISBN 978-0-252-08034-0 (pbk. : alk. paper)
ISBN 978-0-252-09673-0 (ebook)
1. Motion pictures—United States—History—20th century.
2. Motion pictures—Production and direction—United States—History—20th century.
3. Motion pictures—California—Los Angeles—History—20th century.
I. Meadows, Michael Theodore. II. Title.
PN1993.5.U6P6713 2014
791.430973—dc23 2014016334

CONTENTS

ACKNOWLEDGMENTS

This book is a revised and updated version of the original Italian edition. As such it has taken shape slowly through a long process of research and writing spanning over ten years. I am grateful to the many individuals and institutions whose generous support has made this project possible.

First, I would like to thank Jim Naremore who has been an invaluable source of inspiration, as a teacher and a scholar, since my graduate work at Indiana University and who has followed this project up to the end. When Jim responded with a super-positive comment on the noir chapter I knew I was on the right track. At Indiana University I would also like to thank Barb Klinger. After taking my first film class, Barb's classical studio system course, I decided to major in film against my original intentions. If I am in film studies today, it is entirely thanks to Jim Naremore and Barb Klinger's exciting film courses. Before then, at the University of Verona I learned from Franco Moretti invaluable research methods as well as the passion for intellectual work. I will always owe him for this.

Over the years I have spent part of my summers doing research in different libraries. I am indebted to the libraries at Indiana University, Wesleyan University, and most particularly the Bobst at New York University. Thanks to Katrina Boyd for hosting me in Bloomington and for watching Hollywood movies together. At NYU, I want to thank Richard Allen, Antonia Lant, David Forgacs, and Ruth Ben-Ghiat for the academic hospitality they have given me many times. Thanks to Kathy Zuckerman for letting me stay with her in New York any time I needed.

Thanks to Mary Ann Doane for inviting me to teach a Hollywood class at Brown University, which has given me the opportunity to test many of my ideas. I am also grateful to Cynthia Lucia; her invitation to write a piece on cinema and the modern woman has allowed me to revise in important ways the first and second chapters.

For suggestions, comments, and friendly support I would like to thank Raymond Bellour, Thomas Elsaesser, E. Ann Kaplan, Neepa Majumdar, Rosanna Maule, Enrico Menduni, Laura Mulvey, and Vito Zagarrio. Francesco Casetti has followed my work and encouraged me at all stages since I have been back in Italy. I am grateful to Francesco for his long-term support and for his important suggestions on the introductory chapter. I also wish to thank my friends at the University of Turin, Giulia Carluccio and Giaime Alonge, for inviting me to contribute to their numerous projects on Hollywood cinema. Finally, I thank Giorgio De Vincenti who, as Department Director has supported my work throughout these years at Roma Tre.

My thanks also go to my translator Mike Meadows for doing such a good job! I am grateful to Enrico Carocci for his help with the frames. Last, at Illinois Press I want to thank my editor Danny Nasset for all his work in getting the project in production.

Finally, as always, I owe thanks to Paolo Bertetto for his patient hours of reading and rereading and for giving invaluable suggestions on the book's structure, but most for his love and companionship all these years. The book is dedicated to Paolo and to our little son Giacomo who after a long wait has unexpectedly enlightened our lives.

CLASSIC HOLLYWOOD

INTRODUCTION

Classical Hollywood Cinema and Film Studies

INTRODUCTORY REMARKS ON METHOD

Classic Hollywood analyzes American cinema from 1930 to 1960 in terms of the convergence between representations of lifestyles on the one hand and film styles and narrative modes on the other. It argues that within the so-called classical period there are distinct cultural moments or social phases, each marked by a convergence with specific formal elements. As such, one of my general aims is to complicate the expression "classical Hollywood cinema" by showing that American film went through such formidable changes that no single descriptive phrase has sufficient interpretative strength.

The expression *classical Hollywood cinema* refers to a seemingly well-defined, perhaps even crystalline, object of study. Yet a close analysis of its most important characteristics only complicates matters. For beneath classical Hollywood cinema's supposed transparency lurk inconsistencies and antithetical traits, such that the term itself acts as a catchall for defining an otherwise extremely diverse body of film.

As with every categorization, the term classical Hollywood cinema is not an object that can be definitively identified or defined but is more accurately understood as a "discursive formation."[1] Its boundaries—i.e., which films do we consider classical?—obviously depend on the defining qualities chosen and their degree of specificity. Although it is not my primary focus, the question of a "classical corpus" is relevant to this study and will be discussed briefly at the end of this introduction. My project aims, first of all, to reveal the *heterogeneity* of the *classical* form. This heterogeneity serves as foundation for one of my central arguments, that classical cinema properly defined exists only in the second half of the 1930s. This thesis sits in contrast with the two most influential theories on classical Hollywood cinema of recent decades: Raymond Bellour's *The Analysis of Film* (1979) and David Bordwell, Janet Staiger and Kristin Thompson's (hereafter B/S/T) *The Classical Hollywood Cinema* (1985). Notwithstanding their enormous differences, which ultimately make their arguments antithetical, Bellour and B/S/T each locate the classical period between the late 1910s and 1960.[2] By contrast, I argue that it is more accurate and productive to break this period down into phases so that differences and changes might emerge from more traditional notions of continuity. Of course, I do not think that Bellour's and B/S/T's theoretical apparatus and analytical tools are unhelpful. But I do think we need to historicize their respective notions of classical cinema, which means that we need to historicize classical Hollywood *tout court*. For example, as I show in chapter 2, it is clear that B/S/T's model, based on motivation and invisible style, aptly characterizes the cinema of 1934–1939, but it is much less successful at describing both the preceding or subsequent eras. Equally problematic is Bellour's thesis that Hollywood's regime of desire from Griffith to Hitchcock is founded on the Freudian-Lacanian model of sexual difference. This model insists that the formation of the couple signifies not only reconciliation of desire and the law but also the domination of male over female sexuality.[3] As I will show in chapters 1, 3, and 4, American cinema in transition from silent to sound, as well as in the postwar period, privileges the representation of lifestyles and identity models incompatible with those of the nuclear bourgeois family studied by Bellour.

Besides Bellour and B/S/T, my work on classical Hollywood is driven by some of the most influential methods of film study on American cinema since the early 1970s: from the theory of the "progressive text," to Feminist Film Theory, to the "cinema and modernity" approach.[4] But for my part, I will attempt to historicize such methods and conceptual frameworks. By focusing on the relation between a history of theory and the corpus of films considered, it will become evident that each approach accounts for only a specific phase or period of classical Hollywood cinema and thus cannot be applied wholesale to such a large group of films. Therefore, one of my concerns has been to *historicize theory*.

I undertake my theoretical queries on previous methods and approaches in the context of a broader investigation of Hollywood cinema as a *mode of representation*. While I believe that the formula of "classical cinema" may indeed define Hollywood's *mode of production* from the 1920s to the late 1950s, in this same period Hollywood's *mode of representation* varies enormously. For this reason, I believe the expression *classical cinema* is unfit to define American cinema for such an expansive time frame.

I define a mode of representation as the convergence of the cinematic imaginary and a film style or mise-en-scène.[5] In this study, I argue that such a convergence changes repeatedly from the early 1930s to the late 1950s and that their tandem development testifies to the weakness of any monolithic or universal notion of classical Hollywood cinema. As such, I place great emphasis on the cinematic imaginary since I believe that viewing processes depend on more than just questions of language or apparatus as many influential scholars have argued in the past. Indeed, the autonomy of filmic language and the cinematic apparatus have often been key elements in film theory, whether we think of the psychoanalytic and semiotic, or Marxist-Brechtian and cognitivist perspectives, as respectively in Baudry and Metz, MacCabe and Bordwell.[6] But this is not the whole story.

My emphasis on the imaginary can also be considered in relation to a counter-tradition in film theory best exemplified by Edgar Morin's *The Cinema, or the Imaginary Man* (1956). For Morin, there is a structural link between cinema and the imaginary. He argues that while visual representations and images are presented as "nonreality," they invade the subject's psyche and become central to his/her process of knowledge making. For Morin, cinema is an "imaginary spectacle" which we experience "in a state of double consciousness . . . you, us, me while intensely bewitched, possessed, eroticized, excited, terrified, loving, suffering, playing, hating—we do not stop knowing that . . . the illusion of reality is inseparable from the awareness that it is really an illusion, without, however, this awareness killing the feeling of reality."[7] Morin's idea that in cinema there is not only a "distinction," but also a "confusion" and "complementarity" between "real and imaginary," and that illusion has a productive and positive effect on spectators is highly suggestive. This idea sits in direct contrast to 1970s theories of the apparatus that interpreted cinema in relation to ideology. For Baudry, the illusory quality of the cinematic apparatus severely questioned the medium's potential for knowledge production. As is well known, theorists later transferred the negative underpinnings of Baudry's apparatus theory onto Hollywood cinema via the concept of suture, best epitomized by the "tutor-code" of shot/reverse shot. At some point it was no longer cinema *tout court*, but only Hollywood cinema that trapped the viewer into an unconscious viewing experience.[8] Like many, I am now critical of this position and consider Morin's notion of "double consciousness" to be more productive.

Starting from Morin's thesis, Paolo Bertetto has argued that cinema does not simply participate in the production of the social imaginary. It has also been able to historically "interpret, produce/reproduce the existing imaginary into multiple forms." In other words, cinema has "amplified the social circulation of the imaginary" through stories, figures, scenarios, and stereotypes. Further, the social and psychic impact of cinema depends on a mechanism of identification and "is related in particular to the relevance of anthropomorphic images and to the articulation of the imaginary into scenes structured in a narrative trajectory."[9] In my own work, I observe the dominant traits of the Hollywood imaginary both in relation to specific human types and figures and in relation to its narrative forms or genres. Thus, I have structured my project around genres because they are not only a foundational element of the imaginary, but because their individual relevance also varies widely over time.

To some extent, what I try to reveal in the Hollywood imaginary is similar to Stephen Greenblatt's notion of the "circulation of social energy" as described in his work on Shakespeare. For Greenblatt, cultural forms make sense for contemporary viewers because they encode the "social energy" of the time. Social energy "is manifested in the capacity of certain verbal, aural, and visual traces to produce, shape and organize collective physical and mental experiences. Hence it is associated with repeatable forms of pleasure and interest, with the capacity to arouse disquiet, pain, fear, the beating of the heart, pity, laughter, tension, relief, wonder."[10] As an aesthetic mode, social energy must be at least in part predictable so that it can be repeated (as with genres). Looking specifically at Renaissance drama, Greenblatt argues that each play "mediates between the mode of the theatre, understood in its historical specificity, and elements of the society out of which that theatre has been differentiated. Through its representational means, each play carries charges of social energy onto the stage; the stage in its turn revises that energy and returns it to the audience."[11] Thus, social energy is "power, charisma, sexual excitement, collective dreams, wonder, desire, anxiety, religious awe, free-floating intensities of experience [for] everything produced by the society can circulate."[12] Although working in a different period and domain, Greenblatt's notion of social energy is patently similar to Morin's definition of cinema and the cinematic imaginary. More precisely, Morin and Greenblatt hold a similar idea about the effect of theater and cinema on spectators. While they believe that the interaction between spectators and spectacle is socially productive, they also stress the power of representation to voice the collective desires, fears, and aspirations of spectators.

In this study, I have retooled these suggestions by considering the dominant traits of the cinematic imaginary and how they transform over the course of three decades. I have tried to understand how cinema has encoded the social energy of the moment through its own means of representation. What are the figures, the images, the narrative trajectories that Hollywood cinema repeatedly present onscreen? What are the social and collective desires and how are they articulated differently for women and men? Which forms of identity were historically possible during the Studio Era? In other words, I have privileged what I think is the primary element of the social and the cinematic imaginary, the representation of lifestyles and existential models. Starting from the assumption that cinema contributes enormously to the emergent "lifestylization in everyday life" in modernity, I have particularly stressed gender dynamics.[13] Undoubtedly, cinema was the period's most popular form of entertainment and thus simultaneously reflected and interpreted the contradictory cultural arenas of modernity, the New Deal, the war, and postwar. But at any particular moment, the stakes were dramatically different for women and men. So while my work on gender considers the previous scholarship in Film Studies at great length, overall I have produced a rather different narrative, which I hope answers Joan Scott's call for "historical specificity and variability."[14]

My investigation of the cinematic imaginary will be pursued in conjunction with an analysis of narrative technique and mise-en-scène as these also go through impressive changes from the early 1930s to the late 1950s. One need only compare the "rhetoric of attraction" from the first years of sound cinema to invisible style and the dominance of dialogue over image from the mid-1930s, or the visual flamboyance of noir style in the postwar period, to get a sense of what I mean. In this way, working on the convergence of cultural and formal paradigms, I am able to historicize Hollywood's modes of representation and better describe its participation in the production and dissemination of ideas, values, and desires in American culture.

HISTORICIZING THEORY, THEORIZING HISTORY

While the primary scope of this work is to historicize classical American cinema's modes of representation, such a project could not be executed without historicizing the different theoretical approaches dealing with Hollywood that have developed since the early 1970s.[15] While space does not allow for an exhaustive survey of the discourse on classical cinema, in the manner, for example, of Rick Altman's study on genre,[16] here my concern is to reconsider previous methods of study only to explain why I think it is necessary to *historicize theory*.

As we know, the convergence between "modernity studies" and cinema studies has had a tremendous impact on American Film Studies and inspired some of the best research of the last twenty years. One of this area of inquiry's strengths—since the pioneering work of Miriam Hansen and Tom Gunning—has been the fruitful imbrication of *history* and *theory*. From a methodological perspective, I have tried to pursue a similar effort rather than discard theory, as several film historians have done in recent years. Instead, I have tried to historicize theory or "theorize historically," as Mary Ann Doane has suggested in a different context.[17]

In addition to Bellour and B/S/T's systematic definitions of classical cinema, my project also draws heavily on Feminist Film Theory and Gender Studies. However, I have revisited the different phases of film feminism, from Laura Mulvey's seminal essay on "Visual Pleasure and Narrative Cinema" (1975), to the impressive contributions of feminist psychoanalytic film theory in the 1980s, to more recent developments in gender, queer, and masculinity studies in the 1990s and 2000s (J. Bergstrom, S. Cohan, E. Cowie, T. de Lauretis, M. A. Doane, R. Dyer, E. A. Kaplan, T. Modleski, C. Penley, P. White, L. Williams, etc.) to remodel them in a historical perspective. Of course, I do not think that *Feminist Film Theory* should be discarded in favor of *feminist film history* as many have done in recent years. In fact, I share Patrice Petro's discomfort (and anger) toward those who dismiss Feminist Film Theory "as a one-dimensional orthodoxy (by way of the shorthand 'seventies film theory' or 'gaze theory' or by referring to psychoanalysis, semiotics, and the ideological analyses that derived from these schools of thought)."[18] But my overall take on gender has engaged both theoretical assumptions and historical trends and frameworks. Thus, I have attempted to understand how Hollywood cinema has represented feminine and masculine identities over the course of three decades and how it has participated in the production of the American cultural imaginary. While I began working under the obvious assumption that "gender matters" immensely, I was not interested in detailing the contradictions of any single epoch. Instead, I wanted to capture the dominant facet(s) of the different eras in order to map out historical changes and transformations *within* the so-called classical period.

Of course, I am well aware that any historical phase is complex and that it envisions for any subject different lifestyles, modes of being, and subject positions (to use more psychoanalytic vocabulary). According to Raymond Williams, any "cultural system" is composed of "dominant," "emergent," and "residual" meanings and values, or "structures of feeling."[19] But such an approach is better suited to a synchronic study, rather than a diachronic inquiry like mine.

When I started to conceive of the broad contours of this project, the existing literature on classical Hollywood could roughly be divided into two sets. On the one hand, there were those scholars who had analyzed the whole period arguing for continuities and similarities in most domains, from production to plot structure, from stylistic procedures to viewing experience, and so forth. Along these lines, Robert Ray's cultural interpretation in *A Certain Tendency of the Hollywood Cinema* (1985) goes along with Bordwell's neoformalist approach and Bellour's structuralist-psychoanalytic paradigm. Ray interprets American cinema from 1930–1980 by selecting one specific tenet of American ideology, the dichotomy between "outlaw hero" values and those of the "official hero." He then looks at the way Hollywood has perpetuated and/or innovated such values. His concern is to place Hollywood cinema in relation to the American cultural past to capture Hollywood's contribution to it. While Ray is totally aware of narrative filmic devices—his analysis of *Casablanca* (M. Curtiz, 1942), *It's a Wonderful Life* (F. Capra, 1946), and other films remains essential to the field—the strength of his study lies in the way it shows how Hollywood has been able to interpret and renew certain founding elements of American ideology.[20]

On the other hand, critical work on Hollywood cinema had more often approached the topic by selecting a specific genre and period and making a statement, broadly speaking, about the peculiar relations between aesthetics and ideology. I am well aware scholars have produced a tremendous amount of very good work in this domain. Often focusing on a specific genre, many investigated especially 1940s and 1950s Hollywood cinema in relation to cultural, artistic, and social dynamics. Indeed, for four decades, film noir, the woman's film, and melodrama have been the locus of such innovative research, from the theory of the "progressive text" in the early 1970s to "cinema and modernity studies" during the last twenty years or so.[21]

My project, however, started from the desire to make a different hypothesis vis-à-vis these two major trends. Of course, such a hypothesis is necessarily imbued with all the scholarship I have mentioned so far. But I proceed in a rather different direction. On one hand, I was dissatisfied with B/S/T's grand narrative and thought it did not adequately explain postwar cinema. On the other, I wanted to work on the convergence of aesthetics and ideology in a diachronic and not synchronic fashion. In other words, I wanted to understand the changes Hollywood cinema and American culture went through without giving up in-depth analysis of films, cultural dynamics, and viewing habits. This brings me back to film feminism. In the effort to historicize classical Hollywood cinema I realized that some of the foundational features of Feminist Film Theory had to be reassessed. Indeed, if one considers the whole issue of Hollywood's representation of woman and femininity in the context of cinema's relation to modernity, the whole conceptual framework needs retooling. Even before modernity studies became fashionable in Film Studies, feminist historians had shown that modernity had been "unabashedly positive" for women. The impact of modernity on the American woman's experience cannot be underestimated. While new possibilities were not available to all, they were at least available to unmarried young women working in urban areas. By the 1920s, young women of all classes living in big cities as well as small towns claimed new sexual and romantic freedoms. Overall, women's modern lifestyles were defined by financial independence and a whole new relation to work, leisure, and sex. The transition from the Victorian ideology of True Womanhood to the modern vision of New Womanhood could not be more evident. While married women's lives continued to be centered around domesticity, single women forcefully entered the public sphere.[22] Such a process moved women toward a pleasure-oriented culture that defied the Victorian ethos of domesticity and sexual purity. As such, media consumption and moviegoing especially represented a fundamental practice of modern women's everyday lives.

Modernity has undeniably changed the American woman's life and experience a lot more than the American man's. While we must be aware of modernity's contradictions, it is even more important to remember that woman gained agency for the first time in history with modernity. Moreover, cinema was completely implicated with modernity, consumerism, and the culture of pleasure and thus contributed to female empowerment, especially in the silent era. In her pivotal analysis of the Valentino phenomenon, Miriam Hansen has shown that movie-going could have an emancipatory function for the young urban women flocking to movie theaters. For Hansen, both cinema and this specific male star helped channel and elicit new forms of female desire.[23]

Following Hansen's research, several studies by feminist film historians in the last fifteen years have increased our awareness about cinema's central status in the lives of modern women. At the same time, while Hansen focused on women as spectators, we now know all professions were open to women in the film industry in its first thirty years, including the most prestigious jobs such as directing, producing, and screenwriting.[24] This fascinating area of research proves women's relevance in the industry beyond spectatorship as professionals and artists. Moreover, this scholarship stands in direct contrast to that of the first generation of film feminists. Indeed, the passive and objectified women of Mulvey's influential piece have finally given way to the active, energetic, and sometimes masculine women that work on the set, enter the screen, or go to the movie theater.[25]

Nevertheless, while my take on history is different from feminist historians of early cinema, such research has contributed to my reassessment of Feminist Film Theory. Once again, it has helped me to clarify the need to *historicize theory*. For example, in chapter 1 I argue that Hollywood cinema was still marked in important ways by ideological and formal trends of silent cinema as it transitioned to sound, especially in relation to the New Woman and modernity. In fact, my whole project attempts to historicize the relation between masculine and feminine subject positions by showing cinema's changing attitude toward gender dynamics. At the end of the 1980s, Janet Bergstrom and Mary Ann Doane stated that "for a while it seemed (and often still seems) that every feminist writing on cinema felt compelled to situate herself in relation to Mulvey's essay." Judith Mayne similarly stated that much feminist work of the decade "has been a response to the assumptions inherent in both Mulvey's and Bellour's work."[26] Of course, my own work also tries to contribute to a reassessment of such gender parameters, but it does so by combining psychoanalytic frameworks with a detailed analysis of formal models, as well as a broader consideration of cinema's social imaginary and its representation of lifestyles.

Most scholarship on Hollywood cinema thus falls within the two opposing paradigms I just described. While a few have argued that a unique form or mode extends from the 1920s to the late 1950s, many considered specific historical episodes without tackling issues of periodization. However, there have also been some contributions that explicitly suggest looking at American cinema as a *heterogeneous* body of films vis-à-vis different modes of representation. To my knowledge there have been two such critical trends: the theory of the "progressive text" and the debate on "the classic vs. the melodramatic/modern" text. Of course, while these approaches have been crucial to my understanding of Hollywood cinema, my study tries to reassess their relevance in a historical perspective. More specifically, one of the aims of my project is to determine how the status of the classic and the melodramatic modes changes from the 1930s through the 1950s.

The theory of the progressive (or subversive) text was highly debated in the 1970s and 1980s, though such furor has since subsided. The debate took root in the British journal *Screen* after the translation of some French contributions from *Cinéthique* and *Cahiers du cinéma*. The most influential piece by far was Jean-Louis Comolli and Jean Narboni's "Cinema/Ideology/Criticism" published in France in 1969, later translated into English in 1971.

The notion of the progressive text is an elaboration of Comolli and Narboni's position within the specific context of classical American cinema. Central to their argument is the relation between ideology and form. According to Comolli and Narboni, while "all films are always already overdetermined as ideological products" filmmakers can intervene at the aesthetic-formal level in order to disrupt the relation between cinema and its ideological function.[27] Comolli and Narboni devised a typology of seven different filmic texts, each built around a different relation between form and content.[28]

Following this paradigm, scholars have looked at Hollywood cinema to uncover the peculiar relation between form and ideology. They have argued that within Hollywood, two modes of representation coexist: the "classic realist text" and the "progressive text." The classic realist text is totally enmeshed with the dominant ideology since it interpellates the spectator through processes of identification that only exploit the viewer's unconscious experience. On the other hand, while the progressive text seems to remain within the realm of ideology to some extent, closer inspection reveals that it is formally incoherent. At key points, then, the progressive film undermines the procedures of invisible style. Through formal incoherence and stylistic excess, the film breaks the circuit of identification and elicits a conscious process of apperception and reflexivity from the viewer. From a theoretical perspective, Hollywood is thus comprised of films that support "bourgeois ideology" and films that undermine it. But to interpret a film according to the theory of the progressive text also meant to read a film symptomatically, as such a reading was based on the psychoanalytic technique first envisioned by Freud in *The Interpretation of Dreams* (1900). In the same way that psychoanalysis translates the bodily symptom into psychic content, the film analyst translates the surface structure of the film into the deep structure of the text.

The first examples of progressive readings were the influential analyses done by the editors of *Cahiers du cinéma* of John Ford's *Young Mr. Lincoln* (1939) and of Josef Von Sternberg's *Morocco* (1932), both published in the journal in 1970.[29] Thomas Elsaesser's "Tales of Sound and Fury" (1972) is, to my knowledge, the first contribution in the English language to address the issue of the progressive text. Elsaesser investigates the relation between form and ideology in 1950s family melodrama by arguing that, just as previous novelistic and theatrical melodramatic forms were based on "discontinuity," so too were Hollywood melodramas insofar as they evinced "fissures and raptures in the fabric of experience, and appeal[ed] to a reality of the psyche."[30] For Elsaesser, the genre's stylistic excess signifies beyond action and verbal language and is a clear indication of melodrama's self-reflexivity, or the conscious use of style. From then on, family melodrama and melodrama in general would remain a favorite topic of investigation among scholars of American cinema.[31] I discuss at length family melodrama and the theoretical debate surrounding it more in chapter 5.

The issue of the progressive text is also approached by feminists and becomes a staple of Feminist Film Theory. In the early 1970s Claire Johnston and Pam Cook refashioned Comolli and Narboni's theory in terms of gender. Looking at the work of Dorothy Arzner and Ida Lupino, Johnston argued that women's cinema within Hollywood is a counter-cinema since it "attempted by formal means to bring about a dislocation between sexist ideology and the text of the film."[32] For Pam Cook, such a break occurs in Arzner's *Dance, Girl Dance* (1940) when Judy returns the gaze of the diegetic audience. In a manner previously theorized by Elsaesser, Cook speaks of a rapture in the film's most pregnant moment. "The place of the audience *in* the film and the audience *of* the film is disturbed, creating a break between them and the ideology of woman as spectacle, object of their desire."[33] Many other critical contributions could be recalled, since most feminist readings of Hollywood were, in one way or another, "progressive." While the notion of a progressive text or reading is no longer fashionable, this approach is implicitly at work, along with other critical tools, in all cultural interpretations of cinema, including my own, subtending a "dramatistic approach" to culture.[34] This method, however, can still be useful if it is applied to the film as a whole rather than to a fragment as progressive readings did.[35]

Retrospectively, one can see a gap between the theoretical apparatus and the analytical work done in those years since no one ever analyzed a classic realist text. In other words, for scholars Hollywood seemed to have produced only progressive films. However, if we look more closely, it appears that with very few exceptions—the most notable being *Stella Dallas* (K. Vidor, 1937)[36]—all progressive films studied were made during the 1940s and 1950s. Critics repeatedly chose films from the same genres: film noir, the woman's film, and family melodrama. To some extent this dynamic implicitly confirms my hypothesis that classical cinema pertains to 1930s Hollywood and not the following decades.

While in the 1980s the theory of the progressive text slowly faded away, I would argue that it was revived in part toward the end of the decade as a response to B/S/T's *The Classical Hollywood Cinema* (1985).[37] The debate on "the classic vs. the melodramatic," which eventually merged with the "modernity thesis," is in fact an attempt to undermine B/S/T's monolithic view of Hollywood and outline the presence of two different filmic modes.

But in order to understand this shift in Film Studies, it is important to recall the reception of B/S/T's work. One could say that *The Classical Hollywood Cinema* had "mixed reviews" in that most critics simultaneously emphasized both its theoretical innovations and limitations. For his part, Bordwell[38] selects very basic elements in order to define the classical mode of representation. In this way, he can define films as diverse as *The Jazz Singer* (A. Crosland, 1927) and *Written on the Wind* (D. Sirk, 1956), *It Happened One Night* (F. Capra, 1934) and *T-Men* (A. Mann, 1947) as "classic." But from a different perspective, Bordwell's definition can also accommodate both masterpieces and "typical films." Indeed, this is the category that interests B/S/T the most and thus serves as the basis for their paradigm. Working on typical films was truly novel because scholars had almost always privileged masterpieces and auteur films. However, this is the only category that the "Bordwell regime" is capable of explaining. Tom Gunning has argued that "by concentrating nearly exclusively on the 'typical' film, the full dialectical play of the classical paradigm becomes, in spite of the author's announced intentions, a bit static." The classical paradigm "is so encompassing that the possibility of a radical alternative seems to lie" only outside of narration. This "broad synchronic slice of film history chosen necessarily leads to an emphasis on the elements of stability within it."[39] Douglas Pye offers an even more poignant critique by questioning Bordwell's main concept of style. According to Pye, Bordwell's notion of style is too rigid and limited since its relation to meaning and content is totally dismissed. This position is also related to Bordwell's narrow notion of spectatorship. Indeed, he limits the viewer's activity to comprehension of the diegesis and "says very little about the relationship between the inferential activity of making narrative sense and the viewer's response to ideological norms." "Bordwell's view lacks what is crucial for a discussion of style and authorship in any art, not just cinema—the recognition that technical devices and formal systems mean nothing outside their contexts—the specific dramatic and ideological fields they present and comment on."[40] Along these lines, Robert Ray also argues that the "ideological *stakes* of such filmmaking—its effects, its epistemic causes—are left unexplored because the book's methodology commits BST to risking only those hypotheses confirmable by empirical evidence."[41]

As this brief overview suggests, there was strong agreement among film scholars in criticizing B/S/T's static model.[42] The view that Hollywood had produced a homogeneous body of films for more than four decades was highly contested. Aside from the exceptionally large synchronic dimension of the phenomenon, Bordwell's critics particularly disliked his description of Hollywood cinema in terms of narrative efficiency and rationality as well as his views on spectatorship. The former aspect—Bordwell's so-called neo-formalism—seemed patently at odds with the development of filmic forms and genres accentuating the aspect of spectacle over narrative. Similarly, the idea that the viewing process of Hollywood cinema could be reduced to understanding plot construction and narrative motivation—Bordwell's cognitive psychology—was equally frustrating.

Around the mid- to late 1980s, these issues began to be addressed directly and indirectly in other areas, for example, in relation to new ways of studying early cinema. More generally, the second half of the 1980s is a key transitional moment in Film Studies when certain approaches reached their climax while others started to emerge.[43]

Rick Altman's essay "Dickens, Griffith, and Film Theory Today" (1989) is a major episode in what I would define the "classic vs. melodramatic" debate. Altman's main thesis is that film theory on Hollywood cinema has shaped up around a major misunderstanding. From Eisenstein to Bazin, from Barthes to Bordwell, theorists have established a continuity between "the narrative technique of the nineteenth-century realist novel and the dominant style of Hollywood" at the expense of popular theater, or melodrama.[44] "This repression of popular theatre has the effect of denying Hollywood cinema its fundamental connection to popular traditions and to their characteristic forms of spectacle and narrative."[45] According to Altman, most theories of the classical, such as those of Bazin and Bordwell, owe their definition "to the neoclassical French literary theorists of the seventeenth century." They borrowed from them "not only a general sense of harmony and order" but also specific tenets such as "the central importance of the unity of action" and "concentration on human psychology."[46] For Altman, such a definition is inadequate to interpret American cinema. The idea that the Hollywood film is driven toward the transformation of tensions and chaotic forces into an ordered and harmonic form hardly explains anything. In order to understand Hollywood cinema's formal mechanisms, one needs to consider both its narrative structure (the classical) and its spectacular component (the melodramatic). Thus, Hollywood cinema may better be understood as a *dual-focus* text. On the one hand, it follows the Aristotelian rule of cause and effect and is goal-driven, moving "through character-based causality toward a logical conclusion." On the other, it *simultaneously* perpetuates "the menu-driven concerns of popular theatre. Spectacle is needed, as are variety and strong emotions." The Hollywood text is thus a "dynamic, multilevel *system* in which coexisting contradictory forces must regularly clash."[47] The popularity of a film is in fact more often linked to its most intense moments, when narrative motivation is weak, than to its plot, which most viewers tend to forget.

Altman's idea of Hollywood as a dual-focus text has had a profound impact on this book. In *Classic Hollywood*, I have tried to historicize the relation between classic and melodramatic modes. While Altman ultimately argues for the coexistence of the two registers in any Hollywood film, I emphasize the changing historical status of the two modes. I argue that in the second half of the 1930s American cinema practically effaced the melodramatic dimension, while in the transition years to sound and in the postwar era Hollywood limited classical tendencies and amplified melodramatic and spectacular components of the image.

While Altman's essay is devoted to classical sound Hollywood, the main terms of his analysis strongly resonate with those introduced around the same time by Tom Gunning in his first essays on early cinema. While conceived autonomously, the convergence between the two positions is both productive and striking. In "The Cinema of Attractions" (1986) and "An Aesthetic of Astonishment" (1989), Gunning argues that early cinema must be considered in relation to the culture of modernity, and specifically to the new mode of organizing vision and sensory perception embodied more clearly in Benjamin's theory of shock. For Gunning, early cinema is an autonomous mode of representation based on an "aesthetic of attractions" and lacks classical cinema's narrative impulse. In other words, the relation between early and classical cinema may be defined by the opposition between attraction and narration. The cinema of attractions "directly solicits spectator attention, inciting visual curiosity, and supplying pleasure through an exciting spectacle."[48] In contrast to "an involvement with narrative action or empathy with character psychology" as in classical cinema, "the cinema of attractions solicits a highly conscious awareness of the film image" and the spectator "remains aware of the act of looking."[49] In a much quoted passage, Gunning further states that when narrative cinema becomes dominant, the cinema of attractions does not disappear "but rather goes underground, both into certain avant-garde practices and as a component of narrative films, more evident in some genres (e.g., the musical) than in others."[50] The thematic affinity between Gunning and Altman's arguments is evident. Gunning's suggestion corroborates Altman's thesis that Hollywood cinema retains a melodramatic component.

Miriam Hansen more fully develops this argument in her essay "The Mass Production of the Senses" (2000). Hansen had, of course, already investigated similar issues in her famous studies on spectatorship and early cinema,[51] but it is here that she finally develops a fully articulated theory of Hollywood cinema within the confines of the "classic vs. melodramatic" debate. Hansen's argument is both an extension of Altman's (and Gunning's) thesis and an original contribution to the topic. For Hansen, American cinema has developed a mode of reflexivity based on strategies of excess. Hollywood's reflexivity is borne out of a "fascination with 'lower genres,' with adventure serials, detective thrillers, and slapstick comedies," which are "concerned with external appearance, the sensual, material surface of American films" and "focus on action and thrills, physical stunts and attractions . . . eccentricity and excess of situations over plot."[52] While reflexivity does not always have to be critical, it nevertheless allows cinema to engage with the contradictions of modernity. Hansen's central argument is that the reflexive dimension of Hollywood cinema in relation to modernity "is crucially anchored in sensory experience and sensational affect" rather than plot and narrative comprehension, and that musical, horror, and melodrama have the same potential as slapstick to ensure reflexivity.[53] Evidently Hansen's notion of reflexivity is not far from the reflexive thrust of the progressive text. While the seemingly oxymoronic definition of "vernacular modernism" is somewhat original, the idea that in Hollywood cinema "the classical"—narrative efficiency and coherence—coexists with "the melodramatic"—the sensual, the spectacular—clearly recalls Altman's thesis. But while Altman seems to imply that *any* Hollywood film is built around these two antithetical registers, Hansen appears to think that only certain genres contain elements of vernacular modernism. However, she does not fully investigate this issue.

These theoretical inputs have been productively employed to analyze specific genres. In an exemplary study on film noir, for example, Jim Naremore has shown that noir is the product of a convergence of experimental-modernist literary art and popular cultural forms, of the modernist preoccupation with individual subjectivity and "an interest in popular stories about violence and sexual love, or in what Graham Greene once called 'blood melodrama.'"[54] In the area of "cinema and modernity studies" Ben Singer's work on silent melodrama, Edward Dimendberg's study of noir and Francesco Casetti's work on the "modern gaze" have also been very influential for this project.[55]

The dialectic between classic and melodramatic and the imbrication of the melodramatic with the modern are key elements of my analysis. We have to account for the changing relevance of the classic and melodramatic in the Hollywood film over the years. For as the melodramatic has transgressive and reflexive potentials, we must also carefully evaluate its status vis-à-vis the classic throughout the whole Studio Era. Similarly, in this project I will test the viability of the opposition between attraction/spectacle to narration and reshape it in a historical fashion. For these reasons this study hopes to make a contribution to the field of "cinema and modernity studies."

CHAPTER OUTLINE

At this point, we can specify the criteria that define the body of films analyzed in the following pages. As I aim to show dominant tendencies, I have worked on a large corpus of films. But for the most part I concentrate on notable titles appreciated by audiences and/or critics. Most of the films discussed in this study may be found in the top box-office statistics, in the annals of pictures that have been nominated for or won Academy Awards, or in critics' Ten-Best lists. In subsequent years, many of these films drew the interest of academic criticism with which this study also engages. My criteria of selection rested on the assumption that the most influential representation of social identities and lifestyles may be found in such films. Thus, my approach is exactly the opposite of Bordwell, Staiger, and Thompson's *The Classical Hollywood Cinema*, which uses a random sample of 100 films for its analysis. As a result, their work is almost always about "ordinary films" that drew no noteworthy degree of public attention, though they represent a statistical majority of films produced in Hollywood. But these are not the films that the public lined up in droves to see, nor are they the ones so often discussed in newspapers and magazines.[56]

Methodological differences aside, it is clear that the circuit between sociality, forms of identity, and modes of representation reach greater symbolic intensity and adopt a more paradigmatic configuration in the more successful films. Therefore, in order to trace the nature and form of the most desired lifestyles, it is necessary to work on the most widely viewed films, which often enjoyed critical success as well.[57] Moreover, given the quantity of films produced each year and the frequency with which people went to the cinema, this is not a small, but rather a notable, number of films. Among the nearly 500 American films produced annually in the 1930s, 380 in the 1940s, and 280 in the 1950s, almost one-third of all these enjoyed a substantial production budget.[58]

As a rule, each chapter outlines its general arguments by referring to many films and then goes on to discuss a few in depth. Each chapter also sets up a dialogue with critical concepts and trends that have developed in the Anglo-American context. I tackle the dominant formal and representative models that define questions of lifestyle and desire by combining film and cultural history, gender and sexuality studies, family studies, American women's history with formal film analysis.

Chapter 1 considers the early sound period and argues that between the end of the 1920s and the early 1930s American cinema privileges plots of female emancipation and images of the New Woman. From a formal perspective, the dominant film style has an affinity with silent cinema; it is filled with superimpositions, extended dissolves, elaborate optical effects, and a wide range of "attractions." Consequently, the films of this period rely heavily on visual rather than verbal devices. As I demonstrate, the figure of the New Woman, combined with the aesthetic of attractions can be interpreted in light of the "modernity thesis."

Chapter 2 argues that in the mid-1930s American cinema perfected a classical form that dominated till the end of the decade. This form arose out of a new convergence between lifestyle and film style: in ideological terms, the period supported normative and traditional images of femininity and masculinity, and its film style privileged unified narratives based on action, dialogue, and continuity editing. I try to show why David Bordwell's influential thesis on the "classicism" of Hollywood cinema perfectly fits such a period but is inadequate to account for earlier and later periods. While films of the 1940s will be dominated by figures of rebellion and alienation in the second half of the 1930s, integration is the key imperative. The return to traditional values is manifested by a renewed interest in masculinity: in contrast to the earlier period, which is dominated by female stars, the most popular figures in the second half of the 1930s are male stars, along with child and teenage actors. This trend influences the most important genres of the period: screwball comedy, adventure, and biopic.

Chapter 3 discusses the transition between the classical war films of the early 1940s and the anticlassical film noirs of the later half of the decade. This period can be roughly described in terms of a dual crisis, seen at the level of representation and at the level of the subject's capacity to act and to know. I examine noir's visual and narrative regime, especially its ability to express in purely visual terms certain modern tenets such as the psyche's split nature, the notion of embodied subjectivity, the failure of vision and seeing. Similarly, noir alters the function of verbal language: the protagonist's subjective narration is often the only key to knowledge and truth, and words seem to take up the role previously assigned to vision and action. Meanwhile, deep focus photography alters the terms of visuality. My analysis stresses the relation between modernity and subjective vision as well as the idea that modern subjectivity is partial and split.

Chapter 4 discusses noir's twin genre, the woman's film. While this genre's formal politics are quite similar to noir's, its focus on female identity entails a representation of female desire. Starting from the rise and demise of the figure of *Rosie the Riveter* in the early to mid-1940s, the chapter details the decade's discourse on femininity, especially on female sexuality and mental illness as understood by pop psychoanalysis. The woman's film is the site of contradictory and antithetical functions: its narrative is structured by twisted plots and tortuous trajectories that often split into two opposite scenarios or styles, one representing the public/male/urban space and the other the private/female/domestic space. The genre's formal convolutions are homologous with the contradictory discourse on postwar femininity, namely the opposition between the need to conform to normative femininity and the relentless effort by women to find new ways of being and new forms of desire. While the genre's proximity to noir's modern concerns cannot be underestimated, its gender interests lead to what I would define as an *excessive* focus on the female body. As I try to show, for woman the body is the locus of negotiation between different modes of being.

Chapter 5 considers 1950s cinema in terms of family melodrama. I begin by discussing the theoretical debate on melodrama in order to show that, notwithstanding different filmic traditions, "the body" remains melodrama's crucial subject matter. I also attempt to historicize the relation between body, style, and social imaginary. I thus interpret the genre in light of the convergence between the decade's new spectacular visual style (color and wide-screen formats) and the image of the suburban family, which is the dominant lifestyle of 1950s America. By discussing in particular the discourse on masculinity, I argue that melodrama's visual style and narrative contradictions endorse the belief that sexuality is an essential component of human nature. Family melodrama can be understood in relation to Kinsey's contemporary researches, but it is not a critique of the suburban ideology, as critics have often argued. Rather, it expresses the "difficulty of gender." The genre's tendency to focus on a community rather than on an individual or a couple is instrumental to the representation of competing models of identity, for men and women alike. Finally, by looking at certain technical and linguistic devices I argue for the genre's innovative, nonclassical visual style.

Chapter 6 continues to discuss the 1950s spectacular style by considering a cycle of musicals in the period. In contrast to melodrama, the musical combines spectacle with reflexive strategies and is able to comment in a sophisticated fashion on the fiction/reality dichotomy and on the relation between cinema and the other media, especially theater and television. Yet musical's reflexive strategies also have a bearing on the status of subjectivity. While noir and the woman's film used expressive techniques to emphasize the split nature of the human psyche, the opposition between conscious and unconscious realities, 1950s cinema, and especially the musical, goes one step further. Many films show that gendered identities are the product of a series of performances, rather than the expression of an intrinsic nature, and that the same character may well embody opposite tendencies and behaviors. In a similar fashion, other films suggest—foremost among them *Singin' in the Rain* (S. Donen/G. Kelly, 1952)—that the opposition between fiction and reality is no longer tenable, and that the performative register has started to invade both the realm of artistic production and of subjective experience. In this final chapter, I argue that the 1950s musical has taken the genre's "theoretical" nature into the realm of postmodernity.

1

THE EARLY THIRTIES

Modernity, New Women, and the Aesthetic of Attractions

American cinema of the 1930s presents two modes of representation, each marked by a convergence between a specific film style and a peculiar cinematic imaginary. The first is more radical and arises with the advent of sound and ebbs around 1933–1934. The second returns to a more classic mode and develops in the years immediately following and continues to the end of the decade. It must be underscored that such delineation marks the rise and fall of *dominant trends*, which almost certainly overlapped, rather than precise chronological divisions. Nevertheless, one has to account for an increasing preference for the classical model over the "anticlassical" as the decade wore on.

By 1943, Robert Brasillach and Maurice Bardèche had already begun to speak of the talkie's classicism, referring to American cinema between 1933–1939.[1] More recently, Robert Sklar has identified two Golden Ages within the 1930s cinematic imaginary. On the one hand, what he calls the "Age of Turbulence" during the Great Depression represents one of the more significant challenges to traditional values in the history of American media. On the other, the "Age of Order," a Rooseveltian countercurrent that emerged during the 1933–1934 season, reemphasized traditional American values, patriotism, national unity, and family.[2] But as Sklar's argument represents a more nuanced and significant contribution to a fuller understanding of this period, nevertheless, he never accounted for questions of film form and gender, which would significantly bolster his already incisive claims.

The dominant configurations of desire and subjectivity are notably different in the two periods, particularly in relation to women. Feminist historians have shown that modernity changed women's lives much more than men's. This scenario also explains Hollywood's craze for stories of female emancipation and images of the New Woman. In fact, between the end of the 1920s and the early 1930s, American cinema continued to focus on the image of the young, self-assertive, and sexy woman, thus perpetuating the cult of New Womanhood that emerged in the early years of the century. This tendency would wane as the decade progressed. From about the mid-1930s, the dominant narrative of female desire was tuned to the formation of the couple and to marriage while the figure of the emancipated woman became marginal. This shift in the representation of gender identity was matched by a concomitant transformation in film style. In the early 1930s, Hollywood cinema extended the use of visual techniques developed during the silent period that we may consider in light of the "cinema of attractions." While early 1930s cinema is overly narrative, at specific moments (especially, but not only, in the opening episode), such film avoids both narrative articulation and dialogue and communicates merely through visual devices. Conversely, around 1934, the classical mode of representation, namely a rational and motivated mode of storytelling based on action, analytic editing, and dialogue, became dominant, while visual attractions and techniques tended to disappear. Thus, one could argue that in 1930s Hollywood the transition from the "Age of Turbulence" to the "Age of Order" is marked by stylistic-formal changes and a diverse cinematic imaginary, particularly in relation to female desires and lifestyles.

CINEMA AND THE NEW WOMAN

The figure of the New Woman can be situated in the context of the American landscape's rapid urbanization and modernization at the turn of the century. For the female subject, this meant an epochal transition from a Victorian conception of the relation between the sexes to a modern vision that implicated her departure from the domestic sphere and entrance into the public. In recent decades, feminist historians have investigated this fascinating episode of American history by considering all aspects of women's everyday experiences. These range from professional to living conditions, to relations between women and with men both during and after work. While new jobs in department stores, large factories, restaurants, and offices provided alternatives to domestic service and sweatshops, the overall relation between work and leisure also changed. Focusing in particular on women's leisure activities, historians have argued that consumption and entertainment were the primary loci of a cultural crisis where new forms of desire and female identity were consolidated. And for its part, cinema, as the period's visual medium par excellence, played a fundamental role in shaping the American modern woman by disseminating her powerful image. Leading into this phenomenon, Nancy Cott has argued that the 1920s brought a cultural standardization without precedent and that mass media fed the creation of a specifically American modern way of life that could also be readily exported. Accordingly, "surveys reported that movie stars had replaced leaders in politics, business, or the arts as those admired by the young."[3]

In the transition years from silent film to sound, cinema was still the most effective form for representing modernity and urban life, as well as women's desire to be emancipated. Surveys of the period and contemporary investigations in audience studies reveal that, in the 1920s and early 1930s, women were the majority of moviegoers. Working in this domain, Melvyn Stokes has noted that audience research studies at the time were rather impressionistic and that the data available are probably imprecise. Yet while estimates might be individually inaccurate, "collectively they suggest an impressive weight of evidence to buttress the idea of a predominantly female audience." Ultimately, whether women really formed a majority of the cinema audience was "less important than the fact that Hollywood itself assumed that, both through their own attendance and their ability to influence men, they were its primary market."[4] Such an assumption had a powerful effect on the industry. In the 1920s and the 1930s, Hollywood produced a vast number of films centered on women, often written by women scriptwriters.[5] During the first half of the 1930s the woman's film made up a quarter of all movies on the "best lists," with 1931 as the year recording the highest number.[6] In a similar way, one can read the greater success of female over male stars in those years as correlative to female movie-going. On the other hand, in the latter half of the decade box-office dominance would shift from adult females to male leads and to child and adolescent stars like Shirley Temple and Mickey Rooney.[7]

Women, of course, loved to see images of the New Woman and accordingly vested their most fervent desires in her strong attractive persona. In her perhaps most innovative iteration, the flapper stood as the primary reference model for the New Woman and drew characteristic strength, energy, and vitality from divas like Gloria Swanson, Colleen Moore, Louise Brooks, Clara Bow, and Joan Crawford.[8] Whether a woman of high society or working girl, for Mary Ryan "the new movie woman exuded above all a sense of physical freedom—unrestrained movement . . . abounding energy—the antithesis of the controlled, quiet, tight-kneed poses of Griffith's heroines." With "dashing spontaneity" these women "rushed onto dance floors, leapt into swimming pools, and accepted any dare—to drink, to sport, to strip," and they moved into social, work, and higher education spheres.[9] Marked by a spirit of independence, self-determination and expressive sexuality, the image of the New Woman thus eclipsed the Victorian model; a pure, weak, suffering heroine epitomized onscreen by the likes of the Lillian Gish character in a number of D. W. Griffith films. Thus, historians have defined this epochal transformation of the female condition as the passage from Victorian "True Womanhood" to a modern "New Womanhood."[10]

The cult of True Womanhood emerged in the first half of the nineteenth century. As Barbara Welter has argued in her pivotal essay, the Victorian ethos prescribed for women a strict moral code based on four traits: domesticity, religiosity, sexual purity, and subservience to men.[11] New Womanhood, on the other hand, overturned all these values by promoting self-determination, entrance into the working world, and relative sexual freedom. Ironically, however, the second half of the 1930s fostered a restorative climate that explicitly condemned these behaviors in an effort to strip women of their newly gained freedoms. The "fallen woman cycle" represents Hollywood's most visible contribution to this phenomenon. Films such as *Stella Dallas*, *Kitty Foyle* (S. Wood, 1940), the lesser known *The Bride Walks Out* (L. Jason, 1936), and many others relegated the rebellious woman to the margins of society. Typically after transgression, the only way a "fallen woman" could redeem herself was by returning to the domestic sphere and renouncing independence and true love for a glamourless marriage (*The Bride Walks Out* and *Kitty Foyle*) or children's happiness (*Stella Dallas*). The New Woman's lifestyle now seemed possible only in a limited window of time, between early adulthood outside the parental home and marriage. As we see in chapter 2, a notable but very limited exception is represented by the rich heroines of the screwball comedy. By the second half of the 1930s, Hollywood cinema granted sexual freedom and independence only to upper-class women.

The New Woman's trajectory could occur only in the urban milieu of modernity, far from the physically and morally constrictive spaces of the family and the small town.[12] Cinema's representation of the modern subject's experience in this period accords with the sociological views put forth by urban theorists such as Simmel, Kracauer, and Benjamin in the first decades of the century save one noteworthy difference: by the early 1930s, individuals had developed the ability to face dangers and the perceptual shocks of an incessantly chaotic urban environment. For example, the typical working girl plotline transpired between the protective environs of the office or shop where she worked with other young women during the day[13] and the livelier but less secure streets, clubs, dance halls, and night spots where she spent her evenings. No less typical were the episodes set in domestic environments. Either the young woman lived in a furnished rented room or she shared a very small apartment with other girls. However, another type of female character was perhaps more common and at the same time more transgressive as it embodied the greatest sexual liberties of the period. Movie screens teemed with show girls, kept women, and gold diggers who were more open-minded about sex. As seen in many films, sex could be the means of a glamorous standard of living or for some modicum of economic security that assured the woman's independence. While sexual openness often secures the woman a good marriage, in these films frank sexual behavior is not the sign of moral corruption, but the clearest symptom of women's force and emancipated status.

THE FEMALE BODY, THE URBAN DISSOLVE, AND THE AESTHETIC OF ATTRACTIONS

The metropolis as a site of continuous movement, energy and transformation finds its fullest expression in films where female subjects fight for self-determination through either work or sex or both. Movement and transformation, however, not only enliven classically linear narrative trajectories, but they are also visually expressed during moments when plot is suspended. These are moments of pure attraction and spectacle. Via specific formal strategies, these episodes offer the spectator a dizzying, turbulent visual experience that culminates in a temporary suspension of cognitive faculties in hopes of eliciting sensual and shocking perceptive experiences.

As mentioned in the Introduction, a research method emerged in the 1990s that grounded itself in the thought of key theorists of modernity, especially Walter Benjamin.[14] These scholars reexamined the advent of cinema at the turn of the century in relation to the changing urban landscape as well as the period's cultural and visual forms. "The modernity thesis," as David Bordwell has called it, "stresses key formal and spectatorial similarities between cinema—as a medium of strong impressions, spatiotemporal fragmentation, abruptness, mobility—and the nature of the metropolitan experience. Both are characterized by the prominence of fleeting, forceful visual attractions and contra-contemplative spectatorial distraction."[15] Accordingly, early cinema, as well as some narrative genres of the 1910s, may be seen as a formal expression of the modern subject's hyperstimulated experience in the metropolis. For Ben Singer, the serial-queen melodrama beautifully develops the theme of female heroism and is thus a paradigmatic example of the image of the New Woman: "within a sensational action-adventure framework . . . serials gave narrative preeminence to an intrepid young heroine who exhibited a variety of traditionally 'masculine' qualities: physical strength and endurance, self-reliance, courage, social authority, and freedom to explore novel experiences outside the domestic sphere."[16] For Singer, the serial-queen melodrama is an aesthetic version of everyday urban life, dominated by excessive visual sensations, in the sense that cinema duplicates the everyday urban experience of women in the audience. Life in the modern city did indeed become more intensely physical and this had a significant impact on aural and visual modes of perception.[17] As a technological apparatus, cinema contributed to such transformations as it produced spectatorial experiences comparable to that of the subject's daily experience in the metropolis.

As we know, Tom Gunning's felicitous formula, "aesthetic of attractions," represents the most productive cinematic framework for this sociological scenario.[18] In order to account for early 1930s cinema, we need such a framework so that we can evaluate this mode of representation against the larger panorama of narrative sound cinema, or the classical mode of the second half of the decade.

In the early sound years, the aesthetic of attractions played a decisively more important role than in the second half of the 1930s. I would argue that such an aesthetic expressed not simply the subject's particular experience of the modern metropolis, as theorists from Benjamin to Gunning have stated, but more specifically the New Woman's plot of self-determination. As such, a dichotomy between story and spectacle emerged on two fronts: one between word and image, the other between "phenomenological" and "visual-dynamic" images. The attractional component was not reducible to either action or story, but inextricably connected to pure perception and visual sensation. Through formal devices drawn from the silent period, American cinema of the early 1930s expressed the New Woman's condition through visual spectacles that cinematically represented the ideas of movement and metamorphosis as well as the experience of excessive visual sensations typical of modernity. More specifically, cinema's mode of representation relied on a convergence between plots of female emancipation and visual attractions.

Following Tom Gunning's suggestion that when the narrative form won out over a cinema of attractions, diminishing but not eliminating the latter's presence onscreen, I would argue that it is necessary to historicize the notion that attractions are an aesthetic solution to the condition of modernity and evaluate carefully the changing relation between attraction and narration. The cinema of the early 1930s is a fundamental episode in this trajectory since it calls for a *gendered reading* of the aesthetic concept of attraction. In the woman-centered films of the period, visual attractions rely on the image of the female body while narratives focus on stories of female emancipation. The convergence between form and content around the woman's body is a very peculiar solution at this historical moment.

The relation between woman and modernity was expressed in particular by two types of visual attractions: the "urban dissolve" and the exhibitionist display of the female body. The urban dissolve is a specific code of silent cinema, a rhetorical strategy developed in particular in the city symphony documentary films such as Strand and Sheeler's *Manhatta* (1921), Ruttman's *Berlin* (1927), Vertov's *Man with a Movie Camera* (1929), but also used in narrative films, as in Murnau's American debut, *Sunrise* (1927), and in Siodmak and Ulmer's *People on Sunday* (1930), a unique hybrid of documentary and fiction. The urban dissolve is an extended dissolve, a series of superimpositions of images of urban life which "cinematically" amplifies the city's dynamism while also testing the spectator's perceptive skills. Shot in the most bustling areas of the metropolis, the urban dissolve shows masses of people walking or waiting; fast-moving lines of cars, trolleys, and trains; and other energized moments of everyday urban life. The metropolis is transformed into a visual polyphony and an aesthetic kinesthesia. Far from being "realistic," via multiple and complex dissolves the image loses its iconic properties and constantly transforms itself to the extent that it may become pure movement, energy, and light. While we are often unable to "read" the image, our perceptive experience registers endless movement and change as the main condition of city life. The urban dissolve is clearly antinarrative and contributes enormously to the opposition between narrative and spectacle that shaped American cinema in the early sound years.

Dissolves and visual polyphonies are often gendered, that is, related to the female body. Because they effectively exemplify the idea of metamorphosis, they are and were particularly fit to represent the modern woman's narrative of transformation. While this device was very common, it also could attain an unusual level of formal complexity and rhetorical force, as it did in *Glorifying the American Girl* (M. Webb, 1929). A second strategy of attraction, female exhibitionist techniques, was also very common. The exhibition of the female body, especially in a performative context, preserved an element of primitive attraction. Indeed, cinema of these years teemed with show girls, ballerinas, singers, and cabaret actresses, and their performances infused narrative with moments of pure erotic spectacle. Much like Gunning's original formulation on early cinema, a charismatic performer such as Joan Crawford, Mae West, and Marlene Dietrich "directly solicits spectator attention, inciting visual curiosity and supplying pleasure through an exciting spectacle."[19]

Glorifying the American Girl begins with a spectacular four-minute prologue composed of a series of superimpositions activating a vertiginous visual experience. The film tells the story of a young woman who wants to be in the Follies; in the meantime she works in a department store sheet-music section, where she sings the latest hits. She will become a successful performer on Broadway, but in the process she will break up with her boyfriend who is unable to cope with her career and who will marry a more "modest" girl. The prologue postpones the beginning of the narrative and visually "demonstrates" the relation between woman and modernity.

The first shot shows a map of the United States with numerous young women superimposed on top. All dressed in the same uniform, they move in single-file serpentine lines that span the entire country. Their little silhouettes have a robotlike shape and the geometry of their movements resembles Busby Berkeley's dancing numbers in his Warner Brothers musicals of the early 1930s. The first sensible transformation of the image shows a young woman putting on a pantsuit. Moments later, she is transformed again by a sequined costume typical of the famous Ziegfeld girls. She then mounts a dizzying headdress, while on the lower part of the image serpentine lines of girls continue to undulate. The shot then changes again as a moving train appears and is superimposed over the serpentine lines of women. In response, they replicate the train's movement, increasing the effect of bustle and confusion. As the image continues to transform itself, we see a young any-woman-whatever overlaid onto a number of symmetrically grouped girls. In the foreground, automobiles move about the city streets. The prologue continues to develop along the same line: dissolves as well as double or triple superimpositions will build up truly spectacular and dynamic visual effects on the theme of "women and the metropolis."

Neither the story of a common girl's rise to the heights of Broadway nor the revue format was very original. One reviewer at the time wrote that the film presented "nothing . . . that has not been done in the talkies many times before," and another similarly said that "Its plot fairly reeks with familiarity."[20] Nevertheless, the prologue is quite stunning. While superimpositions and extended dissolves are indeed a typical trope of the period, this case is certainly radical in relation to the common use of the device. The visual imagery compellingly raises the question of female desire and emancipation. On the one hand, through multiple dissolves, the sequence suggests the idea of movement and transformation. On the other hand, it provocatively ties these ideas to "the American girl" announced in the title. While a feminist ahistorical interpretation might take the film as the epitome of the representation of woman as commodity, "so that Gloria's middle-class occupation in the world of display showcases is a stepping-stone to the high-class showcase of the Ziegfeld revue,"[21] I believe, on the contrary, that the heroine's career as a Ziegfeld girl should be seen historically, namely, as a successful emancipation from the trappings of Victorian America.

Though dominated by visual sensations, the prologue activates not only a sensual experience but also an intellectual process. As Francesco Casetti has pointed out, one of the challenges of modernity was to reconcile the hyperstimulation of the senses—which defies meaning—with the possibility of making sense of everyday urban life. Cinema provides the means for negotiating such a duality.[22] In the prologue of *Glorifying the American Girl*, all the human figures are female—better, the prologue alternates collective images with shots of individual subjects. The film seems to evoke in a rather precise fashion the historical condition of the modern American woman in the 1920s. In the same way that the title refers to "any" American girl, the robotlike figures are devoid of any individualizing trait and connote a collective experience. The serpentine lines going toward the urban areas express quite literally the young women moving to the big cities in search of jobs. The robotlike figures walking on the map are, at the same time, anonymous and universal, recalling the thousands of stenographers and telephone operators, washerwomen and nurses, secretaries and sales clerks populating the workplace: According to historical research, these were the most common jobs held by American women at the time.[23] Overall, the prologue makes a historical comment on the condition of the working woman by exploiting a typical formal device of the period, while the plot concentrates on the trajectory of the protagonist.

Engaged to Buddy, who thinks only of marrying her, Gloria (Mary Eaton) dreams of doing something important before settling down. While the young woman starts a career as a traveling performer and leaves her hometown, she remains in love with Buddy. Eventually she returns to New York City for an audition and Buddy is there at Grand Central waiting for her. He then accompanies Gloria to the theater where she gets the part. But in the end, the young man understands that his fiancé will not give up her career and settles for Barbara, a long time mutual friend and colleague who had also always been in love with Buddy in spite of his commitment to Gloria. The film then concludes with a diegetic show eponymously called "Glorifying the American Girl," which in turn validates the protagonist's success. Among the public who attend Gloria's happy and triumphant success are Buddy and Barbara. And while in the dressing room between numbers, Gloria receives their telegram congratulating her and announcing that their wedding was celebrated that same day. Incredulous, Gloria bursts into tears. Still, however, she musters the strength to go out on stage for the next number, gazing on the crowd with teary eyes as they applaud. It seems that Gloria has little time for regrets, and the film's last shot ultimately validates her success once more. Through the opposition between the two women, the film dramatizes the dialectic between True and New Womanhood. While Gloria's stardom might also mean "personal misery and sacrifice"[24] we nevertheless see her masculinized autonomy and dignity upheld in the face of a far more traditional female passivity (Barbara).

A more famous example is George Cukor's *What Price Hollywood?* (1932). This film tells a similar story—that of a young girl starting as a waitress and ending up as a Hollywood star. Cukor's film shares themes and traits common to the era's cinema, such as female "social climbing" while also focusing on show business. As in *Glorifying the American Girl*, the metamorphic trajectory of the heroine is anticipated in the opening sequence through a very effective use of dissolves and offscreen space. The first shots, all linked through lap dissolves, play around the dialectic between onscreen and offscreen space by hiding the protagonist's face/identity. In this fashion, the film emphasizes the impression of movement and change rather than action and character identification.

The film starts with the shot of an unfolding fan magazine: a pair of hands is flipping through and reveals photos of glamorous divas and beautiful women. The image then dissolves into a pair of sexy legs: a woman's body is framed from the waist down while she puts on a pair of stockings. The link between the two shots is still not explicit and remains purely associative as the elegant female legs only allude to the beauties photographed in the magazine. But then, a second dissolve assumes a more subjective view of the magazine as the still unseen woman leafs through it. Further on the dissolve returns us to a female body. Now the woman, framed from the knees to the neck, perhaps the same one, is putting on a dress. After another quick shot of the magazine, the camera focuses on a woman's mouth, while invisible hands apply lipstick. At this point, a slow tracking shot reveals the woman's face, the actress Constance Bennett. She continues to put on makeup by peeking at a magazine in order to imitate the style of her favorite stars. When we see a medium shot of the protagonist's whole body we realize that she is the same woman we saw in the previous shots: the dress is indeed the one seen earlier in partial view on the fragmented body.

At this point the film develops into a classical narrative and the associative editing of the first shots is substituted by invisible editing style. The young woman is getting dressed to go to work. She lives in a cheap room and works in a restaurant in Hollywood, hoping to get a chance to start a career in the movies. In the restaurant she will eventually meet a famous actor who will help her to get her first audition. While the episode is less elaborate than the opening sequence of *Glorifying the American Girl*, it relies on a similar anticlassic rhetoric in suggesting the close association between female desire, change, and modernity. Like the earlier film, it also points to the collective thrust of its message: the woman we see getting dressed lacks any individualizing trait and can thus stand for all the young women moving to the big cities in the first decades of the century. Additionally, the generalized sensation of dynamism and transformation of the beginning is a perfect prelude to the plot of emancipation that follows. Significantly, at the moment in which the protagonist realizes her rise to stardom, the film has recourse to the same cinematic composition through a series of spectacular urban dissolves. Illuminated neon signs out in front of the theater proudly announcing her starring roles are superimposed to close-ups of the diva. And this paradigmatic image of urban modernity makes explicit commentary on the privileged relation between the New Woman, modernity, and cinema itself.

But Cukor's film is also a commentary on the relation between cinema, the star system, and female audiences. In the beginning, for example, the described sequence concludes with the protagonist taking the female's place in a magazine image of Clark Gable and Greta Garbo. Bennett folds the magazine in half, puts her face next to Gable's and in an exaggerated manly accent says: "Darrrrlink, how I looove you, my darrrlink." On the one hand the woman seems to make an ironic commentary on her own imitation. On the other, she takes great pleasure in constructing her own image and style by imitating the female role model. As Sarah Berry has shown, this example is in harmony with several ideas about female audiences at the time: "the concept of star emulation" Berry affirms, is "represented in terms of both calculation and fantasy, but rather than being discussed as a matter of psychological identification with particular stars, it is often presented as a conscious move to adopt a particular set of fashion and behavioral codes." In any case, it is never about passive marketing imperatives, but rather a process "connected to both the imaginative activities of women's fan culture and women's conscious use of fashion's social semiotics." Finally, the episode shows how the construction of female identity occurs through a conscious and personal reworking of specific models and lifestyles—those of Hollywood's great divas. As an admirer of Greta Garbo, Constance Bennett is clearly a consumer of fan magazines. She does not passively imitate the glamorous stars she loves, but learns to construct her own identity through a process of negotiation between unconscious desires and a conscious understanding of the way the Dream Factory works.[25]

In a somewhat unusual case, the lyrical-poetic prologue of *Rain* (L. Milestone, 1932) takes up the city symphony's visual-dynamic strategies once more. The opening sequence is directly inspired by Joris Ivens's eponymous poetic documentary *Rain* (1929) and reenters the "fallen woman" cycle by characteristically drawing on a strong literary tradition. Typically, the protagonist transgresses norms of Victorian morality through unconventional sexual behavior. She is often a prostitute or a mother outside wedlock much like Hester Prynne in Hawthorne's *The Scarlet Letter*.[26] Here, Milestone's film is the second cinematic version of Sadie Thompson's similar story. Joan Crawford plays a prostitute who arrives in the Samoan village of Pago Pago and resists every effort at her moral rehabilitation. In fact, Pago Pago is a sort of military outpost where soldiers mix with natives and liberal American civilians take refuge from a culturally conservative trend sweeping the nation.

The beginning of the film, however, foreshadows none of this. In a bizarre opposition to the plot, *Rain* opens with a sequence of clouds, drops of water, and rain in an associative montage clearly codified by lyric documentaries of the preceding decade. The antinarrative beginning is then followed by a brief episode that transitions from nature to the real story as the camera focuses on water gushing from a tube. It then moves into the tube and reveals a tub collecting the runoff. Next we see a group of singing soldiers marching in the rain against the backdrop of a group of natives moving in unison in the opposite direction as they transport wood. Thus, as the nature-themed lyrical prelude ends, the film substitutes a collective human presence as a group of actors enters the scene. With precise control of its representational repertoire, the film passes from evocation to narration, that is, from associative montage, graphic matches, and lyrical music, to an articulation of the relation between on- and offscreen space as well as dialogue.[27] This initial lyrical fragment will also follow both the episode in which Sadie enters the scene and once more, just before we learn of the Davidson couple who have temporarily taken up residence on the island with an eye toward moral reform.

But more than the lyrical sequence's precise meaning, I am interested in drawing a parallel between its formal register and that of those sequences already discussed earlier. All are founded on associative devices and a style of editing that are both deeply antinarrative and truly spectacular. And yet, the most radical visual attractions of the film concern the sexual display of the female body. Milestone's film, in fact, is yet another cinematic example in which female emancipation hinges entirely on sexual liberty. Through an exhibitionist technique that combines acting style, camerawork, and editing, Sadie purposefully presents her body as an attraction. This performance is an active gesture, particularly if it is read in the overall context of the film, which is decidedly sympathetic to Sadie's lifestyle.

In Pago Pago, having fun is the focus and Sadie spends her time drinking and listening to music in the company of soldiers. But Sadie catches the attention of Mr. Davidson, a missionary who has arrived with his wife on the same boat and who wants to reform Sadie. At some point he seems to succeed: Sadie is enthralled by his preaching and begins a process of redemption. But the spell he has cast over Sadie sinks with Davidson when he mysteriously drowns in the ocean. In the end she goes back to her previous life and the whole island seemingly resumes its usual habits and routines.

Throughout the film Sadie's sexual identity is registered on her body. Her sexy outfits give way to modest black dresses during her conversion, but, finally, after the spell wears off, she returns to her excessive wardrobe, heavy makeup, and flashy costume jewelry.

The most interesting visual attraction is related to Sadie's appearance when she is framed by a door and stands in front of the soldiers. Sadie is described through an explicitly erotic and exhibitionist rhetoric twice, when she is first introduced, and at the end, when, after Davidson's death, she accepts Sergeant O'Hara's courtship. Crawford's performance is not inscribed within the active male/passive female dichotomy. On the contrary, the woman's appearance is quite literally an assault on the viewer and on the male protagonists, who are forced to experience Sadie's excessive sexuality. While the male look is part of the rhetorical construction of each performance scene, the active agency is Sadie's. While the two scenes are structured in the same way—Crawford emerges from an offscreen space to meet the boys' looks—what is most striking is the choice to show her body by literally repeating the same five shots. Both episodes start with the soldiers' looks and then present fragments of Sadie's body: first a bejeweled hand, then the other, then an ankle, then the other, and finally her heavily made-up face. If we look carefully at the camera position and characters' looks, it is clear that only the first of the five shots represents the subjective point of view of the diegetic male characters. The scene is clearly shot and edited for the extra-diegetic spectator. Crawford's exhibition actively confronts the viewer rather than the soldiers. As Gunning argued in relation to early cinema, through the use of close-ups the film "aggressively subjects the spectator to 'sensual or psychological impact.'"[28] This type of sequence is repeated at the end of the film when Sadie rejects her brief foray into a reformed lifestyle. After Davidson's death, Sadie wastes little time before returning to her old look and habits. Thus, in many ways similar to *Blonde Venus* (Von Sternberg, 1932) which, as we will see, ends on a contradictory image of Marlene as eroticized mother, *Rain*'s ending is just as problematic. Dressed "as a prostitute," Sadie seems to accept and return the love of a soldier who helped her resist Davidson's efforts at her conversion.[29]

Ultimately in the three films considered, exhibition and spectacle of the female body do not represent the subordination of woman but rather the site of her emancipation. The eroticized female body can thus be seen in opposition to Feminist Film Theory's initial formulations. As Jane Gaines has argued, the eroticized female body does not have to be considered a sign of "the pathology of the male spectator," but may be indicative of the woman's "gratification."[30] Naturally, I do not propose a general extension of this hypothesis to all Hollywood cinema. Instead, my aim has been to carefully evaluate its validity for the transition era as I believe such an idea explains the industry's and the audience's substantial investment in sexuality and the female body between the end of the 1920s and early 1930s. This phenomenon was the extreme ramification of sweeping social and cultural transformations, as the American woman left Victorian morality behind and adopted the new attitudes toward sexuality, so provocatively represented in Roaring Twenties cinema. Accordingly, Hollywood cinema contributed enormously to the "veritable discursive explosion" "around and apropos of sex" that Foucault has spoken about.[31]

In *Intimate Matters*, historians John D'Emilio and Estelle Freedman have described the events and the practices leading up to the American public's radical shift in attitude toward sexuality at the beginning of the previous century. They trace the signs of a "new sexual order" beginning in the early 1910s through the decline among doctors, theorists of sexuality, and middle-class cultural radicals of behavioral models of continence and self-control and the emergence of "a sexual ethic that encouraged expressiveness." Here, we can begin to speak of Freud at a time when "Americans absorbed a version of Freudianism that presented the sexual impulse as an insistent force demanding expression."[32] In reality, however, English sexologist and psychologist Havelock Ellis's work was far more influential. For despite its nineteenth-century pre-Freudian conceptual framework, Ellis's work boldly defended unorthodox practices generally considered perverse, such as self-gratification and homosexuality. He believed that passion, not repression should rule the day.[33] But more generally, opinions on sexuality expressed by other authors of the period also foreshadowed a sea change, inasmuch as defending "sexual expressiveness" indicated the arrival of a larger trend that "was taking sex beyond a procreative framework confines of reproduction . . . [and] attributed to sexuality the power of individual self-definition." In other words, "sex was becoming a marker of identity, the wellspring of an individual's true nature" and its expression had to be encouraged for the sake of a more stable social order.[34]

This initial reception of Freudian thought, however, failed to recognize the existence and function of the unconscious, thereby making it incompatible with successive trends that inextricably linked the issue of identity with the subject's unconscious, that is, with his/her personal history. In fact, this second version of Freudian thought came to dominate the American sociomedia scene beginning in the 1940s on through the early 1960s and took its place as a constitutive element of the cinematic imaginary of those years. This is a phenomenon that is addressed in chapters 3 and 4. Here, however, my aim has been to underscore the importance of the passage from a positivistic idea of "sexual expressiveness" to that of a psychoanalytic split according to which the subject irredeemably falls prey to a conflict between his/her conscious and unconscious processes. Indeed, cinema of the 1930s is a cinema that basically believes in the former. This is not to say, however, that anticipatory fissures of the succeeding phase are not also present—for example, in the Von Sternberg/Dietrich films and, more generally, those productions directly linked to Weimar style cinema, and especially horror. Yet the dominant model of desire and subjectivity underpinning 1930s cinema is in tune with the positivistic ideas on sexuality we have examined.

SEXUALITY/MATERNITY/EXHIBITION: THE EXCESS OF *BLONDE VENUS*

Blonde Venus represents a radical case in the representation of the female subject. In fact, it is one of the most revelatory films because of its complex symbolic investments in the image of woman. Here, the protagonist moves between numerous conflicting female identities. In a dizzying metaphorical and spatial trajectory, she goes from wife/mother, to lover/performer, to mother-on-the-run/prostitute, to great artist/solitary woman, and ultimately to the highly contradictory and bizarre combination of mother/diva. In this way, the film fuses diverse antithetical lifestyles, available to women at that time, investing Dietrich's body with contradictory impulses. First she is sexually virtuous, then transgressive. Later, she dedicates herself to home and family, and then she returns to work as a singer and performer. By contrast, similar films of the period tended to feature more homogeneous or consistent characters. They dealt singularly with a fallen woman's past, or a gold digger in search of a husband, or a Cinderella kissed by fortune, or a working girl trying to better herself.[35] *Blonde Venus*, however, adds them all up in a contradictory vision of the relation between vice and virtue, between maternity and sexuality. As E. Ann Kaplan has argued, the film is based on "the contradiction between sexuality and mothering," which undercuts "the ideal nuclear family."[36] Moreover, Dietrich's character demonstrates that motherhood and prostitution are not necessarily mutually exclusive lifestyles. Rather, prostitution is a means of financially sustaining motherhood. Likewise, Dietrich's singing salary and allowance from lover

Nick Townsend/Cary Grant allow her to pay for her husband's expensive medical treatment back in Germany. And in this way, Dietrich/Helen Faraday demonstrates her ability to provide for her family while at the same time expose her husband's inadequacies. As Kaplan has remarked, "the female spectator may read the masculinized female image as a resisting image."[37]

Among the numerous Von Sternberg/Dietrich films, *Blonde Venus* is the one that has principally inspired feminist scholars. One could even make the case that various strains of film feminism have perennially returned to this film because it represents an ideal case for Gender Studies.[38] In fact, the work's richness and complexity go well beyond Marlene Dietrich's presence and can be attributed to many of its peculiar visual and structural elements. For example, it substitutes elliptical narrative structure in place of classical linearity, plastic images in place of the usual dynamism, and visual sensuality in place of classic sobriety, and it remarkably intertwines notions of femininity, animalism, and the exotic all in the same character.

In one such study, Gaylyn Studlar has claimed that the film's elliptical and repetitive structure is antithetical to classical principles of causality and linearity. For her, this opposition must be seen as a formal and aesthetic solution to the kind of masochism founded on suspended and unsatisfied desires.[39] Moreover, according to Lea Jacobs, even instances of censorship have contributed to the film's elliptical form, with important episodes or details being omitted and thus rendering less than clear the motivation of certain characters. In fact, contrary to the idea that the Hays code was introduced in force in 1934, the Studio Relations Committee, or section of the MPPDA in charge of censorship, was already fully operational by 1929. In particular, Los Angeles offices were in charge of monitoring screenplays before they entered production. By 1931, this practice had become practically obligatory and took the form of intense negotiation between the studios and the censorship office directed by Jason Joy. Thus, Jacobs claims that *Blonde Venus* actually shows how censorship aided the director in his pursuit of "elliptical or indirect modes of representation" by eliminating scenes where female characters underwent explicit processes of "moral degradation." Ultimately, then, it was the production house that was dissatisfied as producers would have preferred an ending more sympathetic to the male lead, ideally swapping out Herbert Marshall for the more attractive Cary Grant. Instead, Sternberg chose to reunite Helen with her less attractive husband, thereby satisfying censor officials and conforming "to the rule of compensating moral values," according to which a character's fall is then compensated by moral rehabilitation.[40]

Nevertheless, the ending is indeed highly contradictory since it condenses the many images of womanhood that can be found throughout the film. For instance, when Dietrich visits her son dressed in an evening gown during the last scene, newspapers have just announced her engagement to Nick. The diva's elegant glamour strikes a sharp contrast with the modesty of her apartment and role as mother. Moreover, in the preceding episode, Dietrich dressed herself in men's clothing at the Paris opera house, cutting the figure of a mannish lesbian and thus establishing one of her signature diva looks.[41] But this diva image—developed since *The Blue Angel* (Von Sternberg, 1930)—could not be farther from Dietrich's return to domesticity at the conclusion of the film. Thus, the film's final transgression lies in its ambition to move beyond antithetical models of womanhood, in which one recognizes both active female sexuality and a mother's willingness to perform self-sacrifice. Such roles are not balanced in equal measure, however. The image of the sexualized mother that closes the film is strong and recalls Dietrich's struggle throughout the film to raise her son on her own. In *Blonde Venus*, the mother/son relation is privileged in a family dynamic that clearly evokes the oedipal triangle. The paternal function, on the other hand, is not only marginalized but declared irrelevant.

Figures 1 and 2. Marlene Dietrich in *Blonde Venus*, 1932.

But the most fascinating and important image that assures Dietrich's autonomy from male hegemony is Marlene's performance as a singer, in particular the famous number "Hot Voodoo." In this sequence, the diva emerges from a gorilla costume and sings accompanied by rhythmic drumming and a group of "savages." This number is an excessive exhibition that renders the relation between femininity and animalism explicit, breaking all rules of decorum. Thus, the episode's transgressive character aligns with what I see as this period's cinematic exhibitory excess, or desire to produce shock in place of "psychological absorption" more common to classic modalities.

Furthermore, the early 1930s can be characterized by multiple forms of cinematic exhibitionism that signal the emergence of spectacular or sensational devices that—as Mulvey had shown with respect to the female body—stop the narrative flow and more directly interpellate the spectator's attention.[42] In fact, the supremacy of the visual and the sensual over the narrative is common to many different film forms and genres of the period: the spectacular aerial shots and colored sequences of *Hell's Angels* (H. Hughes/J. Whale, 1930); the monsters in *Freaks* (T. Browning, 1932); and horror films like *Dracula* (T. Browning, 1931), *Frankenstein* (J. Whale, 1931), *Svengali* (A. Mayo, 1931), *Dr. Jekyll and Mr. Hyde* (R. Mamoulian, 1931) and *King Kong* (M. Cooper and E. Schoedsack, 1933). But of particular interest are Mae West's excessive displays in *I'm No Angel* (W. Ruggles, 1933) and *She Done Him Wrong* (L. Sherman, 1933).[43] However much she differs from Dietrich in personality and style, the two share much in common, especially as *Blonde Venus* relates to *I'm No Angel*. In this film West's persona is constructed by emphasizing the artist's "sensationalism" as she performs at the circus. In fact, when Tira/West offers herself to the anxious all-male audience, the dynamics between object and subject of the gaze seem to reverse themselves. Tira imposes her excessively sexualized body on the spectator, minimizing the distance between performer and audience. And just as Dietrich did, Tira will augment her powers of seduction and attraction by associating femininity with animalism as she tames lions and ultimately puts her head inside a lion's mouth. But the attractional matrix of the film is most readily evinced through a peculiar representation of the artist's public. The high-ranking New Yorkers that attend Tira's show visibly express their desire to be "excited" as they anxiously await the show's climax. After the show, they even file into her dressing room to thank her: "What a thrill you gave us." Thus, as their excessive sexuality borders on animalism, Mae West and Marlene Dietrich not only represent strong and transgressive images of female self-determination, but their performances also accord with procedures common to early 1930s cinema, drawing on the techniques of the aesthetic of attractions of preclassic cinema.[44]

SPECTACLE AND SOCIAL MOBILITY: *GOLD DIGGERS OF 1933*

The visual dynamism and pyrotechnic spectacle of Warner Brothers (WB) musicals directed by Busby Berkeley are probably the most radical of the period. After its initial popularity in the early sound years—above all thanks to the revue format—the musical went through a crisis period during the 1931–1932 season. When the fate of the genre seemed all but sealed, Broadway choreographer Busby Berkeley burst onto the scene in Hollywood. He arrived on the west coast in 1930 for *Whoopee!* (T. Freeland, 1930), but remained behind with the encouragement of Mervyn LeRoy who saw his great potential. Berkeley started off 1933 with three films that came out in quick succession. And in a few short months, industry executives had a new star on their hands as well as a new musical form, the backstage musical. First *42nd Street* (L. Bacon), then *Gold Diggers of 1933* (M. LeRoy), and then *Footlight Parade* (L. Bacon) invaded American screens and revived the dying genre. Berkeley's contribution cannot be underestimated, because the backstage musical was the first truly "cinematic" musical that liberated itself from its theatrical roots. Berkeley brought about important innovations in language and filmic mise-en-scène. For argumentative coherence, we acknowledge only some of the most significant aspects of the Berkeley/Warner Brothers musical.[45]

If Fred Astaire/Ginger Rogers films (RKO, 1933–1939) were in perfect harmony with the classical mode, the WB musical was one of the most radical departures from that mode of mise-en-scène. Between story and spectacle, the backstage musical is a dual text in the sense that each register has a different style of directing, or better, an autonomous mode of representation. Granted, the presence of musical numbers and dances was motivated by the dramatization of a show business production, but the peculiarity of this subgenre came out in the opposition between the style of the plot (story) and the style of the musical scenes (spectacle). Different from musicals of the preceding years in which the narrative material was extremely limited, here it was rich with events. Such films depicted the difficulty of daily life for Broadway performers in the darkest years of the Great Depression. And as they hoped to find a producer who would put them in a show, we also saw their on- and off-stage love stories. Thus, the depiction of events on- and off-stage followed two different strategies: while the love stories were founded on a classical unity of scene and analytic montage, the Busby Berkeley show numbers were a visual wonder and inspired dizzying camera movements. And it is precisely this energetic camera that increased the dynamism of the dance numbers. With dozens of male and female dancers moving on self-propelled platforms and dizzying staircases, the camera spectacularized their bodies. Right next to the dancers' open legs in one instant, as in the famous crotch-shots,[46] and then held on high to shoot the floral geometries of the dance from an "impossible position" in the next, Berkeley's innovative camera contradicted the fundamental rules of classical cinematography. Thus, a clear division between diegetic and extra-diegetic audience emerged insofar as the former could not possibly observe what the latter was seeing. In fact, Berkeley's famous floral compositions came to life only thanks to the camera, whether shot from above, or even underwater, as in *Footlight Parade*'s "By a Waterfall."[47] As such, Berkeley's work stands as an extreme anticlassical tendency in cinema of these years and still very much indebted to the visionary qualities of silent cinema. As in *The Last Man* (F. W. Murnau, 1924), *Metropolis* (F. Lang, 1927), *Napoleon* (A. Gance, 1927) or *Man with a Movie Camera*, Berkeley refused to use the camera as a human eye. Instead, he emphasized the greater possibilities of cinematic technique and tried to augment human perception. Here, the aesthetic of attractions was achieved through the inhuman or superhuman devices that did not perpetuate narrative development, but stimulated perception. At the polar opposite of psychological absorption, the visual experience of Berkeley's choreographies activated wonder and amazement as audiences marveled at complex compositions in which bodies lost their humanity and individuality in order to perfect his geometric and mechanical patterns.

Gold Diggers of 1933 is a final example that combines spectacle and the question of female subjectivity in a particularly interesting way. Such a question is unexplored or at best secondary in *42nd Street* and *Footlight Parade*. But in this film, the gold-digger figure is central and her presence renders the plot much more complex and revelatory than the other two films. Such complexity is the result of fusing the backstage musical's semantic materi-

Figure 3. Busby Berkeley's choreography in *Gold Diggers of 1933*, 1933.

als—the dancers' lives outside the theater, the dynamics of dating, and so forth—with those of comedy—the male/female dialectic in conjunction with questions of class that fuels misunderstanding on characters' identities. But rather than focus on the issue of courtship and the relation between male and female dancer (here and in other films interpreted by Dick Powell and Ruby Keeler),[48] my aim is to explore the centrality of the female question in historical terms such that it leads us to a deeper understanding of the female body's function in such spectacular roles. Thus, beyond its construction around a classical/anticlassical, narration/attraction dialectic, I will focus on how the film dramatizes a bifurcated discourse, which is then articulated on the female body and subject. The film, in fact, accumulates dualities and oppositions, whether it be in relation to the era's social imaginary or to cinema's aesthetic mode, and summarizes many of the most innovative dynamics in cinema of this period.

The film begins in a Broadway theater as police interrupt rehearsals to close down a new musical, "We're in the Money," ironically on the verge of bankruptcy. Three penniless female dancers then retire to their little furnished apartment waiting for a new show. Across the hall, an out-of-work pianist interpreted by Dick Powell plays sweet melodies directed at Ruby Keeler, one of the three roommates. A friend named Dixie then informs Keeler that a producer is about to begin a new show and is looking for artists. It is a musical about the Depression, a litany on hunger, on forgotten men who march and sing about their pain. The pianist, hired together with the three girls, then mysteriously procures the $15,000 needed by the producer to begin rehearsals. We learn that Powell does not want to appear on the stage but is forced to do so after the lead singer injures himself the night before the opening. The show has all the characteristics of Berkeley style choreography. The number "Petting in the Park" initially focuses on Powell/Keeler but then gives way to a collective performance that becomes the most spectacular part of the show.[49] The fusion of spectacle and sexuality is particularly noteworthy during the episode in which the female dancers wear tin bodices and then open them with can openers, a true striptease. But the most interesting part of the film happens after the show when newspapers reveal Powell's identity as the descendant of a rich family from Boston. The pianist's family is scandalized by seeing his involvement with popular entertainment and even more so when they come to realize that he has proposed to one of the dancers. His brother and his family lawyer arrive in New York to convince Powell to return and leave the girl or lose his inheritance. Before even meeting her, they judge her to be a "parasitic gold digger" only interested in their fortune. At this point, Keeler's two friends

Figure 4. Ginger Rogers, Ruby Keeler, Joan Blondell, and Aline MacMahon in *Gold Diggers of 1933*, 1933.

decide to hold true to the cliché and take full advantage of their presumed gold-digger reputations. As such, they begin to solicit gifts and invitations from the two elderly aristocrats. But the two Bostonians, at the beginning proud, aloof, and snobbish, soon allow themselves to wallow in "popular" entertainment and end up behaving exactly as the young Powell.

The film concludes with a triple marriage and makes an ironic commentary on the relation between sexes. The cliché of the gold digger as a girl without scruples is subverted. The two young women, who indubitably prefer wealthy husbands, become more than just positive characters. They are lively, nice, of good heart, and profoundly loyal to their female friends. And while it is true that they are motivated by economic security, they also represent an invaluable source of regeneration for the pallid Bostonians, the best thing that could happen to them. Thus, while the image of the oppressive and repressed northeast aristocratic is re-dimensioned, the enterprising and self-determined young woman, whether gold digger or working girl, is once again validated as she enriches the lives of all around her. After all, it is men who benefit the most from the encounter.

2

NORMATIVE DESIRES AND VISUAL SOBRIETY

Apogee of the Classical Model

THE CLASSICAL FORM

Hollywood's classical mode of representation coalesced during the mid-1930s and dominated as such until the end of the decade. For us, classical cinema properly defined is limited to this brief period. As mentioned earlier, the classical period should not be defined in terms of modes of production, so much as representational parameters. Hollywood classicism must be understood as a narrative form in harmony with Aristotelian poetics, such that narrative model itself is based on "the fable or plot." For Aristotle, the fable is "the combination of the incidents, or things done in the story; whereas character is what makes us ascribe certain moral qualities to the agents."[1] In tragedy, "peripeties and discoveries" play fundamental roles. Action determines the nature and quality of characters, but not vice versa: "the first essential, the life and soul, so to speak, of tragedy is the plot."[2] Further, tragedy is an *organic form* since it must represent "a complete whole, with its several incidents so closely connected that the transposal or withdrawal of any one of them will disjoin and dislocate the whole. For that which makes no perceptible difference by its presence or absence is no real part of the whole."[3] Suffice it to say, classical Hollywood cinema owes a considerable debt to Aristotelian poetics. For beyond the few corresponding elements mentioned here, it should be noted that Hollywood screenplay writing manuals have directly referred to the *Poetics* since the early 1910s.

Traditionally, critical discourse has analyzed classical cinema from this perspective. Even luminaries as diverse as Bazin and Bordwell share this foundational point of departure. At bottom, each defines classicism as a restyling or simplification of the Aristotelian model. Indeed, Bordwell acknowledges his debt to Bazin, underscoring how the French critic's notion of classicism resembles the way Hollywood defined its own cinema. In the opening remarks of his work on classical style he states that "the principles which Hollywood claims as its own rely on notions of decorum, proportion, formal harmony, respect for tradition, mimesis, self-effacing craftsmanship, and cool control of the perceiver's response—canons which critics in any medium usually call 'classical.'"[4] While the New Wave's future directors were claiming authorship for some of the Hollywood directors, Bazin's thinking was going into a different direction. In "La politique des auteurs" (1957), Bazin states that Hollywood's global superiority could not be credited only to a select group of influential directors. Its success was due primarily to "the vitality and, in a certain sense, the excellence of a tradition. Hollywood's superiority is only incidentally technical; it lies much more in what one might call the American cinematic genius, something which should be analyzed, then defined, by a sociological approach to its production." As such, "it follows that directors are swept along by this powerful surge; naturally their artistic course has to be plotted according to the currents—it is not as if they were sailing as their fancy took them on the calm waters of a lake."[5] Thus, one can easily make the case that American cinema is a classical art, and as such, more admirable as a system than for its singular auteurs.

In "The Evolution of the Language of Cinema" (1950–1955), Bazin argues that American (and French) cinema between 1930 and 1940 "has reached a well-balanced stage of maturity." Moreover, by 1938 or 1939 the talking film "has reached a level of classical perfection as a result, on the one hand, of the maturing of different kinds of drama developed in part over the past ten years and in part inherited from the silent film, and, on the other, of the stabilization of technical progress." The main feature of classicism is the standardization of montage techniques in constructing a scene through analytic decoupage. Accordingly, we witness "the almost complete disappearance of optical effects such as superimpositions and even . . . the close-up." Bazin seizes the distinctive strokes and effects of such practices, not only finding a "verisimilitude of space," as spectators understand the exact position of characters "even when a close-up eliminates the décor," but also in the "exclusively dramatic or psychological" intentions of montage itself.[6] Thus, Bordwell's later formulations on the construction of classical space and articulation of stylistic indexes appear as amplification and enrichment of Bazin's ideas, even if not merely reducible as such. But while we do not have space for a more detailed analysis of Bazin and Bordwell's paradigms, a fundamental difference between them must be underscored. For Bazin, the use of depth of field and the long take after 1940 presented a challenge to classicism. For Bordwell, however, these same innovations—as with Technicolor, panoramic formats, and stereophonic sound, which will come later—did not invalidate classical form but rendered it stronger. In fact, according to the American scholar, "the classical style promptly assigned the new techniques to already-canonized functions; reciprocally, some of the new devices extended and enriched the classical paradigm."[7]

But in order to satisfactorily define classicism as a mode of representation, we need at least one more element overlooked by both Bazin and Bordwell. At the analytic crossroads between semiotics and psychoanalysis lies the question of the film's meaning as it is produced for the spectator. We are not interested in an abstract discussion of narrative device and codes or stylistic indexes, as in Bazin and Bordwell, but rather analytically verifiable pathways of meaning, which are neither infinite nor univocal. Such pathways inscribe themselves in the horizon of desire and make classical film a mode of narrating and representing the world in which the spectator puts his/her desire to the test. In other words, the spectator achieves knowledge and an idea of her/himself through and in relation to the other on the screen. Here, the subject is not involved in empty or abstract mechanisms of mere cognition as Bordwell would say, but encounters desires, lifestyles, and historically bound forms of identity through the film. A film's meaning can therefore be cultivated only through an analysis that considers style, narrative, and the imaginary in relation to the particular dynamics of material and cultural history. Finally, the spectator is not neuter but gendered and engages with a film accordingly. Thus, whether it be the notion of subject or that of text and narration, each implicates *processes* and not fixed structures. Or as Teresa de Lauretis has argued, subjectivity is "constituted in the relation of narrative, meaning, and desire; so that the very work of narration is the engagement of the subject in certain positionalities of meaning and desire."[8]

THE AGE OF ORDER AND THE DEMISE OF THE NEW WOMAN

The classical mode of representation dominating American cinema in the second half of the 1930s may be described as a convergence of normative desires and lifestyles and a mode of storytelling founded on action and dialogue. With respect to cinema of the early 1930s, this change is significant in that it sanctioned a renewed trust in order, rationality, and the possibility of objectively explaining all human action and behavior. Consequently, the classical text's organic quality lay not only in the functionality of each part with respect to the whole but also in the understanding of individual action with respect to social norms. Because the subject of classical cinema has not yet lived through the Freudian split, and is therefore unaware of any sense of lack, the quality of his/her desire is not linked to individual psychic experience, but is explainable in rational and social-collective terms.

Classical cinema mainly supported traditional forms of identity and lifestyle, especially for women. While a major figure like the New Woman was relegated to the margins, a renewed trust in masculinity emerges in the cinematic imaginary of the period. Indeed, it was the combination of a purely invisible style and a rational mode of storytelling with a new set of images concerning female and male desire that accounted for the shift in Hollywood's ideological project. What Robert Sklar has called the "Age of Order" implies a reversal vis-à-vis the gender discourse of the previous years. Transgressive sexual attitudes were no longer supported and women's working careers were similarly negated. The only trajectory available for women was marriage. More generally, while in the previous years cinema preferred to focus on working women and their social rise, now women's experience was mainly framed within marriage and the home. Emancipatory plots often had a negative outcome, while the formation of the heterosexual couple became the new model of reference, the era's dominant lifestyle. The classical status of cinema thus relied on a specific ideological project. In contrast to the earlier period, as well as to post–World War II cinema, classical cinema generally narrated plots of integration: that is why comedy is such a key genre in the period. Comedy provided the framework through which this new couple could be easily inserted into a preexisting social order. While it is true that the screwball heroine usually enjoys sexual and social freedom, the narrative nevertheless develops within the precincts of marriage or remarriage in an upper-class scenario.[9]

At the end of the chapter we discuss the politics of desire of the screwball comedy and argue that the genre expressed Hollywood's only progressive stance vis-à-vis women at that historical moment. The scenario had in fact dramatically changed in relation to the earlier years, both in the social and the filmic context. While in the early 1930s women had dominated the industry at all levels—onscreen, at the box office, in the audience—now the values of masculinity and family came back with a vengeance. For instance, an analysis of late 1930s box-office returns clearly shows a renewed interest in images of order, normalcy, and masculinity. We have already mentioned the inversion of gender in the divistic system, when male *divi* once again topped the charts. But other data also show great public interest in traditional images of family and family values. Take, for instance, child-star Shirley Temple's triumph at the box office, four years running from 1935 to

1938. There was also Temple's male adolescent counterpart Mickey Rooney who dominated from 1939 to 1941. And not to be forgotten, Norwegian Olympic ice-skating champion Sonja Henie starred in a series of extremely popular sport films. At the same time, the virile Clark Gable was not far behind, second only to Temple. Likewise, the public adored adventure films—a typically male genre—and costume dramas, while another male genre—the biopic—was highly praised by critics and a favorite at the Oscars.[10] As we will see, such genres were not only adequate to address the classical thrust for linear structures, but they all focused on male agency and relegated female characters to marginal roles.

Popularity of the Astaire/Rogers partnership also reached its height during the mid-1930s. And here, it is enough to make a superficial comparison between their musicals and the Busby Berkeley films to see the shift in the representation of gender identity. It is easy to note how the hyperbolic elements and visual excesses of Berkeley's films, in relation to both female sexuality and mise-en-scène, are totally tamed in the Astaire/Rogers films where female body as well as shooting and editing techniques follow classical precepts.[11] Therefore, while male genres and stars had a greater impact than their female counterparts, romantic couples and child or adolescent actors developed the theme of marriage and family in a forceful way.

In this scenario, it is not surprising that, outside the screwball comedy, female independence is typically frustrated. In fact, in 1930s cinema strong women were often nasty so that they could rightfully be punished. Bette Davis, for example, was the prototype of the "Hollywood Bitch" and had her nastiness toward weaker men usually turned against her. It is enough to think of *Of Human Bondage* (J. Cromwell, 1934), *Jezebel* (W. Wyler, 1938), and later *The Letter* (W. Wyler, 1940) and *The Little Foxes* (W. Wyler, 1941).[12] But perhaps the best example of the dynamics here described is *Dark Victory* (E. Goulding, 1939) in which a rich and pampered Davis concerns herself with anything but marriage. In the habit of passing her days at horse races and parties, she suddenly discovers that an incurable disease will cut her life short. As a result, she begins to reflect on the "true values" of life. Her doctor falls in love with her and she returns that love, agreeing to marry him though she has little time left to live. Together, they leave the city—a place of cultured entertainment and diversion—for the countryside in Vermont. There, she learns to be a good wife, tending to her hardworking husband and leading a simple life. After making sense of her life as a dutiful and passive wife, Judith will die alone in her bedroom while her husband is away at a conference. One can easily speculate that her early death is the direct effect of her modern lifestyle: had she spent less time in having fun and paid more attention to her symptoms, Judith could still be alive. Marriage is a sort of redemption for her past "sins," the choice she should have made from the start. The change in lifestyle is complete and involves every aspect of her everyday experience: Judith starts as a single, independent, and urban woman and ends as a married housewife in the countryside.

But Dorothy Arzner's films also tackle the question of female independence. In *Christopher Strong* (1933), Katherine Hepburn plays a successful aviatrix who has a relationship with a married man. Upon becoming pregnant, however, she crashes her plane to commit suicide. In *Craig's Wife* (1936), the protagonist chooses marriage for fear of ending up in poverty like her mother. But as she develops an obsessive attachment to her house, she totally alienates herself from the affections of those most dear to her. Thus, in Arzner's films, the autonomous or unconventional woman remains single in the best of circumstances or dies young in the worst.

The shift in representation of female desire is further evident if we look at Barbara Stanwyck's career throughout the decade. Perhaps even more than Joan Crawford, no one embodied the role of a poor girl aspiring to glamour and riches better than Stanwyck. In the early 1930s, both actresses had interpreted key roles as young women attempting to raise their social status through hard work and/or sex. Crawford and Stanwyck played working-class women who moved to the big city in search of a job, as well as a variety of fallen and/or redeemed women. In *Ladies of Leisure* (F. Capra, 1930), Stanwyck plays Kay Arnold, a party girl hired by Jerry Strong, a young aristocrat, to become his model. The two fall in love but the man's parents strongly disapprove of their relationship. Jerry does not allow his parents to persuade him to leave the woman, but Kay sacrifices herself to free the man. She initially decides to resume her old life, but her feelings are so strong that she later decides to commit suicide by jumping into the ocean. After being rescued and brought to the hospital, she is joined by Jerry and the two declare their mutual love. In *Night Nurse* (W. Wellman, 1931), Stanwyck is Lora Hart, a determined young woman who arrives in New York to look for a job. Lora begins to train as a nurse in a hospital and becomes close friends with B. Maloney (Joan Blondell), a more experienced nurse who helps her get adjusted to the new situation. The two women, who share a room in the hospital to save money, build a strong friendship and show little interest in men. In *Forbidden* (F. Capra, 1932), Stanwyck has a married man's baby, and in *Shopworn* (N. Grinde, 1932), she is a hard-working waitress who falls in love with a college student. Her social rise will take place after several dramatic twists. In *Baby Face* (A. E. Green, 1933) one of her most famous roles, Stanwyck plays Lily Powers, a strong young woman who tries to cope with her abusive father, a violent man who runs a speakeasy where Lily serves drinks. A famous censorship case in pre-Code Hollywood, the film contains among the most explicit of sexual content during the period. Lily's father has prostituted his daughter to his customers for a few bucks since she was fourteen.[13] Lily's life is miserable; her only comforts are Chico, the African American maid who works for the family, and Mr. Cragg, one of her father's customers. Mr. Cragg is a cultivated man and is very fond of Lily. He urges her to leave the place and "go to some big city." Indirectly quoting Nietzsche's "Will to power," he tells her "to use men, not be used by them, to get things."[14] After her father accidentally dies, Lily and Chico leave Pittsburgh and go to New York. Lily will indeed follow Mr. Cragg's suggestion *à la lettre* and use men to climb the social ladder. While the film resorts to a sentimental tone only at the very end, it provides a harsh and cynical representation of sexual relations in urban America. Yet it is far from critical of Lily's behavior. On the contrary, *Baby Face* shows that sex is the only means a woman has to attract men's attention. Lily, in fact, is very good at her job, but it is only when her bosses realize she is pretty that they consider her for promotion. Similarly, when the new president of the bank she works for sees her in the Paris agency, he is very surprised to hear that her division has improved its business by 40 percent since he can only judge her by her good looks. But Lily is very capable at her job and is also a hard worker. If she needs powerful men to succeed, it is because women can, on their own, be only secretaries at best.[15]

In the following years Stanwyck continued to play working-class characters struggling for upward mobility. But then her desire would be repeatedly frustrated. In *The Bride Walks Out*, she is Carolyn, a fashion model forced by her husband (Michael Martin) to quit her job after they get married. As she realizes that her husband's salary is not enough, Carolyn goes back to modeling. She keeps her work a secret to protect Michael's pride. But her decision will seriously jeopardize her marriage. Once her husband finds out about her job, he leaves her. After their divorce, Carolyn dates a rich man and is about to marry him when she learns that Michael has accepted a dangerous job in South America. In a comic ending, Carolyn will prevent her husband from taking the boat but in the process will get herself arrested. From inside the jeep, she promises Michael she will quit her job.

In the more well-known *Stella Dallas*, Stanwyck plays Stella Martin, an attractive young woman living with her working-class family in a factory town.

Stella wishes to improve her social status and meets the rich Stephen Dallas, who manages the factory where Stella's brother works. Stephen, who has been forced to end his engagement, is lonely and appreciates Stella's company and lively manners. He falls in love and asks her to marry him. After their daughter Laurel is born, their marriage begins to crumble. Stephen seems to love Stella, but he cannot tolerate her uneducated manners and crude behavior. When Stephen is offered a better job in New York, Stella decides to stay in their house with Laurel, knowing that she'll never be a part of her husband's social circle. From then on, the two will lead separate lives. In New York, Stephen meets his ex-fiancée, Helen Morrison, who is now a widow with three children. As Stephen and Laurel visit Helen's elegant house and attend her parties, the film's discourse on class becomes clear. While Laurel is extremely attached to her mother and Stella cannot think of anything but pleasing her daughter, the film's heartbreaking narrative unfolds, making their relationship impossible. Stella is a loving mother, but she is also cheap and vulgar, most obviously in her choice of clothes, accessories, and friends. On the other hand, like her father and his new fiancée, Laurel is polite and understated in her behavior and mannerisms. The film's ideological project focuses precisely on taste. Stella's bad taste is the visible sign of her working-class status and is evidenced in her clothes, her home, and her raucous company. In the same way, Helen's proper behavior and controlled manners are reflective of her upper-class status, which is similarly evidenced in her clothing, her home, and her polite friends. When Stella realizes that Laurel will be better off in life without her, she sacrifices her love so that her daughter can attain the social status she once wished for herself. In the much discussed ending Stella gazes up at her daughter's wedding framed by the wrought-iron stakes of the fence behind which she is made to stand, and by the window through which she sees the wedding taking place in Helen's lavish home. As Ann Kaplan has stated, the film's closure "pulls the spectator toward dominant patriarchal class and gender ideology."[16]

Having sketched the broad contours of the era's new politics of desire, I now investigate the relationship between formal order and subjective normativity by looking closely to one of the decade's most famous comedies, Frank Capra's *It Happened One Night*. Capra's film shows a hidden reality lurking behind the freshness and independence of Claudette Colbert's flapper, i.e., a strong desire for marriage and the male protection-domination that goes along with it. Then we consider classical cinema's turn to masculinity by analyzing William Dieterle's biopic *The Life of Emile Zola* (1937) and Howard Hawks's male adventure film *Only Angels Have Wings* (1939).

IT HAPPENED ONE NIGHT: THE FLAPPER GETS MARRIED

It Happened One Night is a film of undisputed critical and popular success. Winning five Oscars, it was not only considered an auteurial text, but also a paradigmatic example of studio style.[17] Having eliminated any vestige of either silent cinema's visionariness or attractionalism of many early 1930s films, Capra's is perfectly classical in plot, camera work, and editing. But here, we are not interested in simply confirming the film's classical form, so much as in analyzing the relationship between its representation of gender and the sociomedial imaginary.

Classical style's core structure is founded on a correspondence between narrative and formal logic, i.e., motivated action or cause-effect relations. In other words, just as each action is caused by the preceding and effects what follows, the same can be said for a film's modes of shooting and sequence of shots. Moreover, as camera work and editing are subordinated to narrative, motivation and causality render them invisible through the enunciative act. And in turn, these driving forces are anchored in characters.[18]

A character's *strong* desire is a fundamental attribute of classical cinema, which further distinguishes it from 1940s cinema, when the inexorable corrosion of a character's unity began. In other words, if the 1930s protagonist is a full subject "without an unconscious" who automatically translates desire into action, the protagonists of film noir and the woman's film are structured around a gap between psyche and body, interrupting the subject's ability to act.

Ultimately, classical cinema's capacity to represent the world is based on dialectics, or the systematic opposition of both semantic and technical-formal elements. Likewise, its power of seduction and ideological impact are founded on the narrative mechanism's ability to obscure both syntactic and semantic operations. In fact, a detailed analysis of formal structures within a given text—as Raymond Bellour and Stephen Heath first taught us[19]—demonstrate how meaning is highly codified. The truly classical text is thus "more closed" than that of the early 1930s or the 1940s, in the sense that it employs formal solutions to more convincingly resolve narrative problems. This important prerogative distinguishes cinema of the latter half of the 1930s from that of preceding and successive periods. Based on the convergence of classical style and normative desires and lifestyles the cinema of these years posed itself as a fundamental producer of identity models. For if it is true that Hollywood cinema is founded on a "system of genres," or plurality of coextensive genres, it is also true that such a system has different connotations in various periods and that "genres of integration" dominated the second half of the decade.[20]

Formal and narrative dialectics are so central to classical style that any interpretation of its textual and spectatorial mechanisms cannot do without structural analysis. Informing the classical text at all levels, these differences systematically converge most effectively in the comedy's traditional male-female opposition. In *It Happened One Night*, such a mechanism is activated through a peculiar regulation of the film's first two sequences or "movements," which introduce female and male protagonists, respectively.[21] Moreover, we also note the depiction of two very different lifestyles. In the first sequence, Ellie Andrews, a young and rich heiress, is in her family's luxurious yacht fighting with her father about her intended marriage. In the second episode, Peter Warne, a journalist who has just been fired, is drunk and also fighting with his boss over the phone. Their juxtaposition immediately establishes two oppositional lifestyles and levels of social standing. Ellie is rich and pampered. Peter is a morally grounded, but penniless, blowhard. The typical work-play dichotomy also reinforces their two contrasting social identities. Their common act of rebellion against a paternal-authority figure, however, also establishes an analogy between Ellie and Peter, formally anticipating their eventual union. But before this can happen, the two must mitigate their strong personal and social differences through change, though mostly on the part of the female character. Ellie is, in fact, an energetic and willful young woman, rebelling against the father who opposes her marriage. But she is also spoiled and unaware of what is going on around her. Thus, the trip from Miami to New York City constitutes her *Bildung*, or maturation into adulthood and exposure to the poverty and misery of Appalachia. Here, Capra succeeds in operating on a double level, both narrative and ideological. He is simultaneously able to motivate the character's personal growth while also injecting the film with a good dose of populism. For example, there is the famous sequence in which Ellie attempts to shower at a motel. A long tracking shot follows the girl as she gets closer to a group of women waiting, depicting a particularly memorable slice of Depression-era life. Indeed, Capra's signature truly lies in his ability to integrate the screwball plot, full of rapid-fire dialogue and male-female physical comedy, with "realistic" representations of subaltern classes. And in this sense, one can also reconcile the numerous bus-interior tracking shots as the camera follows the protagonists' movements while at the same time capturing the bodies and faces of poverty.[22]

The film's narrative trajectory focuses on the couple's evolving relationship, from their initial mutual disdain to their ultimately reciprocal affection for one another. And right from the beginning, its mise-en-scène also shows a synthesis of dialogue and the rules of classical continuity. The quick rhythm of shots—the bickering between father and daughter, for example—and precise connections between ensure invisible style. There are also no moments of visual spectacle, which in turn draws attention to the film's perfect narrative functionality. The story can therefore unfurl according to principles of motivated action and causality. Thus, Ellie's desire to marry Westley in New York City also affords Peter the chance to regain his job because of their coincidental meeting. From the outset, Peter helps Ellie to keep sight of herself. But in the process, he falls for her just as she him. As in other important films of the period—*Stagecoach* (J. Ford, 1939), for instance—the trip is the paradigmatic form of the classical narrative's defining characteristic of forward movement. This idea manifests itself here as the protagonists complete a voyage, both literal and metaphorical, each incrementally evolving as they go from a point of departure (Miami) to arrival (New York City). As a result, the film's final resolution can be constructed through exquisitely classical formal strategies from the very beginning. First, the film anticipates the finale by establishing a formal union between the protagonists in opposition to their diegetic separation. As mentioned before, Ellie and Peter come onscreen separately, but unite in their common act of rebellion against paternal authority. Then, although upon meeting they will have a mutual disdain for one another, the camera formally unites them without their knowing. After having shot Ellie with her ticket for New York City, the camera moves with combined tracking and panoramic shots from the woman directly to Peter who is talking in a phone booth, *formally intertwining* their destinies in the same shot before the story really even begins. And finally, the "wall of Jericho," or hanging blanket that preserves Ellie's virginity as they share a bedroom, ultimately reveals the unstable and fictitious nature of their separation.

Different from the sophisticated comedies of Hawks, Cukor, and McCarey, Capra's film maintains a traditional vision of sexuality and male-female relationships in line with a "return to order" rooted in the New Deal.[23] As a result, most critics label Capra's work as "utopian cinema." However, by reanalyzing the film in the context of its contemporary images of gender identity, a strong grounding in the period's social imaginary emerges. This is much less true of the screwball comedies that followed. And here, we refer not only to the well-studied representation of Depression-era realities and misery but also the male and female figures that were anything but utopian. In fact, such figures were decidedly conservative according to both the cultural imaginary and iconography of the time.

Christina Simmons has analyzed American theories on sexuality that emerged in the 1920s and 1930s, not only looking at work done by sociologists and psychologists, but also lettered scholars and journalists in those same years. Through her research, she has been able to define a spectrum of male and female typologies present in the collective imaginary, ranging from traditional modes of being to innovative and more modern lifestyles. Simmons underscores that despite the indubitable gains of women—culminating with the right to vote in 1920—advances in the female condition attenuated over the course of the 1930s, and may have even regressed to the point of renewed levels of subordination.[24] Moreover, Blanche Wiesen Cook has also shown how the political economy and inequitable Rooseveltian social policy contributed to this state of affairs. It is enough to think of the early measure that mandated the dismissal of all married women who, like their husbands, worked for government administration. Despite the First Lady's untiring commitment to women's condition, federal assistance for female employment was almost nonexistent.[25]

According to Simmons, there are four female figures that dominated the period. The new value given to sexual expressivity corroded the image of the "respectable married woman," cornerstone of Victorian morality. Likewise, the "prudish Victorian matriarch" who "disciplines her children harshly and dominates her husband as well" also appeared as an inheritance of a bygone era, mostly because she ignored male sexual needs.[26] The career woman or feminist on the other hand, was little admired for opposite reasons. In thinking of herself, she too showed little interest for men, but also scared them off with her excessive independence. Often, the career woman was depicted as "hostile to sexuality but secretly frustrated and desperate for male attention. Other writers suggested that such women could be lesbians."[27] It was the flapper, however, that captured public interest and became the ideal positive female figure since she "both embodied the popular notion of the free woman and retained a softness that did not threaten men." In fact, the flapper was an ideal combination of different elements that succeeded in satisfying male desire. On the one hand, she was active and perspicacious, venturing into the male world and fleeing the domestic environment. On the other, she "cared more about men and babies than about her paid work or her development as an individual through work." At the same time she was interested in sex, which she saw as a normal element of life. But her behavior was never libertine. Ultimately, the flapper was a romantic girl who wanted to be protected by her chosen man.[28] And as such, she was as much the ideal female role model as ideal companion of the "healthy male" or

Figure 5. Claudette Colbert in *It Happened One Night*, 1934.

analogously positive image of masculinity that emerged during the period. But in exchange for this renewed attention to female sexuality, the male had to be reeducated to better understand the needs of his updated companion. He had to reject any remnant of the "sexual brute." Yet he could not be weak either. In fact, just like the excessively independent female, the sexually timid man was often branded homosexual. Thus, the "healthy male animal" not only had to relate to women but embrace their newly expressive sexuality. Sensitive and at the same time decisive, he therefore assumed the function of guide toward matrimony as the flapper gladly ceded him command.[29] In other words, the "flapper marriage" "can best be understood as modernizing male dominance through unions in which vital, modern, yet pliant flappers' sweethearts formed relationships with sensitive yet still masterful men."[30]

As protagonist in previous films, for example C. B. De Mille's *Cleopatra* (1934), Claudette Colbert seemed a natural choice to play the flapper in *It Happened One Night*. Ellie Andrews had all the verve of this almost mythic figure, defined by Fitzgerald as "lovely, and expensive, and about nineteen."[31] She had a will of steel, strong desire for independence, and an athletic body. But if the occasion arose, she could also be sexy. For example, Ellie escapes from her father's yacht by agilely diving into the sea, a little like the heroines of the serial-queen melodramas of the 1910s. Later after having missed her bus and not a cent on her, she does not hesitate to raise her skirt in hopes that someone will stop to pick her up. But in spite of her autonomy, Ellie does not know how to get around in the working-class environments where Peter seems to find himself at home. Further, he wastes no opportunity to gain an edge over the beautiful aristocrat, even showing her how to eat breakfast "correctly." Thus, Ellie's autonomy is once again limited and never throws Peter's leadership role into question. She is simply a romantic girl, as can be seen in the exterior-shot scene under the moon's reflection. She desires a strong man's protection and, in spite of her independence, thinks only of marriage. Peter/Gable, on the other hand, embodies the figure of the healthy male animal, having attenuated the brutish sexual aggression that characterized his first films. In *A Free Soul* (C. Brown, 1931), for example, the actor showed a crude and excessive physicality, which was at the same time also captivating and extremely sexy. As one critic noted, in his first films Gable is "a celebration of cruelty. . . . Gable embodied a masculine cruelty, and somehow this, combined with the gorgeousness of his face, became unjustifiably, incorrectly, and inarguably sexy."[32]

In *It Happened One Night*, the flapper's subordination is rather more pervasive and deep than the relation between New Woman and New Man. Not only is the sanctity of marriage reestablished, but also that of family and parent-child relationships. Different from many sophisticated comedies in which parental figures are either absent or indecisive at crucial moments, in Capra's film the parental figure is fundamental. Narrative structure and intersubjective relationships overturn the initial conflict between father and daughter. And not only does Ellie's father change from oppressive tyrant to benevolent patriarch,[33] but he allies with Peter in the literal implementation of the symbolic process described by Lévi-Strauss in which men exchange their women to preserve social order.[34] Thus, at the end of the film when marriage between Ellie and Westley seems inevitable, Peter finally succeeds in meeting with Mr. Andrews and confessing his love for the man's daughter. Mr. Andrews, who had finally come to accept Ellie's marriage to Westley, now understands that his daughter is in love with someone else. Father then invites daughter to be a runaway bride and catch up with Peter who just went out the back door. Thus, if he initially functioned as an obstacle to Ellie's desire, he now facilitates her ultimate happiness. And in this case, much like the primitive societies analyzed by Lévi-Strauss, the woman functions as a go-between or intermediary of communication between men. In turn, she also functions as a sign that assures and maintains the symbolic order. For unbeknownst to Ellie, the conversation between her father and Peter appears as a pact through which men ensure the intergenerational continuity of family and social order, ultimately celebrating the underlying values of American tradition that require female subordination to male.

STRONG MEN AND BIOGRAPHICAL FILM: *THE LIFE OF EMILE ZOLA*

The Life of Emile Zola (W. Dieterle, 1937) was one of the most acclaimed and prized films of its day. It received ten Oscar nominations and won three, including Best Film. It also won the New York Film Critics Circle Award for Best Film, lead the charts of *Film Daily*, placed second on the National Board of Review, and made the *New York Times* Top-Ten film list. Immediately heralded as a masterpiece, it was even more successful than Dieterle's previous biopic, *The Story of Louis Pasteur* (1936). Together with Paul Muni, Dieterle's films thus contributed to making the biopic a "prestige film" on par with the Errol Flynn costume adventure epics. In fact, in the latter 1930s adventure epics and biopics were two of the most important trends to come out of Warner Brothers. The former brought commercial success and the latter critical, transforming Warner Brothers itself into a "prestige studio" like MGM and Paramount.[35] Just as with comedy, adventure epics and biopics were genres particularly representative of classical form and thus vital to our analysis.

In contrast with the leading women in comedy films, epic-adventure films and biopics were typically masculine genres that relegated women to peripheral and secondary roles. In fact, this sort of discrimination was the cornerstone of a *philosophy* that promoted linear and unequivocal representations of the social and historical milieu. Moreover, only a strong male subject was perceived as capable of dominating wild places or complex historical dynamics through physical action and intellectual charge, respectively, thus producing significant change for the common good, his brethren, and country. As such, there are no better examples of a return to order and traditional values than can be found in these genres. In them, trust in human capacity to influence world events appeared exceedingly strong. For on the one hand, the world was legible and its inner dynamics comprehensible. On the other, man was able to change the course of world events provided that he drew on the right values and ideas, or a clear humanistic matrix of truth and justice.

Dieterle's biopics, and especially *The Life of Emile Zola*, also became a hot commodity for critics on the Left struck by the antifascist stance of the film. Recently, Chris Robé has investigated radical film culture of the time and shown that leftists' love for historical biopics betrayed a very reactionary stance toward gender dynamics. In fact, their praise of progressive films such as Dieterle's was implicitly a tribute to masculinity since it developed along with a profound critique (and distaste) for the flapper film and its representation of modern femininity. This belief "highlighted the extent to which America's new found postwar materialism allowed women to occupy new social roles that defied older, Victorian standards." In 1939, Lewis Jacobs stated that the flapper's lifestyle "not only emancipated modern girls from 'woman's passive role' but freed her for masculine pursuits as well."[36] While on the surface the problem seemed to reside in the link between women's desires and consumer culture, deep down for Robé critics were "personally unsettled by the films' representation of powerful female figures who challenged their patriarchal authority and heterosexual assumptions."[37]

The Life of Emile Zola is the second of the four most famous biopics directed by William Dieterle between 1936 and 1940 for Warner Brothers.[38] Most notably indebted to *Disraeli* (A. E. Green, 1929), which originated the biopic, the film exhibits core traits of the genre. The historical character is "a foreigner, an independent thinker, a human rights fighter, an eccentric genius."[39] Zola's life is almost entirely narrated, from his penniless youth in a "typical artist's attic" shared with Paul Cézanne in Paris, all the way to his death just hours before Captain Dreyfus's public rehabilitation. The film focuses on two particular experiences. First, we witness Zola's success as a writer with the publication of his novel *Nana*. Then we have the Dreyfus affair that consumes Zola's mature age. In fact, the film dedicates a significant amount of time to it, focusing on the trial immediately following the writer's dismissal and sentencing to a year in prison. Yet, if it is true that the film is narratively discontinuous at times because the Dreyfus affair is introduced apart from Zola's life and thus irrespective of classical rules of cause and effect, the film nevertheless embodies a truly "classical" faith in truth and objectivity with respect to human actions. Indeed, Zola is a notable public figure who fights his whole life for truth and rectitude in the case of injustice or abuse of power. Moreover, if this dose of populism is rather pronounced, traces of the social-problem film are just as evident. For this genre, along with the backstage musical, constituted the primary mode of production for Warner Brothers in the early 1930s. Thanks to Paul Muni's presence and earlier breakout role, Dieterle's film clearly reminds us of *I Am a Fugitive from a Chain Gang* (1932). In Mervyn LeRoy's famous film, the unjustly accused protagonist spends many years in prison. Then, after having escaped and transformed himself into a model citizen, he is sadly reincarcerated. Finally, after having escaped a second time, Muni arranges a meeting with his former fiancé. Frightened that he will be recognized, however, he takes cover in the darkness. His fiancé then asks how he has been able to get by, to which he responds: "I steal." As such, the film closes on a pessimistic note. Not only is the justice system unjust, but to paraphrase the title of another Warner Brothers social-problem film, *They Made Me a Criminal* (B. Berkeley, 1939), it makes an honest citizen into a criminal.

Accordingly, if social issues remain almost intact in *They Made Me a Criminal*, the protagonist's transformation is then a clear indication of changing attitudes with respect to films of the early 1930s. Incidentally,

They Made Me a Criminal is almost a remake of *I Am a Fugitive from a Chain Gang*, given that the protagonist gains a new lease on life after being erroneously convicted of homicide. But here, when the detective finds the escaped convict in an Arizona town, he comes to realize the man's innocence and decides not to send him back to prison. While the institution would have done differently (i.e., send him back to prison), the detective performs an unrecognized act of human kindness and justice. In Dieterle's film, however, the injustice suffered by Captain Dreyfus is made whole in the end by the institution. His innocence, as with the preceding guilt, is publicly exhibited and the falsely imprisoned military officer not only receives restitution but is also promoted. Here, it must be underscored that acknowledgment of the truth can happen only when the institutions in charge are willing to come clean. Thus, if Zola's detractors prefer government cover-up to save the nation's honor, it becomes incumbent upon Zola to show that the revelation of truth cannot but reinforce national identity and unity. Ultimately, the film drives home a strong patriotic message via moments of national rhetoric—such as Anatole France's commemoration of the writer—firmly in line with Rooseveltian sociopolitics.

The film's classical center then lies in the fact that justice is rendered possible by the action of a single uniquely moral individual. In the film's opening scene, Zola notes to Cézanne that "people prefer lies to the truth." This declaration, pronounced during the hardship of winter while unsuccessfully attempting to plug a draft, is an example of Zola's morality that will become the film's leitmotif. Zola wants to become a singer of human miseries and contribute to the redemption of the most humble while denouncing abuses of power. The plot is constructed along these lines and thus divided into two halves. The first half narrates the writer's popular success in publishing *Nana* after a bout with censors. From then on, his fortune is unstoppable. Zola publishes novel after novel and wins recognition and prizes such as the *Légion d'Honneur*. Nevertheless, his works still provoke resentment in some spheres. As he tells the Chief Censor, who had complained about Zola's critique of the Army, "the facts can be bothersome, but they are true." By now, Zola is rich and famous, having fought and won many battles. He even confides in Cézanne that he would like a little rest. But it is at this point, when both protagonist and film seem to be winding down that the Dreyfus affair inaugurates the second part of the film.

While the writer's friends do not believe the charges, Zola is at first convinced of the captain's guilt. In reality, however, he simply does not want to become involved in the case, vacillating in his most fervent ideals. But his reticence does not last long. One night, with his wife he reads a letter from the *Académie Française* about his probable nomination to the prestigious institution. Then suddenly, Dreyfus's wife arrives. Zola begrudgingly receives her and appears reluctant to consider the evidence she presents that would exonerate her husband. Just as in his youth, he is startled by the news that truth is being covered up. But strangely, no reaction follows and the woman goes away dispirited, forgetting her documents on the table. In the most psychologically pregnant moment of the film, Zola reconsiders and regains his old conscience. This is an interesting juncture in relation to the construction of identificatory processes. Zola is seated at the table. First he looks at Cézanne's self portrait, implicitly remembering the criticism his friend offered him during their last meeting. The painter scolded him for having become "too rich and fat," for having forgotten the ideals of his youth. Then Zola reflects, holding the *Académie*'s letter in one hand and the documents proving Dreyfus's innocence in the other. Looking at the portrait again, he then tears up the *Académie* letter and begins reading Madame Dreyfus's papers. In the following scene, Zola meets his intellectual friends in a bookstore to read them his famous *J'accuse*. His letter insists on "truth," marking a classical reprise of his comment to Cézanne at the beginning of the film. Not only is Zola able to demonstrate Dreyfus's innocence with impeccable evidence, but he also reveals the conspiracy amongst high-ranking military officials to cover it up. The film's second half will therefore be dedicated exclusively to the writer's quest to bring out the truth, while Dreyfus languishes in a cell on Devil's Island. But neither the captain nor his wife ever give up hope, and their frequent intercutting assures a classical transmission of all the necessary information for plot development.

The strong moments of Zola's trial, and in particular his defense, are a reminder of his having done everything in the name of truth and not to discredit France. But pleading to the jury does not solicit their desired sympathy and Zola is sentenced to a year in prison. Friends convince him to flee to London, and from there he continues to sound off with his articles. In the end, however, the new Minister of War grasps the situation and dismisses all the high-ranking military officials. Soon after, London headlines read "Truth Is on the March" and inform Zola of his having won the hard battle. Dreyfus is then liberated and Zola reiterates to his friends on the train back to Paris that, once again, the facts confirm the rule of "cause and effect like roots and trees." It is difficult to find in a film a more explicit definition of the classical narrative device and its central tenet. Ultimately, such a declaration affirms that reality indeed functions according to the principle of cause and effect. Moreover, from the mouth of the protagonist and perhaps its author, the film maintains that by obeying the same rule

Figure 6. Paul Muni in *The Life of Emile Zola*, 1937.

classical cinema also aims to faithfully imitate reality. And this affirmation is also linked to individual action once more at the end of the film. For only the human subject can be the primary agent of such a dynamic, as Anatole France commemorates Zola's unique love and sacrifice for others. According to the film's concluding line, Zola exemplified "a moment of the conscious of man."

The film appears as an anthem for traditional humanistic values thanks to its grandiloquence and pomposity, exacerbated by Muni's good but excessive performance.[40] It is also a tribute to a "great man" in line with the Rooseveltian populism of those years.[41] Therefore, we have nothing of the modernity discussed at length in the previous chapter. Ironically, if cinema gave voice and body to contemporary urban men and women—the same subjects that populated the movie theaters—the biopic brings us back to a premodern social model devoid of transformation and dynamism. To this end, camera work and editing construct the image of a "bigger than life" man. Although Zola is almost always shot in the company of his wife or friends, the camera tends to center the protagonist excessively, often leaving other characters to occupy marginal screen space. In fact, Zola almost always steals the scene and the camera favors him with close-ups, leaving most shots formally unbalanced. The Zola-Cézanne relationship represents an exception in the first half of the film. But in comparison, Alexandrine Zola's visual marginality is much more interesting and relevant to our concerns. Though almost always present with her husband, she is relegated to a secondary role within the shot. And even when the two share screen space, as happens rather frequently, the camera still shows preference for husband rather than wife. Alexandrine certainly provides vital moral support during her husband's fight. However, she is never the subject of action. There is never even any explicit mention of their marriage. Based on the film, one could suppose that she has always been a part of Emile's life—we see her enter the attic with the writer's mother at the beginning of the film—but her role is never rendered explicit, neither through dialogues nor actions. Thus, she appears more like a paid companion than a wife, present but always silent. Certainly these choices support the film's overall image of a man whose entire life qualifies him as an "official hero," or embodiment of the classical American cinema archetype. According to Robert Ray, the official hero was "normally portrayed as a teacher, lawyer, politician, farmer or family man, [who] represented the American belief in collective action, and the objective legal process that superseded private notions of right and wrong."[42] As a defender of law and culture, the official hero also believes in progress and civilization, his polar opposite being the "outlaw hero" who advocates individual freedom from institutional, social, and familial strictures. For just as President Lincoln in *Young Mr. Lincoln* trusts in the written word of the Law, so too does Zola privilege the word as a means of seeking truth. In fact, the film is a triumph of logocentrism. Thus, whether written in novels, published in provocative articles in *L'Aurore*, read in *J'accuse* or proclaimed in Anatole France's final celebration of Zola, words exert a radical dominion of reason over sensation in the world of 1930s cinema.

STRONG MEN AND ADVENTURE FILM: *ONLY ANGELS HAVE WINGS*

Like the biopic, the adventure epic also enjoyed ample public success and represents another fundamentally classical genre. In fact, each genre had a similar mode of articulating gender relations. The agent of action and diegetic space were noticeably masculine, while females played marginal or subordinate roles. In the case of *Only Angels Have Wings*, women were even transformed into foreign bodies, intruders to be expelled by any means necessary. But while Hawks's attention to gender is an auteurial mark—for example, think of how banal *Gunga Din* (G. Stevens, 1939) is in terms of gender relations vis-à-vis *Only Angels Have Wings*—his "excessive" gender politics actually allows us to better understand how male genres of the period support the "containment of desire." Furthermore, comparing the work of "contract directors" like Dieterle with films by auteurs like Hawks is a necessary step if one wants to make a full account of classical style. For as many scholars have noted, the most successful, important, complex, revelatory, and intriguing Hollywood films of the era came from both studio and auteur directors alike.

Just like other Hawks' films of the period, such as *Bringing Up Baby* (1938), *Only Angels Have Wings* is a film with an excessively "obvious style," as Bellour would say citing Rivette. But obviousness or invisibility, far from being only an auteurial characteristic, as Andrew Sarris has also argued, must be seen in its historical context.[43] I would argue, in fact, that Hawks was an auteur with a "permeable style" and he allowed himself to be influenced by whatever modalities of mise-en-scène and shooting techniques happened to be current at the time. Thus, he repeatedly changed his style throughout his career. In fact, it is mostly his films of the 1930s that have an obvious or invisible style, while those of the 1940s and 1950s were more in line with their respective periods. Take, for example, *Gentlemen Prefer Blondes* (H. Hawks, 1953), a musical in Technicolor; or *His Girl Friday* (H. Hawks, 1940), which has evident traces of film noir; or *Red River* (H. Hawks, 1948), which owes its expressive style to contemporary cinematographic trends.

Hawks's duality systematically converges through his representation of male-female relationships. These are not inflected according to uniform, but multiple, parameters. According to Peter Wollen, Hawks's auteurial nature resides in the relationship between adventure film and screwball comedy. In fact, "his real claim as an author lies in the presence, together with the dramas, of their inverse, the crazy comedies. They are the agonised exposure of the underlying tensions of the heroic dramas. . . . Whereas the dramas show the mastery of man over nature, over woman, over the animal and childish; the comedies show his humiliation, his regression."[44] Thus, the excess of female domination in a film like *Bringing Up Baby*—vis-à-vis other comedies of the period—can only be explained in an auteurial context.[45]

In line with the genre dynamics, *Only Angels Have Wings* narrates the classic oedipal trajectory of a male subject who must psychically come to terms with his own masculinity. In contrast to the comedies, male-female relationships are defined in terms of conflict and mutual exclusion. The film's double narrative line deals with Jeff/Cary Grant's effort to save his airmail company from financial ruin and his evolving relationships with men and women along the lines of a classical oedipal trajectory. Thus, the film depicts male friendship inflected with homosexual traits at first that impede movement toward a "correct masculinity," or union between man and woman. For example, whether it be Bonnie/Jean Arthur or ex-fiancé Judy/Rita Hayworth, each female upsets Jeff's precarious homeostasis among male companions in the distant and wild port of Barranca. Surrounded by his fellow pilots and best friend Kid, Jeff is incapable of seriously taking up with a woman because they frighten him and threaten his freedom. In fact, he consciously avoids commitment; he is the typical American hero "in flight from woman and home" as Leslie Fiedler would say.[46] But by necessity, the film aims to contain deviant desire while simultaneously promoting heterosexuality. Jeff and Bonnie's relationship is made possible by means of a classical visual-formal substitution, swapping Jeff's best friend Kid for the woman.

The film's beginning establishes a structural and formal analogy between Kid and Bonnie. For example, the first evening concludes with Bonnie and Kid looking off-camera toward Jeff who goes to meet an airplane out on the runway. In the sequence immediately following, the next morning Kid is awakened by the sound of the plane. He looks out of the door-window and sees Jeff return unharmed. Repetition of the same gazing-subject/watched-object paradigm in two adjacent sequences establishes first an analogy between Bonnie and Kid—the two contenders both look at Jeff—then gives Kid a temporary advantage. When Jeff returns, Kid is waiting for him. But by the end of the film, Bonnie will watch Jeff embark from exactly the same position previously occupied by Kid. Finally accepted by the other pilots, Bonnie is granted access to the male-dominated space of Jeff's office. In another example, Kid interrupts a dialogue between his friend and the woman. Visually, Jeff is squeezed in the middle between the two rival lovers. Later, the same triangulation is evoked in Jeff's absence. In an on-and-off camera dialogue, Bonnie turns to Kid as if he were in love with Jeff and asks: "What do you do when he's late?" Kid replies: "I go crazy." As such, the two declare their mutual love for the protagonist and structurally demonstrate the "formal criterion of recognition" that Deleuze defines as "local or positional."[47]

If the film lingers on dynamics of masculinity, more generally it underwrites the essential Freudian conflict between the sexes. Through an attentive articulation of different spaces, the film shows that a subject's occupation of certain spaces depends on its sex. For example, only male pilots are allowed in Jeff's office while the bar is a mixed place that grants access to women.[48] Moreover, in this game of inclusion and exclusion, the local population is also marginalized and kept separate from white people. Spatial relations are constructed via a very effective use of the door. In this film, the door is clearly both an object and a *dispositif*: it constantly articulates passages and separations, in particular between the bar, Jeff's office, and the runaway.

Indeed, *Only Angels Have Wings* is a model film for structural analysis. The relationship between self and other is organized according to a system of oppositions in which the social-spatial dimension constructs the self and not vice versa. The fact that the subject's status depends on his or her position within the structure is often so obvious that one wonders whether Hawks was conscious of it. As is always the case with classical cinema, articulation of these basic dualities (male/female, occupier/native) is introduced in the opening episode. Thanks to the usual (and congenial) dynamism combined in impeccable dialogues, Hawks can simultaneously animate three characters—protagonist Bonnie Lee and two pilots Joe and Les—in a liminal space at the South American port of Barranca. And it is here, in the space of a few shots, that female identity takes on antithetical modalities. Moreover, the discursive dimension of gender identity is placed in relation to cultural and national identity through a North/South America dichotomy. For the female character has a highly flexible status compared to her male counterparts, able to approach the native and exotic by virtue of her femininity.

The initial episode is subdivided into three parts. Such segmentation draws a clear ideological path that structurally undergirds the film. After several establishing shots aimed at presenting the setting, an unspecified location in South America called Port Barranca, the affair begins with shot number 12. Two young men, carrying several packages walk energetically onto the port. They occupy the very center of the screen, their every movement followed by a tracking shot. The opening continues for a total of 40 shots combined, lasting a little more than four minutes. During that time, Joe and Les go to the pier where the boat has just anchored to deliver postal packages. But their conversation also indicates that they hope to find some attractive passengers and spend some time with them. Shortly thereafter, we learn that the two work as pilots for Jeff's airmail company. As they walk, they constantly look offscreen in hopes of seeing something interesting. Finally, their gaze comes to rest on a young woman who is disembarking for a brief stay. In fact, the boat will leave just a few hours later. Then begins a series of shots in which Les and Joe follow the woman through a crowd of market stands and street vendors as she tries to avoid them. Suddenly, the woman is attracted by music coming from a locale right in front of her. This initiates the second part of the episode. Bonnie stops to enjoy natives performing in a mixture of dance, song, and music. The mise-en-scène emphasizes both the woman's alterity to the group and her proximity, via a connection between her femininity and the exotic. Woman and native are linked by a similar position of alterity with respect to norms of maleness and cultural hegemony. With the pilots temporarily out of the picture, the scene alternates between shots of spectacle and the gazing female protagonist. At the end of the dance, Bonnie leaves, only to run into Joe and Les again. This begins the third and final part of the episode. As she takes flight a second

Figure 7. Noah Berry Jr. and Allyn Joslyn in *Only Angels Have Wings*, 1939.

Figure 8. Jean Arthur in *Only Angels Have Wings*, 1939.

time, Bonnie comes to realize that they are Americans. Excusing herself for running away, she ultimately joins up with the two. But more than that, she is so happy to hear a language that does not resemble "pig latin" that she offers to buy them a drink. Arm in arm, the three happily walk into a bar.

The female protagonist carries out a clearly articulated trajectory in this episode. In the space of a few minutes, Bonnie successively assumes three antithetical identities through three different formal strategies. As such, the opening sequence of *Only Angels Have Wings* reveals a rather convincing qualification of Laura Mulvey's expression-content relation theory. For it is true that the meeting between Joe, Les, and Bonnie in part is shot according to the voyeuristic paradigm and depicts a perfectly classical gender dynamic. However, this paradigm is problematized and overturned by part three when Bonnie shows herself to be a strong woman, more inclined to become a buddy or partner in crime than submit to male domination. In fact, the woman's new status is formally expressed by nonvoyeuristic shots reflective of Hawks's well-studied signature auteurial style. As Wollen's reading emphasized, if a woman endangers survival of male groups in adventure epics, for Hawks she must be neutralized in some way. In *Only Angels Have Wings*, male friendship seems a stronger and more important sentiment than heterosexual love. Thus, Bonnie's masculinization is necessary to the male group's survival.[49] Moreover, we can observe Bonnie's double status when the three sit down to drink something, planning to have a "real American steak" in the evening ahead. Just as before, when Bonnie discovered the nationality of the two men, the three were then able to commiserate over their shared "American" identity. Here, nationality supersedes gender and enables the woman to become a buddy through a sense of shared cultural belonging. This equilibrium is upset, however, by Jeff's sudden entrance onto the scene. In fact, his office opens right onto the bar where the three are having drinks, and Jeff brusquely interrupts their conversation, ordering Joe to prepare himself immediately for departure. Jeff's arrogance provokes Bonnie to demand that Jeff be more cordial and respectful. With intent to diminish her, he turns to her and asks: "Chorus girl?" Though slightly humiliated, Bonnie gathers her wits to fight back: "I do specialty." The brief exchange is filmed in shot/reverse shot and newly reinscribes Bonnie in the film's earlier conflicted gender relation with Joe and Les. In effect, the beginning episode of *Only Angels Have Wings* classically links woman, spectacle, nature, and the exotic. But to gain the full significance of this point, the function and form of its voyeuristic dynamics must also be analyzed.

The episode begins with the classic-voyeuristic articulation described by Mulvey in "Visual Pleasure and Narrative Cinema." On the one hand, the male is introduced in a dynamic fashion, combining action, a walk followed by a long tracking shot, and gaze. On the other hand, as the female asks for the action to stop, she is captured in a fixed shot that initiates a contemplative act. But it must also be noted that while the two pilots constantly look offscreen, the camera shows what they look at only when the woman appears. Only at that point does their gaze become a subjective shot. In this film, whatever comes from offscreen space poses a threat to male integrity: besides women, the birds that cause Kid's death while flying also emerge from offscreen. Likewise, Bonnie emerges from invisibility to threaten the stability of the male group. And later, Rita Hayworth's entrance from offscreen will be even more mysterious, erotic, and threatening than that of Bonnie.[50]

In the second part of the episode, the camera's articulation of the gaze constructs a discourse that links woman to nature and the exotic. In the heterogeneous world of the port, "the natives" ironically remain apart. Only Bonnie gains access to their social space, which makes her position both double and liminal. The native's spectacular performance happens in a separate place, establishing a sort of opposition between colonized and colonizer. In fact, this spot will among other things sit in opposition to the "white" bar, frequented by the protagonists. However, Bonnie's entrance into native space is not left off-camera, but becomes visible. As Bonnie looks at the couple dancing, the reversibility of their gaze implies the possibility of changing roles and therefore a structural similarity between Bonnie and the native couple. For Bonnie's approval is reconciled in the following sequence when we discover that she is a showgirl. Now the film's discourse becomes clear. At the beginning, Bonnie is a spectacle for Joe and Les. In fact she is someone who regularly exhibits herself for the pleasure of others. Then she observes the natives' spectacle. But the most significant element is the structural relation between the two sequences set back to back, effectively drawing a parallel between woman and native. And in this way, we can also understand the camera's exclusion of the two pilots as they follow Bonnie, for American males cannot occupy the space of the other as she can. Thus, they only reappear just as Bonnie diverts her gaze away from the native's spectacle.

This opening episode is so rich that by its conclusion we witness a new reversal of the paradigm. When Bonnie discovers that Joe and Les are American, cultural and national identity supersedes gender and the woman immediately identifies with them. Arm in arm, a preceding tracking shot follows the three as they walk together. A sexy woman but also a comrade, Bonnie becomes an active accomplice to the men. But Jeff's entrance into the scene sets the film's core plot in motion and brings the female's ambiguous status to an end. Thus, from their very first verbal exchange, the woman is positioned as other to the man. In fact, Bonnie's function, along with the film's narrative trajectory, follows Freud (and Mulvey) to the letter in establishing the classical paradigm. The woman reactivates the male subject's fear of castration, cornerstone of the pre-oedipal male phase, and constitutes a threat to the unity of his homosocial group. As in *Red River*, Hawks shows an interest and perhaps a predilection for homoerotic relationships. Such a tendency is nicely furthered by a whole series of collective shots. At the same time, Bonnie's presence constitutes an undeniable push for Jeff to overcome his oedipal complex. Despite Hawks's attention to elaborate forms of identity, his film concludes with the affirmation of normative masculinity and subordination of the female subject that goes along with it. Ultimately, *Only Angels Have Wings* stands partially apart from other adventure films, evoking alternative gender identities before a more definitive affirmation of order and norms in line with the era's dominant trends.

A NOTABLE EXCEPTION—RICH AND (THEREFORE) FREE: WOMEN AND SCREWBALL COMEDIES

While from the mid-1930s the demise of the New Woman was undeniable, the genre of screwball comedy represented a partial exception. If comedy's main ideological project aims at integrating the couple within the social structure through marriage, several comedies of the period presented progressive forms of sexual interaction and female desire. Moreover, in contrast to the sentimental tone of *It Happened One Night*, a rather traditional film in terms of gender politics as we have argued, films such as *Sylvia Scarlett* (G. Cukor, 1935), *The Awful Truth* (L. McCarey, 1937), *Bringing Up Baby*, *The Women* (G. Cukor, 1939), *My Favorite Wife* (G. Kanin, 1940), *His Girl Friday*, and *The Philadelphia Story* (G. Cukor, 1940) expressed a deep understanding of the social nature of heterosexual love and of the unbridgeable gap between sexual drive and the legal bond of marriage. In comedies of the late 1930s, two adults would generally decide to get married, not in order to form a family, but to satisfy their sexual impulses. As such, marriage was the institution that both contained and allowed the expression of sexuality.

The screwball comedy contributed to the symbolic production that gave voice to the new paradigm of sexual life and behavior that emerged at the beginning of the century. While it may have begun as a medical discourse produced by professionals, the debate around sexuality became part of the broader shift focused on the subject's experience in modernity and became a topic of discussion in various media, whether it be popular literature and press, women's magazines, or cinema. As noted in chapter 1, the change pointed toward acceptance of a sexual ethic that encouraged expressiveness rather than containment. While such a discourse made possible a whole set of social dynamics, from the suffragette movement to the creation of radical and bohemian forms of living, it also explained the progressive and transgressive elements of some screwball comedies.

In *The Awful Truth*, for example, the female protagonist Lucy Warriner (Irene Dunne) has three male partners. Her promiscuous behavior, which causes some hilarious moments, especially when the three men are in her apartment, each unaware of the other two, can only be tamed by marriage. The viewer knows that Lucy loves only her ex-husband, Jerry (Cary Grant), and that she uses her lovers to make him jealous. It is also evident that their marriage ended because of their mutual betrayal. At the beginning of the film Jerry makes the point that in marriage each partner needs to trust the other. Marriage, in other words, is not based on fidelity per se, but on the lack of suspicions. In *My Favorite Wife* Cary Grant, as Nick Arden, and

Irene Dunne, as Ellen Arden, ultimately choose to remarry, thus breaking up their triangular relation with Steve Burkett (Randolph Scott). But one clearly senses that the two are extremely attracted to Steve. Ellen has continued to have a long relationship with him since they were shipwrecked on a desert island. When she returns home, Nick, who believes her dead, is engaged to be married to his new fiancée. He is still in love with his wife but does not know how to handle the situation with his current partner. As he meets Steve, he is struck by his beautiful and athletic body and feels both inadequate and attracted to him. Both films solve, in a rational way, the problem of desire and sexuality: marriage is a necessary institution if one wants to preserve the social order. In other films, sexuality is addressed in a different way. In *Bringing Up Baby*, for instance, Susan Vance (Katharine Hepburn) rescues her partner, David Huxley (played, once again, by Cary Grant), from a married life devoid of fun and sex. A serious paleontologist totally devoted to his work, David prepares to marry his prudish and boring assistant when Susan plunges into his life and drives him away from his plans. Susan is the epitome of the screwball heroine. She is funny, crazy, entertaining, extremely energetic, and contagious. Her desire to marry him is a true blessing for David: Susan will allow him to experience the joys of married life, especially sex.

In the screwball comedy, the dynamics between male and female subtends a clear equality of the sexes in line with the model of "companionate marriage" that emerged in urban areas in the 1920s. In this new model of gender relations, a young man wanted a woman "he could sleep with and talk with too" and he wanted "it to be the same girl."[51] As in the new marital ideal, which "boosted marriage as more appealing than ever to women," in comedy sex is central: "the sexual adjustment and satisfaction of both partners [are] principal measures of marital harmony" and social order.[52]

The comedy of the second half of the 1930s presented the most advanced and progressive model of gender relations of the period, one that continued the modern thrust toward female emancipation from Victorian passivity and domesticity. However, the convergence of gender and class identity had strikingly changed in relation to the earlier years. In the classical era, only the rich and aristocratic heroines of the screwball comedy enjoyed sexual freedom. The New Woman's lifestyle survived only for them. While in 1940, the genre produced some of its best examples, that same year a film like *Kitty Foyle* (S. Wood, 1940) depicted, in a poignant fashion, the demise of the model of the New Woman for working girls. In that film, subtitled "The Natural History of a Woman," Kitty (Ginger Rogers) must choose between two men, and her choice is articulated along the lines of class difference.[53] She will eventually choose a poor but idealistic doctor and refuse her aristocratic suitor. But the film begins with a nondiegetic prologue commenting on the trajectory of women in the early decades of the century and "explaining" the "cause" of the film's outcome.

The prologue's title announces that we are going to see the story of the white-collar girl, a novelty in American society. In the first scene, set in 1900, men in a crowded cable car rise to give their seat to a woman; we then see a courtship scene on a porch and the same man who offered his seat asks the same young woman to marry him. In the following sequence, a group of suffragettes protest and ask for equal rights. Then we are presented with its "direct consequence": in a crowded cable car, nobody rises to offer his seat to the woman. The last title of the prologue states that men have gotten so accustomed to seeing women during the workday that, in 1940, white-collar women suffer from a new malady: "that five-thirty feeling" of not having a date for the evening or a man waiting at home. At this point, the prologue unfolds into the diegesis. This is the problem afflicting the young women working with Kitty in a luxurious boutique in New York. As the story develops, the relation between the prologue and the diegesis becomes clear: Kitty's problematic choice is the consequence of women's emancipation and working careers.

The trajectory of the modern woman has thus ended miserably. If in the early 1930s, class difference could be overcome and women's upward mobility (and sexual freedom) was one of Hollywood's favorite topics, in the following years working-class women were denied social rise while spoiled aristocrats enjoyed romantic and sexual freedom. As Sam Wood's film sadly shows, at the end of the decade a girl of humble origins could not but marry a poor (and boring) doctor. But the viewer cannot forget that Kitty's only moments of happiness are those spent with Win, the charming Philadelphia aristocrat she could not have.

3

THE MALE SUBJECT OF NOIR AND THE MODERN GAZE

CRISES OF THE SUBJECT AND REPRESENTATION

While affirming its value and originality, critical literature on *The Classical Hollywood Cinema* stresses the fact that Bordwell's discussion of film noir (and 1950s melodrama) unwittingly reveals the limits of his theory of classical cinema. Bordwell rejects the notion that noir is a subversive cinema when compared to that of the 1930s, claiming that it can be perfectly integrated into his classical paradigm. He argues that noir's innovations were motivated by the genre's historical relationship with detective fiction or "new forms of realism." But these purely formal criteria are of little use in defining noir's subversiveness, for as Douglas Pye argues, such a task would require consideration of cinema in terms of representation, of "how dominant institutions and values are refigured" and what material forms representations take. Discussing a film's subversiveness thus requires an examination of "representative and stylistic parameters in the narrowest sense."[1] Likewise, R. Barton Palmer suggests that Bordwell's neoformalist approach does not grasp the "noir question" insofar as these films, as a "socially collective unit in the Bakhtinian sense," interrogate the dominant structures of Hollywood cinema by proposing new ones. Ultimately, such differences have a social relevance in that they must be considered in relation to ideology and reception. Yet, much like structuralism itself, this neoformalist model lacks a semantic component and thus obfuscates issues related to "meaning."[2]

We have already discussed the centrality of representation in chapter 2, in which the style and formal structures of classical film were placed in relation to certain models of subjectivity and sociocultural scenarios. The dominant role of omniscient narration and objective shooting expressed a unified representation of the world in perfect agreement with the story's narrative causality. Such strategies represented highly legible worlds, in which a subject's identity conformed to codified roles and functions. The classical character expressed his/her essence through action that enacted his/her desire in an unproblematic way. Moreover, the legibility of the world and individual actions was further supported by dynamics of conflict and dialectic, which were constructed by precise narrative and directorial choices. Finally, spatial and individual relationships were resolved whereby the latter controlled the former.

The noir and the woman's film overturn all of these paradigms. Often the two genres are rightly seen as two sides of the same coin in 1940s Hollywood symbolic discourse. The first aimed at representing a crisis of the male subject, and the second that of the female.[3] The genres parallel each other in both visual and formal structures. For example, first-person voice-over narration by the protagonist, the flashback, and the relation between present and past are almost invariably present in each. Frank Krutnik argues that "the 'tough' thrillers tend to treat the drama of their 'dislocated' heroes seriously. . . . Just as the dramatic representation of the realm of women—issues of the family, home, romance, motherhood, female identity, and desire—has been approached (by the film industry and by film critics) in terms of the generic category of the 'women's picture' melodrama, one could consider the 'tough' thriller as representing a form of 'masculine melodrama.'"[4] In my opinion, however, there is a fundamental difference between the two genres. In the noir, the male subject carries out an investigation of the world and often of a woman, which stand in for an investigation of the self and of his desire. In the woman's film, on the other hand, the female subject's investigation is often onto herself and focuses on her sexual identity. Between the two genres, the relation between public and private is thus reversed, confirming the traditional division of gender roles.

Whether rooted in male or female sexuality, the oedipal scenario dominates both genres. Narrative discontinuity follows the nonlinear paths of a protagonist's desire, which in turn is dominated by the "return of the repressed." As such, it is impossible not to address 1940s cinema through psychoanalytic discourse, insofar as it is the product of an era that witnessed "the substitution of the Protestant ethic by the Freudian ethic,"[5] or America's "rite of passage from childhood to adulthood."[6] This passage is critical and when properly articulated, helps us to resolve the irreducible difference between the cinema of the 1930s and that of the following decade.

Cinema of the latter 1930s was indeed dominated by a Protestant ethic, which could often be found in a film's narrative structure and objectivity as well as spatial and character relationships. But one can also insert notions of class difference and gender to explain this paradigm. The primary category of difference here seems to be that of class even though the screwball comedy also insists on the relevance of gender conflicts. In some ways, however, these gender conflicts were only a narrative pretext, and overall the genre's politics of desire was mildly subversive because equality between the sexes was available only to upper-class women. Furthermore, in most films of the period, the subject simply accepts the position into which he or she was born. There is no demand for an alternative class or gender identity. Thus, the question of positioning is crucial because it takes identity as a given, by means of the symbolic order. It does not depend in any way upon the individual. Moreover, this acceptance of a given position also explains why the 1930s subject seems "to lack an unconscious." He or she is defined only by his or her own actions and is completely unaware of him or herself as a desiring subject. Thus, the characters of 1930s films can be taken as pre-Freudian subjects who do not experience the split between conscious and unconscious processes.

The emergence of subjectivity as a process, rather than a fact or given, is visible only in the cinema produced during the war and subsequent years. Here, the experience of the self is no longer a question of unconscious positioning, but rather takes shape through a continual and closed dialectic between individual drives and social demands. It cannot be traced back to a generalized structural or even collective identity, but rather is carried out on the level of the self's absolute singularity. As in psychoanalysis, in which "to the question that grounds every cure, 'who am I?' the analyst responds, 'You are your history,' thus inaugurating the narrative construction of the modern subject,"[7] so too do the noir and particularly the woman's film narrate obsessively individual stories. In both genres, an adult character must come to terms with his or her own desire in a continual oscillation between past and present, between traumatic experiences and attempts to break free of them, between the imposition of a correct masculinity or femininity and the desire to be something other than this. These conflicts play out according to scenarios that take up Freudian formulations, albeit in simplified forms. In the noir and woman's film, however, repression is never totally successful in the sense that the repressed returns to the surface to trouble the subject's psyche. Such scenarios develop not only according to discontinuous or contorted temporal trajectories, but also in specific spaces. For example, both the noir and the woman's film are urban genres. The noir usually takes place in the neon-lit nighttime streets of the city, and not just any city, but usually New York, Los Angeles, San Francisco, Chicago, or

Las Vegas. Moreover, on these streets we often find ourselves in venues of popular entertainment: nightclubs, restaurants, gambling houses, and boxing rings. But we also frequently encounter the impoverished detective's office in run-down buildings near noisy train stations, much like that of Bradford Galt in *The Dark Corner* (H. Hathaway, 1946), located near the elevated Third Avenue Station in New York,[8] or diners like the one in Hopper's *Nighthawks* (1942). There are also housing developments far from the city center, like the tenement in *Where the Sidewalk Ends* (O. Preminger, 1950), and big dehumanizing markets, like the one in *Double Indemnity* (B. Wilder, 1944) where the protagonists walk between aisles and "talk about murder in public, but the big store makes them anonymous, virtually invisible to shoppers."[9]

But in the woman's film, noir's urban locations are cross-pollinated with the domestic spaces of protagonists in such a way that the private space of female melodrama sits alongside the public space of the male noir. At times, the difference between the two spaces is only one of degree, above all when noir elements invade the woman's film or when the story itself is divided into urban and domestic spaces. In extreme cases, this procedure leads to a veritable hybridization of genres, the most famous being that of *Mildred Pierce* (M. Curtiz, 1945), in which noir and melodrama play an equal part in the (dis)adventures of the protagonist (played by Joan Crawford). This duality is expressed by a dialectic of spaces, between the domestic environment of house and family and that of crime and passion typical of noir and criminal environments, which also work out the relation between past and present. *The Damned Don't Cry* (V. Sherman, 1950) also demonstrates a similar dynamic, although in this case the noir element prevails. With exemplary narrative technique, the police investigation of a famous Las Vegas Mafioso's murder is quickly transformed into an investigation of a woman, photographed beside a swimming pool in home movies found at the scene of the crime. In an extremely long flashback narrated from the protagonist's point of view, an incomparable Joan Crawford explains how she became involved in mafia activities after leaving her family. In fact, she had come from a small backward town, subject to the domineering will of a cold husband and father in an unloving household. By comparison, even with its reputation for illicit activity and alienation, the freedom of the city seems preferable.

Among the urban spaces linked to the female experience is the dress shop, where before placing their orders, well-off female customers could see the latest creations of their favorite designer donned by young models. Indeed, the figure of the model is a recurring topos in both noir and the woman's film. Like artistic performance, the techniques of exhibition characteristic of modeling make it a privileged site for defining the status of the female body. Usually the job of a model was temporary, an absolute necessity for the income of a protagonist who came from a working-class background. In *The Damned Don't Cry*, it is the first job that a penniless Crawford finds upon her arrival in the city, as well as Gene Tierney's in *Where the Sidewalk Ends*. In *The House on 92nd Street* (H. Hathaway, 1945) meanwhile, an elegant atelier serves as a cover for a group of German spies under investigation by the FBI. Urban genres par excellence, the noir and the woman's film admirably exploit entertainment venues and the meeting places of the modern metropolis where marginal, or illegal, ways of life develop, and in which sex, violence, and alienation arise unchecked.

VISION/SUBJECTIVITY/MODERNITY

In comparison to classical Hollywood style, 1940s cinema developed an explicit visionary quality and patent sense of narrative discontinuity. *Citizen Kane* (O. Welles, 1941) clearly played an important role in the transition between these two forms as a work that ruptured the link between narrative and point-of-view structures as well as classical composition and visual structures. Indeed, Welles's principal innovations were the fragmentation of narrative and the denial of an objective perspective, leading to a radical form of subjective point of view. Visually, *Citizen Kane* carries out a similar reorganization of the human subject, by subordinating it to space through depth of field, frequent use of the wide-angle lens, and extreme angles of framing. The sequence shot and the long take, meanwhile, highlighted the emergence of a temporal dimension in flux. This brief description is sufficient basis for demonstrating that *Citizen Kane* is a limit case and an eccentric film, and it differed from most Hollywood cinema.[10] Yet its influence on 1940s cinema is indisputable. All of the innovations introduced or radicalized by Welles would be incorporated in the most "extreme" cinema of subsequent years, but in attenuated form as noted by Bordwell. As for depth of field, Bordwell argues that Welles's film was an anomaly and therefore not a valid model for understanding the function of this technique in American cinema. Nonetheless, "If it had not been made, many Hollywood directors would have continued to combine occasional, moderate depth with cutting and camera movement. But *Kane* probably did more than any other film to persuade directors that inflated foregrounds and great depth of focus could intensify a scene's drama."[11]

The integration of this technique is strongest and most evident in the noir film. Noir is not only a macro-genre, but it is also a visual style that contaminates other genres, which undergo a kind of "noirization" during this period. One can see this contamination in the western, both in *films d'auteur* like Ford's *My Darling Clementine* (1946) and Walsh's *Pursued* (1947), and in studio westerns. For example, it takes on a notable narrative efficacy in *Ramrod* (A. de Toth, 1947), featuring a formidable Veronica Lake, and *Station West* (S. Lanfield, 1948), in which Dick Powell plays a military intelligence officer sent by Washington to investigate the murder of two soldiers. The woman's film makes use of similar visual and narrative technique, as does even the genre of the musical, seemingly incompatible with noir. In *Cover Girl* (Ch. Vidor, 1944)—a teaming of Rita Hayworth and Charles Vidor predating the better known *Gilda* (Ch. Vidor, 1946)—flashback, high-contrast lighting, mirrors, and reflecting surfaces are all employed. The noir look of the film is particularly strong in the episode in which Hayworth returns to the now-closed Brooklyn theater where she performed at the beginning of her career. This list of hybrid films could easily go on with countless examples, both well-known and obscure.

Noir's capacity to express concepts and sensations purely in visual terms is a radical innovation with respect to classical style. Equally innovative is its redefined use of verbal language. In the progression charted thus far, the new status of the image might seem to have much in common with the visual-dynamic register of the first years of sound film. Film noir, however, does not simply reemploy expressive modes already used in the past. Rather, it carries out a new articulation of the relationship between "narration" and "attraction" and between "word" and "vision," in which the second term dominates the first. The noir produces a new mode of representation and is responsible for inaugurating a new model of subjectivity, fully enmeshed with modernity. This is no longer the modernity theorized by Simmel, Benjamin, and Kracauer, but rather one tied to Freudian analysis and psychoanalysis more generally, highlighting the impossibility of a whole integrated subject.

Classical cinema is based on such a perfect system of narrative causality that visual and attractive components seem comparatively irrelevant or absent. As such, the effectiveness of classical framing depends on a highly legible image that essentially acts as a double for words or dialogue, a means of communication par excellence.[12] The hegemony of the image's narrative function is also linked to its high degree of objectivity. Cinema of the 1930s favors an omniscient point of view, albeit one marked by human characteristics much like that of the nineteenth-century novel.[13] This technique produces a particular kind of identification, as classical cinema engenders such a process with both the diegesis and characters that inhabit that world. Such strategies can be broadly interpreted as Hollywood's way of seeing the subject/world relationship, as individuals are integrated into social space and governed by precise codified norms. The trajectories of these characters are attempts at integration into an environment, structured by an ideological and moral point of view. It is in this sense that one can explain the primary function of comedy, in its manifold forms and variations. Films narrating the subversion of dominant ways of life, meanwhile, are less numerous in this period. The absence of challenges to dominant models holds particularly true for gender relations, as stressed in the previous chapter. Thus, here I want to argue that there is an explicit relationship between formal and social trends. Objective narration and organic space can be linked to the stability of inescapable social and moral norms. The ideological work of the film then consists in showing that such norms do not function so much to assure social stability but rather allow for individual happiness. Rebellious figures are undoubtedly altogether marginal in the second half of the 1930s, while they become dominant in postwar cinema.

But 1940s cinema is not monolithic. While the noir and woman's film are the most innovative and modern forms, dominating the postwar period, they are not the sum total of Hollywood production at the time. In *Power and Paranoia* (1986), a study that after almost thirty years remains an indispensable point of reference on 1940s cinema, Dana Polan discusses the copresence of two incompatible models, the war film and film noir. He argues that if a war film works "to institute a logic of temporality that would bind all moments of the social totality into one master synthesis, another side of the forties equally suggests that this dream of totality is a fragile, reversible, unstable one." Such vulnerability "is figured especially in film noir where objects resist control, where our familiar world can turn on us . . . where the opening of a car door can kill, where temporal progression dilates and becomes a nightmare of coincidence and alogical repetition."[14] The historical significance of the two models, however, is not the same. The war film, of course, dominates the early 1940s, while the noir begins to make its presence felt in 1944 and only flourishes between 1945 and 1948.[15]

By 1943, certain signals and tendencies anticipated the end of the war. For example, in July of that year, *Variety* reported that studios were beginning to move away from war stories due to a 40 percent drop in box-office returns.[16] Another sign was the debate over what women would do after the war. According to Michael Renov, already in 1944 many government agencies began to discuss the "problem" of female work, and more specifically how to send women back to the home now that soldiers were about to return from war. Studying government papers and documents, Renov states that women's jobs were now defined as a "workforce in excess." Moreover, agencies tried to induce women to retire voluntarily and used major newspapers and magazines to sway public opinion in this direction.[17]

Analogous to the shift between nineteenth-century and modernist novels, one notes a passage from objective storytelling in classical cinema to the subjective in noir. Omniscient narration in which the camera acts as an external observer to the diegesis is abandoned. Instead, we now see a privileged individual point of view that is, by necessity, limited. This is a material subjectivity in which the body becomes ground for the inscription of identificatory signs and sensory experience. Perceptive acts and actions are shown in their material physicality. These acts, however, are almost always failures and the protagonists' trajectories are marked by defeat and lack. Kaja Silverman notes that in a certain number of films from the mid-1940s, the paradigmatic example being Wyler's masterpiece, *The Best Years of Our Lives* (1946), the male subject is metaphorically castrated, while in a clear inversion of traditional roles, the control of narration and of the look is attributed to the female character. Silverman emphasizes that in many cases the condition of the male subject's lack is "the symptom of broader historical crisis," linked to the World War and the immediate postwar period.[18] Nonetheless, I would note that the woman's power is more of a rhetorical strategy than a sign of real power. During the same period, the woman's film shows a parallel castration of the female subject. As we will see in the following chapter, women's attempts at self-determination are often doomed to failure or fall back upon more traditional parameters of behavior. In contrast to the integrated character that dominates in the 1930s, the 1940s sees the strengthening of the rebel or alienated figure, both in male and female characters. In this sense, modern subject's centrality is reaffirmed. In the noir and woman's film, the self is split, conscious of itself as a nontranscendent subject, and irremediably marked by lack.

The emergence of subjective vision as a symptom of modernity is one of the major themes of the philosophical reflections on the *specificity* of western culture, and one in which the cinema has played a fundamental role. Indeed, apparatus theories of the 1970s interpreted classical cinema as a transcendent system of vision and representation in the tradition of Renaissance perspective, the camera obscura, and photography. The cinema, in its dominant form, would represent the apex of this tradition and a paradigmatic form of the twentieth century. Following this argument, the nature of vision, the kind of subject it constructs, and the relationship between observer and image instituted by classical cinema would fall in line with aforementioned elements of the western visual tradition. Stephen Heath argues that "The conception of the Quattrocento system is that of a scenographic space, space set out as spectacle for the eye of a spectator. Eye and knowledge come together: subject, object, and the distance of the steady observation that allows the one to master the other."[19] Despite the fact that cinema is based on movement, unlike photography, classical narrative cancels this mobility and transforms the movement and temporality of cinema into spatial dimensions. Thus, "the ideal of space remains that of photographic vision which brings with it the concern to sustain the camera as eye; in the sense of the detached, untroubled eye discussed earlier; an eye free from the body, outside process, purely looking." In this system the spectator becomes "a ubiquitous observer" endowed at each moment of the action with the best possible viewpoint.[20]

Although this argument was later called into question, it can still be useful for a study of American cinema, provided that it is refashioned in a more historical perspective. Indeed, linking classical cinema to premodern forms of vision is not at all inappropriate, although such a linkage is not, as it might seem, a mere tautology. If we abandon the ideological underpinnings of Heath's interpretation and consider the historically perceptible changes in film language and mise-en-scène, then we can ascribe these qualities to the American cinema of the second half of the 1930s.[21]

In contrast to the transcendental and detached subject of late 1930s cinema, a pure eye deprived of corporeality, a subjective and embodied vision emerges in 1940s narratives. In other words, because the narrative and perceptual acts it represents are those of a specific individual, 1940s cinema makes a corporealized self visible. We might recall the frequency of cases in which a character loses consciousness or the ability to see clearly, and how this loss is depicted by way of a detailed description of diminished physical sensations. One of the earliest examples is Philip Marlowe/Humphrey Bogart's loss of consciousness and subsequent coming-to after being assaulted by Sidney Greenstreet's thugs in *The Maltese Falcon* (J. Huston, 1941). This shot is depicted with an out-of-focus framing that slowly becomes clear and legible. Similarly, the protagonist of *Murder My Sweet* (E. Dmytryk, 1944) has bandages over his eyes for the entire film, but is also drugged, knocked out, and subject to intense dreaming. In *Notorious* (A. Hitchcock, 1946), Alicia Huberman/Ingrid Bergman is drunk at the beginning and poisoned at the end. At first she sees in an out-of-focus, doubled, or upside-down manner, and finally, before the last minute rescue, is nearly blind. In each of these cases, vision takes on a strongly subjective quality which is then imprinted on the character's body. But these images are also visionary and highly spectacular, constructed through complex superimpositions and dissolves or manipulations of the perspective and photographic dimensions of the image. In the case of dream sequences, loss of consciousness, hallucinations, or blockages of a physical or psychic nature, the filmic image no longer records the profilmic. Rather, it expresses the psychic and subjective experience of the character. It is in these cases that we see a fundamental difference from dissolves employed during the early 1930s. While in the early sound years, superimposition acted as the filmic analogue of the modern city's dynamism and energy, here it expresses an individual's crisis and split self. In the first case, visual dynamism is not linked to an individual instance, but rather it expresses the collective dimension of the urban subject, especially modern women. Furthermore, this earlier use of dissolve is linked to the possibility of female self-determination in the chaotic jumble of the metropolis. In the noir, however, everything is turned upside down. On the one hand, the subject lives out his own alienation in solitude. On the other, the city becomes a sinister, mysterious, two-faced place in which the individual struggles and loses his way without any real hope of integration.

The changed status of vision in noir parallels broader trends in western culture. In *Techniques of the Observer*, Jonathan Crary argues that in the early 1800s, before the discovery of photography, a paradigm shift occurred in western culture in relation to the structural function of sight, ways of seeing, and the status of the observer. Crary, who works within an explicitly Foucaultian framework, is concerned with retracing the genealogy of modernity through the emergence of new modes of visual experience in relation both to certain optical systems and devices and to certain forms of the observing subject. According to Crary, what takes place "is an uprooting of vision from the stable and fixed relations incarnated in the camera obscura. . . . In a sense, what occurs is a new valuation of visual experience: it is given an unprecedented mobility and exchangeability, abstracted from any founding site or referent." The perceptual act becomes autonomous from reality and loses "the apodictic claims of the camera obscura to establish its truth."[22] The incorporeality of vision engendered by the camera obscura is replaced by a vision that is resituated within the body. The nineteenth century, as Foucault has shown, witnessed the proliferation of disciplines and institutions that investigated the body and human activity, while science explored the sensory possibilities of the human eye. There is, in short, "a new arrangement of knowledge about the body and the constitutive relation of that knowledge to social power." This reorganization is the effect of the emergence of a "remaking of the individual as observer into something calculable and regularizable and of human vision into something measurable and thus exchangeable."[23] The modernization of vision entails further changes. The perceptual act is dissociated from touch, and a new regime of separation between the senses emerges in which vision becomes more and more autonomous. But it also becomes abstract in relation to space and tangible objects. Modernity transforms vision into a temporal and kinetic activity and makes contemplative observation impossible: "There is never a pure access to a single object; vision is always multiple, adjacent to and overlapping with other objects, desires and vectors."[24] At the beginning of the 1800s, the observer is repositioned "outside of the fixed relations of interior/exterior presupposed by the camera obscura and into an undemarcated terrain on which the distinction between internal sensation and external signs is irrevocably blurred."[25] In conclusion, Crary argues that the new model of vision would be characterized by two main trends: vision becomes subjective (and no longer objective), but also measurable in a rational way.

Film noir is the privileged cinematic site to test the convergence of discourses on subjective vision and modernity. Through the figure of the Private I (Eye), the mise-en-scène of vision in relation to knowledge displays the aforementioned features and appears irreconcilable with the cinema of previous years. But noir also demonstrates the emergence of a quantifiable and scientific vision made possible by recording techniques, most importantly those of the cinematographic apparatus itself. For example, in the "police procedural thriller" subgenre[26]—*The House on 92nd Street* and *The Street with No Name* (W. Keighley, 1948) immediately spring to mind[27]—intelligence succeeds thanks to the most sophisticated investigative techniques in which the sense of sight is central to solve any case with scientific precision. Indeed, stylistically these films venture far afield from the more famous noirs and use a series of objectivizing techniques to create an expository tone, such as a cold and scientific voice-over in place of the usual emotional one; or a documentary look derivative of real FBI training films; or the use of real FBI offices, locations, and so forth. The techniques that describe procedures of identification such as fingerprinting, meanwhile, are worthy predecessors to the filmic and investigative techniques of the TV series *CSI (Crime Scene Investigation*, 2000–). This subgenre, although not well-studied, includes Mann's masterpiece *T-Men*. The "police procedural thriller" emphasizes certain traits of the noir, such as the protagonist's solitude and work in urban spaces, while eliminating or marginalizing any female presence.

GAZE AND KNOWLEDGE: *MURDER MY SWEET* AND *DARK PASSAGE*

In *Murder My Sweet* and *Dark Passage* (D. Daves, 1947), knowledge-vision and subject-space relationships constitute two poles of a formal discourse. Adapted from hard-boiled novels by Raymond Chandler and David Goodis, respectively, the two films have many elements in common, such as the path toward proving the protagonist's innocence and the representation of urban space. The first scene in both films foregrounds the question of vision. In *Murder My Sweet*, Philip Marlowe/Dick Powell sits in a police station with bandages around his eyes. Accused of two homicides, the detective recounts the events leading up to his arrest in a long flashback and ultimately succeeds in proving his innocence. In the few scenes set in the present, Marlowe never removes the bandages from his eyes, and in the final shot, he walks away from the police station a free man, still bandaged and temporarily blind.

In some ways, the beginning of *Dark Passage* almost mirrors that of *Murder My Sweet*, though here the obstacle to vision lies with spectator. The viewer is denied vision of the protagonist's face, who is introduced as he escapes from San Quentin prison. Indeed, the film cannot show Humphrey Bogart's face until he undergoes plastic surgery, as dictated by the plot. Thus, we see Bogart only in the final part of the film, as his face goes unfilmed in the first part and is bandaged in the second. Indeed, the actor's celebrity status and the narrative need to hide his face affect the film's form in a manner entirely befitting noir philosophy. Just as it had happened many times before at Warner Brothers,[28] Delmer Daves succeeds in transforming an apparent lack into an aesthetic and expressive resource. But the impossibility of showing the star obviously limited options for the mise-en-scène. In fact, the director adopted a subjective camera much like that of *The Lady in the Lake* (R. Montgomery, 1946). The effects of this technique, however, are somewhat mitigated through the use of other devices to ensure identification. For example, Daves used a new lightweight handheld camera that allowed him to film the movements of the protagonist up close, thereby placing the spectator alongside the character. This effect is most visible in the first episode in which Vincent Parry moves through the bushes. The camera films his approach to the thicket, touching leaves and hedges as the actor's body does. Later, in the memorable taxi scene in which the protagonist is driven by the man who refers him to the plastic surgeon, Daves resolves the problem of hiding Bogart's face through a masterful use of lighting. With the protagonist seated in the back seat, a shot from his point of view would

Figure 9. Tom D'Andrea and Humphrey Bogart in *Dark Passage*, 1947.

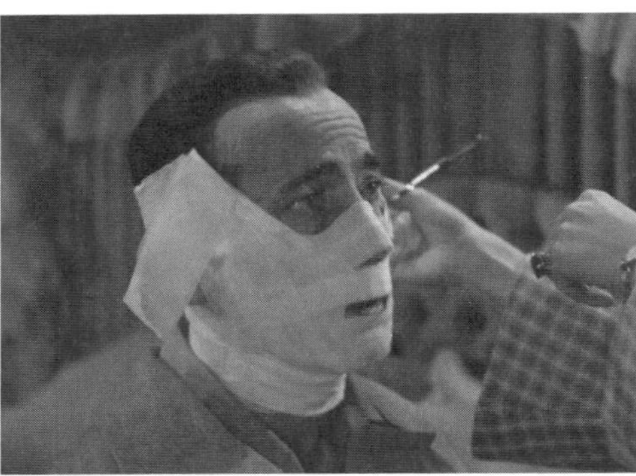

Figure 10. Humphrey Bogart in *Dark Passage*, 1947.

have shown the neck of the taxi driver. This would not have been effective, however, given that it is the taxi driver who suggests the operation. Instead, Daves opts to shoot the two frontally. On the left, Bogart remains in shadows, while the taxi driver, on the right, is lit. The opposition between light and shadow creates a tension in the shot, which is divided into two parts. But it is also adapted to narrative and technical demands. The protagonist must not only not be seen by the spectator, but he also does not want to be recognized by the driver, who nevertheless soon realizes who he is. This episode represents a characteristic example of noir's melodramatic tendencies, in which the contrast between darkness and light elicits a perceptual, affective, and cognitive reaction on the part of the spectator.[29]

The other episodes of dialogue are generally filmed in subjective shots. In place of the usual shot/reverse shot we see closely framed long takes of Vincent's interlocutors, shot from his point of view. First, the man who transports him in the car, then Irene/Lauren Bacall, and then the surgeon, are filmed while speaking with Parry as they look into the camera. The subjective shot only partially limits storytelling possibilities, but there are moments of obvious artificiality. While the use of the subjective shot is initially motivated by the protagonist's attempted escape, the lack of reverse shots in interior sequences seems unmotivated and artificial, as in the long dialogue with Irene in her apartment. The spectator, however, is reassured of the star's identity. In part, the presence of Bogart's voice compensates for his visual absence, while in the taxi sequence we see an outline of the actor's face. But the absence/presence of Bogart, more than disrupting the usual process of identification, creates a different type of spectatorial positioning. Our point of view is that of an alienated figure, unjustly condemned and on the run. As such, "there is a level on which the misidentification Parry feels as an unjustly convicted murderer models our own unease at the forced union of our perspective with his."[30]

In both *Murder My Sweet* and *Dark Passage*, the dynamics of vision seem to move between two poles. On one hand, as we have seen, the subjective gaze is embodied but also limited, while on the other the capacity to look appears to be available to all. In many noirs, each character of any importance is at once the object and subject of the gaze, and one often has the feeling that everyone is looking at everyone else. This mechanism does not produce clarity or truth, nor does it make the facts any more legible. Rather, it complicates the status of knowledge and often renders the narrative implausible and difficult to understand. The plot may be dominated by tactics of pursuit or hiding, or attempts at disguise or flight, in which the motive or identity of the implicated subjects is not always clear or even important.

Edward Dimendberg has interpreted the noir vis-à-vis the subject's changing relationship to modern urban space and transportation, while at the same time considering new apparatuses and regimes of vision in the way of surveillance, photographic models for filming urban space, and new modes of traveling through metropolis. Indeed, after World War II the relation between individual and collective radically changes in urban spaces, as increasing numbers of bodies aggregate, move, and circulate together. According to Simmel, "socialization in the modern city entails learning to ignore other people and developing a calculated indifference to the bodies with which one shares public transportation and the street." Yet at the same time, attention is necessary inasmuch as the techniques of surveillance developed near the beginning of the twentieth century become fundamental for locating criminals among the teeming masses. As a result, Dimendberg suggests that a "balance between noticing and disregarding other people [is] required by urban life."[31]

The use of real locations has led some to speak of noir in terms of "realist cinema." But it is perhaps more accurate to see the genre as a photographic historical document or a visual testimony to the architectural reality of urban America. This documentary function is particularly acute in the case of many filmed sites that no longer exist, such as New York's elevated train station on Third Avenue or Bunker Hill in Los Angeles.[32] Nevertheless, it is clear that questions relating to vision and perception call for strategies that have little to do with "realism." The complex plots of noir and the complicated movements of characters in urban spaces depict alienated intersubjective relations, in which everyone seems to watch over everyone else in a vertiginous movement destined to implode. *Dark Passage* is emblematic in this sense. To prove his innocence, Vincent Parry, wrongly sentenced for the murder of his wife, must find the real killer. Parry's investigation, however, is made difficult not only because he himself is being hunted by the police, but because he also does not seem to have any idea who the guilty party might be. Even when he thinks he is safe, hidden in Irene's apartment, he is in fact being watched. He is not only being sought by the police, but also by the man who offered to help him, but whom he punched after being recognized. While investigating Madge/Agnes Moorehead, who will turn out to be the killer, the protagonist is himself sought by bounty hunters. Madge, meanwhile, is trying to find out the identity of the man who Irene is hiding (Vincent). Finally, when Madge accidentally dies from a fall, there is no longer anyone who can prove the protagonist's innocence. The interweaving of multiple searches within the same group of characters, as subject and object repeatedly interchange, creates a whirl of movements that turn the city of San Francisco into a trap for Vincent. In the diner scene, for example, the policeman intuits from a "mistaken" question and from his unseasonal clothes that Vincent is a wanted man, preventing Bogart once again from leaving the city. When in the end, we find the protagonist in a South American country, the solution seems to be more a celebrity gimmick—the Bogart/Bacall couple can be reunited—than a narratively credible solution.[33]

The case of *Murder My Sweet* is somewhat different. While Marlowe is both the subject and the object of the investigation and initially suspected by the police, unlike Parry, he is never at risk of being convicted of a crime. What is striking about Marlowe is his inability to understand signs and clues and his limited ability to make progress in his investigation. He is not only bandaged for the entire time, but he also complains that everyone is manipulating him. On the other hand, he is capable of producing remarkable imaginings, as in the hallucination sequence brought on by drugs. In

Figure 11. Dick Powell and Mike Mazurki in *Murder My Sweet*, 1944.

this film, we also find an excellent and truly spectacular example of how, in Crary's opinion, the distinction between internal sensation and external reality becomes irremediably indistinct in modern vision. The beginning of the flashback is one of the most memorable episodes of the genre.

At the police station, Marlowe tells how it all began one night in his office. The scene opens with a shot of the seated protagonist looking out his window. It is night, and the city is an array of lights that stand out against the darkness. While he looks outside, his face is reflected in the glass. After a few moments, another face appears, reflected above the detective's face. The image now seems ambiguous and the glass becomes the ideal surface for breaking the clear division between interior and exterior space. On the one hand, the exterior and lights seem to penetrate into the room through the transparent surface. On the other, the interior reflected in the glass seems as though it wants to move outside. This situation of uncertainty intensifies with the appearance of a second face. Perhaps because Marlowe appears pensive, the new face seems to be an image emerging from within his mind, a memory or a nightmare. In a subsequent shot, however, we realize that the face is in fact that of a client who has come to seek the detective's services. When the camera cuts to the man, the ambiguity vanishes.[34] The indeterminacy of this reflected image—where is its source?—parallels the detective's difficulty in correctly interpreting what he sees. This inability is shown most clearly with respect to Velma, the girl the client is after and thus the object of Marlowe's investigation for the rest of the film. In one of the first scenes, Marlowe is shown a photo of an attractive woman signed "Velma." Overvaluing the nonindexical power of the word, he will continue to believe throughout the film that this is Velma's picture. On the other hand, Marlowe seems more capable of interpreting voices, words, and smells. At one point he realizes Ann's identity because she speaks the same phrase that she did earlier in the woods, and in the end, he recognizes her again as a result of her perfume. Ann goes to the police station to take Marlowe home. He is still bandaged, but in the taxi he recognizes the scent of the young woman and can, now that the mystery is solved, begin a love affair with her.

WORD/TRUTH/OEDIPUS: *DOUBLE INDEMNITY* AND *PURSUED*

Compared to the previous decade's cinema, film noir's subjective vision involves a diminished capacity for reading the world's signs. This limitation becomes especially significant in investigative plots that involve seeking out truth. The emergence of the embodied look, with all its limits, in some ways indicates the end of a "transcendent" and objective vision. While much more powerful than the vision available to the characters of film noir, such transcendent vision is revealed as a mere illusion, something that the human subject has never really possessed. Without treating this question in greater depth, I simply want to draw attention to noir's role in this process, leading to changed forms of vision. According to many, the ontology of vision and its relationship to knowledge and truth dominated western culture from the time of the Ancient Greeks until the late 1800s. Martin Jay hypothesizes that the "ocularcentric tradition" enters into crisis with Bergson as a result of two radical innovations. In Bergson, perspective loses its transcendent character—the cognitive process of the individual is no longer abstract or transcendent, but corporealized—and the temporal dimension takes primacy over the spatial.[35] A further component of this paradigm shift is underlined by Hans Blumenberg, who points out a fundamental difference between Greek and Jewish cultures. For Greek thought, all certainty is based on visibility: "Logos is a collection of what has been seen. . . . For the Greeks, 'hearing' is of no significance for truth and is initially nonbinding. As an imparting of doxa, it represents an assertion that must always be confirmed visually." Conversely, for the Old Testament literature, "seeing is always predetermined, put into question, or surpassed by hearing. The created is based on the Word, and in terms of its binding claim, the Word always precedes the created."[36]

Film noir seems at least partly comprehensible in light of this new paradigm. On the one hand we find the centrality of speech. It is not a means of intersubjective communication, as in the case of dialogue in classical cinema, but rather a means of narrating one's own story, an indispensable instrument of knowledge. In other words, speech is subjective here. It is charged with the subject's personal experience and through the act of narration, posits itself as the only means of agency available to a character to either diegetically understand his doomed fate or save himself. Examples of the two cases would be, respectively, *Double Indemnity* and *Murder My Sweet*.[37] Here, we might say that speech in the form of monologue or narration takes on a function of knowledge unavailable to sight and the gaze. For example, when Walter Neff/Fred MacMurray in *Double Indemnity* enters the Dietrichson house for the first time, the sight of Phyllis/Barbara Stanwyck at the top of a staircase wearing only a bath towel blinds him to the "truth" about her, though it is obvious to the spectator. In noir, sight is often deceiving, especially when the man sees a woman, and above all when the detective (or his equivalent substitute) meets the femme fatale. This topos of noir has rightly become a topos of critical studies of the genre, especially in Feminist Film Theory.[38]

At the beginning of Wilder's film, a limping and bleeding man enters the insurance office where he works late one night. Upon reaching his office, he begins to record his confession into a Dictaphone, addressing himself to his boss Barton Keyes/Edward G. Robinson. Neff confesses to having killed Mr. Dietrichson "for money—and for a woman. . . . It all began last May." At this point his voice and the image give way to a flashback of his meeting with the woman one warm and sunny afternoon in Los Angeles. The opening is staged to give the impression that the protagonist has understood his actions only in the face of his impending death. The urgent need to tell his story before it's too late drives him to run to the office after everyone else has left. Walter's act, however, also expresses a desire to tell his story and confess his misdeed to his symbolic father himself before anyone else has a chance to do so. Walter's hoarse and trembling voice, full of halting pauses, expresses emotion and pain at having to confess his terrible and unpardonable guilt to a man whom he has clearly disappointed and loves even more than his own father, as is so often the case in noirs in which the protagonist

Figure 12. Fred MacMurray in *Double Indemnity*, 1944.

seems to have no past. In his analysis of the film, Jim Naremore argues: "One of the ironies of Walter's crime is that in betraying his employer, he is also betraying a friend and a father substitute; hence his interoffice message, which is not only a confession of guilt but also an admission of love."[39]

Verbal narration and flashbacks are common strategies in noir and emphasize the genre's tendency to bring the protagonist's repressed desire to the surface. Noirs structured around these strategies bring out their oedipal content in clearly articulated forms, creating narrative trajectories that demonstrate the male subject's difficulty in overcoming the pre-oedipal phase. In *Double Indemnity*, the paternal function clearly represents the Law, while the symbolic son is incapable of identifying with the father, which according to Freud is a necessary condition for the formation of the Superego. Keyes himself describes his function as that of a doctor, a policeman, a father confessor (truly Symbolic figures in Lacan's terminology). In a clear oedipal conflict, Walter transgresses the law, attempting to devise a perfect plan that defies the father's power.[40] Keyes's moral and institutional function is even stronger in Billy Wilder's original ending where Walter Neff is put to death in a California gas chamber.[41]

Similar dynamics inform the noir western *Pursued* in which the function of speech is even more marked, almost excessive in relation to the image. Here, the role of oedipal and familial dynamics is also stronger and more clearly articulated than in Wilder's film. Like that of the female characters in the woman's film, the male subject's experience is problematized as the result of a repressed childhood trauma that haunts and prevents the protagonist from establishing healthy familial and romantic relationships. The centrality of the home and domestic environment brings the story of Jeb Rand/Robert Mitchum into proximity with those of the heroines of women's films, and to some extent feminizes his character. As in *Duel in the Sun* (K. Vidor, 1946), the film incorporates traits of melodrama, contributing to the development of a vein or subgenre of melodrama-western hybrids, of which *Johnny Guitar* (N. Ray, 1954) is perhaps the most famous example.[42] Like the protagonist of *The Snake Pit* (A. Litvak, 1948), whose insanity derives from an excessive love for her father, Jeb recalls nothing of his biological family and does not know why he was adopted by Mrs. Callum, who raised him along with her own two children.

At the beginning of the film, Thorley/Teresa Wright joins Jeb in a ruined hillside house, bringing him provisions and a map. Being followed, Jeb must escape before he is found and killed. The woman, however, says that she will not go with him even though she loves him. In fact, he should flee but is unable to leave the house because he is convinced that his psychic problems began here. Now, in the face of death he wants to understand what has been haunting him and why he has been unable to live a normal life. "This is where it started, this is where it's going to end," he tells his beloved. He is convinced that the mystery of his unhappiness is hidden here and thus begins to recount what he does not understand. His memory is partial, only remembering the image of boots and spurs and the flash of a firing rifle, after which Thorley's mother (Judith Anderson) arrives at the house. Finding him frightened and hiding, she takes him away with her.

Like Walter Neff with Barton Keyes, Jeb feels the irresistible need to tell his memories to his wife Thorley in the hopes of discovering the truth through storytelling. Obviously this is an almost absurd narrative situation, seeing that he seems to be gambling away his only chance to save himself. But as happens frequently over the course of the film, Jeb is compelled to bring his past to light. It is this act alone that seems to make sense to him. The flashback dwells on the important episodes in the lives of Jeb and the Callums, and in particular on the revenge sought by Grant Callum, brother of the adoptive mother's dead husband. He holds Jeb's father responsible for his brother's death and wages a vendetta against his son. Callum's plan entails convincing Jeb's stepbrother, and then Thorley's suitor, to kill him. But Jeb is too clever and in both cases manages to save himself and kill his rival. These acts, however, estrange him from his beloved Thorley, who begins to hate him and eventually plots to kill him herself. She accepts his marriage proposal and marries him with the intention of killing him on their wedding night. At the crucial moment, however, she cannot resist her desire for her husband and instead of killing him, fully devotes herself to him. At this point, Callum arrives with his gang, hoping to take Jeb by surprise and to do away with him once and for all. Jeb manages to escape and seeks refuge in the ruined house. Here, Jeb's account and the flashback conclude and the action of the film returns to where it began. Then, as if by a miracle, Jeb finally remembers the missing pieces of his past. The boots and spurs belonged to his father who shot at his enemies to defend himself in the same house where Jeb is now hiding. Soon, he will have to do the same as his father, as he remembers the bodies of his brother and sister dead on the floor. Then, he sees his father get shot and die. While witnessing the frightful scene, Jeb sees Callum enter, dragging his future adoptive mother to confront her with the death of her lover. Now all is clear. Mrs. Callum's initial reluctance to disclose the facts now becomes understandable. She cheated on her husband with Jeb's father, with whom she was very much in love. The shoot-out, in which both men died, was a settling of scores.

Figure 13. Jeb (Robert Mitchum)'s nightmare in *Pursued*, 1947.

Figure 14. Robert Mitchum in *Pursued*, 1947.

While the film implies that Jeb probably witnessed the primal scene, the sexual intercourse between his father and Mrs. Callum, it also dictates his fate as a man forced against his will to repeat the errors of his father, leaving a trail of violence and death in his wake. In a finale that repeats the scene of the trauma, Jeb must defend himself, just as his father did, against the attack of Callum and his gang. But ultimately, he decides to surrender instead. Just as he is about to be hanged, his adoptive mother shoots her brother-in-law, putting an end to the violence that she herself caused. While she is not the main protagonist, Anderson's character—as compelling here as in her more famous role as Mrs. Danvers in *Rebecca* (A. Hitchcock, 1940)—is in fact the key to the film, the cause of and solution to the problem. While the crisis of masculinity is signified by a clear feminization of the male character, placed in a passive role, it is interesting to note how, in contrast to more orthodox noirs, his path to knowledge is directed more toward himself than toward the outside world much like that of the female protagonist in a woman's film. The structural use of domestic space, which provides a link with melodrama, can be understood in light of this fact. The house is the site of childhood trauma, but also that in which the trauma is relived and cured. As in the psychoanalytic talking cure, speech is the means through which the subject can overcome his own trauma. In this case, Thorley takes on a role comparable to that of the psychoanalyst. She encourages Jeb to remember, listens patiently and attentively, and ultimately decides to remain at his side. Having initially joined him with the intention of helping him escape, she decides to stay with him after having learned the truth, knowing all the while that death awaits. Speech and verbal narration have succeeded where actions, and years of life lived together, had failed.

DEPTH OF FIELD AND URBAN SPACE: *WHERE THE SIDEWALK ENDS*

More than any other genre, noir makes systematic and radical use of depth of field. As noted, this technique was the subject of much theoretical debate about the status of the filmic image and became a privileged site for defining the aesthetics of cinema, the ideological-materialist interpretation of film, and the neoformalist theory of cinema (in the cases of Bazin, Comolli, and Bordwell, respectively).[43] As with other important theoretical and critical concerns we cannot, in this context, consider the argument in all of its complexity. It should be noted, however, that Bazin's position is of little use for this study insofar as it is irreconcilable with the idea of cinema as a mode of representation. Bordwell, meanwhile, is useful in his suggestion that the "'impression of reality,' whether in the hands of Bazin or Comolli, will not be an illuminating guide to every matter of style that we might want to study."[44] On the other hand, the American theorist's hypothesis that depth of field should be seen as a technique that makes the image legible and guides the attention of the spectator, which aligns with his neoformalist and cognitive approach, seems to me altogether insufficient.[45]

The use of deep focus in the noir seems to be linked to a greater redefinition of the visible and visibility throughout American culture of the period. Filming on location, especially the exteriors in large American cities, and more generally the depiction of lower-class and marginalized urban reality, attests to the fact that the iconographic models of 1940s cinema are very different from those of the previous decade. So while the stage of bourgeois theater is an important influence in 1930s classical cinema, with the characters speaking in a room at the center of the frame, the noir turns to and also influences a completely different visual scenario, especially photography. The space of the huge metropolis represents a radical rupture with the closed space of the studio set, which in its imitation of the theatrical set also mimicked the rooms of domestic interiors. In the classical system, dialogue and conversation dominate, while the conflicts and solutions are structured around intersubjective relations. In the new iconic system of the 1940s, dialogue takes on a secondary role and meaning is expressed visually. For example, urban spaces seem to dominate human subjects and the noir atmosphere consists of clarifying the individual's solitude and alienation through certain shooting and lighting techniques or through a different treatment of the function of objects. Similar interests and strategies inform the work of several photographers of the time. Esther Bubley, for example, obsessively shoots women alone in furnished rooms, waiting in a diner, or sleeping in the waiting room of a bus station. Thanks in particular to lighting techniques, as Paula Rabinowitz has shown in reference to a series of photographs from 1943, the similarity between Bubley's works and noir iconography is clear.[46] The style of Weegee, a photographer and journalist who specialized in crime scenes and nocturnal violence, is also characterized by high-contrast images that place their illuminated subjects against a dark background. According to Edward Dimendberg, Weegee, especially in his photographs of New York in *The Naked City* (1945), aspired, as with many noir films, "to humanize faceless citydwellers, to restore an experience of place to an urban realm becoming increasingly homogenized through abstract space, and to recognize the lived dimension of mass cultural seriality."[47]

In contrast to the neutral space of the interior room in which human figures are central, the space of noir is divided between two opposing poles. On the one hand, interiors appear claustrophobic, full of objects and characters, as well as zones of darkness, with a tendency toward centripetal composition. On the other, characters move through multiple exterior spaces. Indeed, film noir is characterized by a multiplicity of urban locations. Different from classical cinema, in which the action takes place in few spaces that tend to be repeated systematically, the action in noir moves frequently through different locations of the city. In place of classical narrative and spatial continuity, here a sense of dislocation and discontinuity dominates. Through precise formal choices, the two spaces of noir express two different modes of the self. The centripetal framing represents a space that inexorably closes in on the protagonist. In interior spaces, lights, objects, and human beings constitute a barrier to his movement, while the limits of the frame seem to block movement toward the outside. In short, the centripetal image shows a character visually in a trap, incapable of moving freely and controlling space. In these cases, depth of field plays a fundamental role. Indeed, it is the total visibility of every object in the frame that assures that such objects become a clear obstacle to the protagonist's movements and actions. But while examples of such scenes are many, the most memorable are perhaps those shot by John Alton in Anthony Mann's *T-Men* and *Raw Deal* (1948) and Joseph H. Lewis's *The Big Combo* (1955). In *T-Men*, for example, several scenes explicitly recall *Citizen Kane*. There are long takes with three different planes of action, all in focus, and few camera movements. In certain cases, the protagonist is at the center of the frame but surrounded by other characters looking at him. The overall effect is that space beyond the limits of the frame is inaccessible to the protagonist.

The multiplicity of exterior spaces and real locations, meanwhile, represents the second spatial modality of film noir. Like the temporal dimension fragmented by flashbacks in which the addition of dreamlike situations makes the story's truth even more ambiguous, the space of noir is fragmented both in terms of the relationship between one scene and another and even within single scenes themselves. The logic of totality is replaced by one of fragmentation, as a character more often finds himself in the wrong place than in the right one.[48] At the same time, however, noir films seem more interested in filming locations than human subjects. The numerous urban shots without any characters, but nonetheless full of life and energy, attest to the lost centrality of the individual, who now must compete for the camera's attention.

The staging of urban space as a site of the subject's alienation becomes particularly effective when framing devices are used, such as the mirror or even the window, which appears frequently and becomes the primary signifying figure in a film like *Where the Sidewalk Ends*. We have already emphasized the effectiveness and seductiveness of transparent glass, the night, the city lights, and the weak gaze of the subject in *Murder My Sweet*, which join together in a highly ambiguous shot, while also being indicative of a changed relationship between subject and space. Indeed, in Preminger's film—in which we find paired once again the two protagonists of *Laura* (O. Preminger, 1944)—the window is the iconographic motif that structures the film and filters the subject's alienated condition.

While investigating a homicide that occurred in a clandestine gambling den, detective Mark Dixon/Dana Andrews, an unscrupulous policeman haunted by his father's criminal past, accidentally kills a suspect. Fearing the consequences of his act, Dixon carries out a plan to conceal his crime, which occurred in the dead man's own apartment in a lower-class tenement house on the outskirts of the city, "where the sidewalk ends." When an innocent taxi driver, the father of the dead man's ex-wife Morgan/Gene Tierney, is accused of the crime, Dixon is divided and helps this woman he loves to find a lawyer to clear her father's name. Dixon continues his investigation of the first murder in the hopes of arresting his father's partner-in-crime, with whom he is obsessed. Dixon's oedipal trajectory is similar to that of Jeb Rand in *Pursued*. Both victims of their father's illegal acts, they have lost any moral reference point and the certainty of stable values. Thus, they fight to extricate themselves from a moral labyrinth in which good cannot be distinguished from evil.[49] As frequently occurs in film noir, Dixon is saved by a woman. At the end of the film, when he has succeeded in escaping detection, he redeems himself by confessing to the murder. Morgan, who loves him, promises to remain faithful and wait for him. The melodramatic use of light, and more specifically the correspondence between visual and cognitive levels, is emphasized. In many scenes, the double nature of the protagonist is shown by partially obscuring his face in shadow, while at the end, when he turns himself over to the law, the shadows disappear.

In addition to showing the most common visual and formal characteristics of the genre in its plot and narrative structure, characterizations, iconography, and use of lighting, the film is marked by a prominent use of the window as a motif. The window acts not only as a frame, carrying out a clear *mise-en-abyme*, but also articulates the difference between subject and urban space and stresses the strong class contrasts of the metropolis.[50] The recurring motif of the window, which always appears perfectly centered in the frame, also indicates a clear authorial signature. The window is not, however, always the same. Rather, the film is punctuated by a series of windows in different locations and spaces through which the protagonists pass. Nonetheless, the configuration of the shots does not change and each window functions in a similar manner. Each is shot at night, opening onto thousands of New York City lights that glimmer in the distance. Each shot of a window underscores the insurmountable distance between the sparkling horizon and the barren spaces in which the camera is placed, between the wealth of downtown and the poverty of the outskirts inhabited by the film's characters. The Third Avenue police station where Dixon works has only rear windows, and the tiny room where he sleeps while on duty opens onto the nighttime lights of the city. While we see Dixon lying on his cot, the window occupies the center of the shot. His disinterest in what appears in the distance makes clear the reflexive function of the shot, reserved only for the gaze of the spectator. The lights are not only unattainable but further blocked by the presence of a grating over the window, which strengthens the opposition between the two spaces and shows that the fate of the protagonist has already been decided.[51]

Figure 15. Dana Andrews in *Where the Sidewalk Ends*, 1950.

Figure 16. Gene Tierney, Dana Andrews, and Ruth Donnelly in *Where the Sidewalk Ends*, 1950.

The function of the window is even more explicit in the scenes set in the apartment where Morgan lives with her father. After her parent has been arrested, Dixon sees Morgan home. The interior scene of the respectable apartment opens and closes with the same shot of the window centered in the frame. It shows us the far-off lights and skyscrapers, underscoring once again the distance between the two spaces that Morgan must traverse each day to go to work. The film is full of marginal places—above all the two tenement houses where Morgan and her ex-husband live—and hard and exhausting lives. Every character seems to be constantly on the verge of poverty and defeat. But in two cases, the gap between the two spaces narrows and the lights seem to move within reach. At the beginning of the film, Dixon is in a car with his partner, driving near Times Square. From inside the car framed by its window, we see crowds of people walking along the sidewalk seeking their nightly entertainment. But the episode in which the characters' space seems to merge most strongly with that of the city is that in which Dixon and Morgan go to a restaurant. The two sit at a table near a large window that opens onto the pavement. While they talk and eat, we see the nightlife going on outside through the glass. At the moment in which the two characters seem to have developed a personal rapport, the urban space no longer seems so alienating and the couple seems to have a chance at integration. This hope is fleeting, but the film's conclusion, as we have noted, does not lack a vision for the future. Preminger's film suggests that love can be the only path to salvation in an alienated and alienating world. While much has been rightly said about the relationship of death that links the femme fatale to the noir hero, perhaps it would be necessary to inquire more deeply into the model of the couple—doubtless rarer, but no less interesting—formed by a man and a woman who are equally alone, but who in uniting are able to save themselves and defeat their endemic solitude.[52]

4

(DIS)ADVENTURES OF FEMALE DESIRE IN THE 1940S WOMAN'S FILM

PSYCHIC DYNAMICS AND FEMALE SOCIAL LANDSCAPES

After the Second World War, female desire took on simultaneously innovative and problematic traits. In the name of national interest, during the war women had been asked to make personal sacrifices at home just as men had been abroad. Indeed, compared to the socially regressive years of the Great Depression, the war was in some ways analogous to the period spanning from the end of the nineteenth century up to the late 1920s, when women left the domestic sphere for the working world in droves. Now women were compelled to inhabit typically male roles. But this time their movement was officially sanctioned through government-sponsored propaganda. The image of *Rosie the Riveter* is paradigmatic. Invented by Norman Rockwell for the cover of the *Saturday Evening Post* of May 29, 1943, Rosie was a white woman in her thirties, muscular, dressed in working overalls in a moment of repose. She eats a sandwich while a tool rests on her lap. A pair of working glasses sits on her forehead. At the same time, she treads on a copy of Hitler's *Mein Kampf*. Rosie thus represents the American woman's contribution to the war effort in support of, and equal to, that of men on the battlefield. In the weeks and months that followed, the image resurfaced on numerous posters, in magazines and in films, inviting even more women to commit themselves to the war effort. But the image also had to negotiate a delicate balance of femininity and masculinity. For on the one hand, it had to convince women to leave the domestic sphere and take over traditionally masculine roles in the war industry on the home front. On the other, it had to ensure that women understood that their participation was only "for the duration" of the war, and no longer. Thus, differences of gender had to be maintained. Rosie appears strong and muscular. But she also retained a concrete and distinct air of femininity, lest she really consider herself a viable substitute for a man.[1]

Historical studies have verified time and time again that many women preferred to remain in the workforce rather than return to the home. That which began as sacrifice out of necessity proved to be much more than symbolic and contributed to a process of female self-determination that began several decades earlier. In August 1944, when the end of the war was imminent, Eleanor Roosevelt gave a speech entitled "Woman's Place after the War" in which she asked whether "women would want to keep their jobs after the war." She speculated that even if women "could continue on in the future," the skills they acquired would likely atrophy "if they had a house and a family that would recall them to a different type of life." Nevertheless, if the First Lady linked a woman's destiny in the public sphere to future availability of work, she also appeared reluctant to sacrifice a collective desire for female self-determination. In fact, in the preceding decade Eleanor Roosevelt was an ardent proponent of women in the workforce, much to her husband's chagrin.[2] In her 1944 speech, she did not advocate that women cede their posts back to men, but upheld that while "the first obligation of governance and economy is to ensure that every man capable of working has a job, and every woman who needs a job should have it . . . we have to fight until . . . every person who wants to work . . . has the possibility of working at something that satisfies them from a creative point of view."[3] Thus, in the space of a few words, this speech encapsulates some of the most important aspects of the female condition and its discourse at the time. Eleanor's rhetorical skill not only reveals her decidedly liberal point of view, but also a countervailing opinion that would come to dominate later on, insisting that women return to the home. Ultimately, however, Mrs. Roosevelt's argument is interesting because it begins with seemingly "objective" reflections on economic and biological order and then moves to different levels of discourse, such as personal fulfillment, which questions the supposed objectivity of her initial observations. Moreover, such a move proposes the female subject as agent of her own desire, beyond both motherhood and the domestic environment.

If national interest was placed ahead of gender exigencies during the war, desire for female emancipation fueled by wartime opportunity persisted in the postwar period. Here, William Wyler's award winning film *Mrs. Miniver* (1942) offers a paradigmatic image of the relation between femininity and war based on "sacrifice." The film begins in Great Britain before the war with Mr. and Mrs. Miniver living in a country house just outside London. The film still bears traces of the screwball comedy. The two are sophisticated,

Figure 17. Greer Garson in *Mrs. Miniver*, 1942.

accomplices, and very close, in spite of many years of marriage. They also share a passion: the Minivers are both avid consumers, having a taste for beautiful and expensive things, which they buy unbeknownst to one another.

In the film's opening sequence, we see Kay Miniver/Greer Garson in central London, unsure about whether to get on a bus or not. Suddenly, she changes her mind, running against chaotic traffic toward a store in hopes of still finding a wonderful and bizarre little hat she did not have the courage to buy earlier. As she enters the store, we come to understand that Kay's impulse is a frequent occurrence. Convinced that she would return to buy it, the shop owner set the hat aside. Moreover, when Kay guiltily admits "I do like nice things," she taps into a legacy of a desire and eccentricity that characterized female protagonists of earlier sophisticated comedies. It is enough to think about Rosalind Russell's hat in *His Girl Friday*, or the insane ribbon that hung twirled from Katherine Hepburn's hair in *Bringing Up Baby*. Nevertheless, cultivating her look was also a way for Kay to carve her own space, to activate her own desires apart from the maternal or domestic. Likewise, Kay's desire can be satisfied only in the "metropolis." The opening shots return to the image of the modern city as the site of movement and transformation. But eventually, the dolly shots cutting through chaotic urban crowds will give way to more sober classical shots of the Miniver family's quiet bourgeois life in Belham. There, Kay's superfluity and attitude of easy consumption will prove incompatible with the necessity of wartime sacrifice. In fact, when the country enters into war, Kay must set aside her passion. But along with it, she ironically loses out on any shred of autonomy she may once have had. The independence she exhibited at the beginning of the film gives way to more traditional and conservative modes of behavior. Her eccentric hats and elegant outfits are gone. Now she dresses plainly as she begins to earnestly inhabit her roles as mother and wife. The most memorable of such images feature Kay as protective mother, at one point huddled over her children in an underground air-raid shelter. Later, she becomes the fearful wife who rises at dawn to wait for her husband's return from a dangerous expedition to Dunkerque. As one scholar has argued, the film depicts "the family unit as an institution worth defending."[4] Ultimately, it is not by chance that Mrs. Miniver's first name is left out of the film's title. For unlike the famous women's films *Stella Dallas*, *Kitty Foyle*, and *Mildred Pierce*, which feature protagonists who rebel against traditional female roles, *Mrs. Miniver* only underscores the condition of a married woman.[5]

We find similar dynamics in *Since You Went Away* (J. Cromwell, 1944), where Claudette Colbert plays Anne Hilton, an "American Mrs. Miniver." Anne lives with her teenage daughters while her husband is at war. While fulfilling her roles as wife and mother she also takes up a job in an ammunitions factory to support her family. As we saw in chapter 2, in the previous decade Colbert had played famous flapper roles, most notably in *It Happened One Night*. Even though, in the end, what she wished most was only getting married, for a while she had shown some desire for independence and transgression. On the other hand, in this war film only her family duties seem to give her an identity. As one critic has stated "Colbert dutifully embodied each tearful situation. Such a nobility . . . required [her] to forfeit any sensuality."[6] In effect, both *Mrs. Miniver* and *Since You Went Away* are sort of antiwoman's films.

During the 1940s, the woman's film depicted a female will to autonomy through psychic dynamics resistant to stabilized norms. Here, I follow Mary Ann Doane's stricter definition of the woman's film rather than the more expansive one formulated by Jeanine Basinger. For Basinger, the "woman's film is a movie that places at the center of its universe a female who is trying to deal with the emotional, social, and psychological problems that are specifically connected to the fact that she is a woman."[7] Accordingly, for Basinger the woman's film is not a genre and must not be confused with melodrama. Otherwise, one would have to discount a large number of films "among them Rosalind Russell's career comedies, musical biographies of real-life women, combat films featuring brave nurses on Bataan," and so on.[8] But as Basinger attributes such a large sphere of activity to the woman's film, she does not allow for differentiation between films that otherwise bear little resemblance to one another, as if all films with male protagonists could be grouped together. Thus, similarly to Doane,[9] I define the woman's film by its manifestation of a female subject's desire in transgressive ways. Here, a woman typically pursues an emancipatory trajectory in an attempt to redefine herself, whether it be in a familial or public context. But this female desire is almost always destined to be held in check, marked by the loss of that which is most dear to her as the price of freedom. In particular, such films center on Freudian scenarios showing the incompatibility between what Freud considered "normal femininity" and other forms of desire. Motherhood and female passivity turn out to be incompatible with modes of active subjectivity in which women sexualize themselves beyond the traditional function in search of economic autonomy outside marriage. Here, a woman may even go as far as divesting her husband of his authority and taking his place. *Mildred Pierce* is a significant film in this respect and among those most analyzed and debated in Feminist Film Theory. Curtiz's film contains all the traits just listed. Mildred is forced to work and maintain her struggling family because her husband cannot find a job. Left on her own, then, she has to work *and* care for her two children. After having begun as a waitress, she soon opens her own successful restaurant. Business is so good she even becomes a real entrepreneur. But her economic success is not enough to win back her eldest daughter's dwindling affection. Eventually, Mildred will lose both daughters, one to prison and one to fatal illness. Thus, despite the fact that Mildred seems to reconnect with her first husband in the end, her personal defeat is total. Moreover, it seems natural to read her overall trajectory metaphorically. Mildred is punished for having refashioned herself in a new and transgressive lifestyle in which, among other things, her true soul mate is her female business partner and trusted friend Ida. As in *Blonde Venus*, *Mildred Pierce* not only marginalizes the male subject incapable of carrying out his duties, but it also envisions the possibility of a "female genealogy" in which women identify with the experience of other women. However, this liberated trajectory is interrupted precisely because mother and daughter fail to connect since Veda is unable to identify with her mother.[10]

The dynamic between Mildred and Veda is a paradigmatic example of Hollywood's tendency to systematically imbue mother-daughter relationships with conflict. As such, the cinematic imaginary unconsciously aligned itself with noted Freudian theses: the Oedipus complex and dynamics of the familial triangle. Through these, Hollywood fashioned simplified versions of psychoanalytic scenarios, which in fact bore considerable resemblance to official disciplinary doctrine. This process allowed for a diffusion of psychoanalytic discourse in the American cultural imaginary on two fronts; not only from doctors and specialists, but also through treatises and do-it-yourself manuals that adumbrated the discipline's core concepts. Pop psychoanalysis is a fascinating episode of American culture and provides a useful frame of reference to be touched upon at various points throughout the remainder of this chapter.[11]

In the woman's film, the representation of female desire is defined by a convergence of textual and contextual dynamics. As such, the genre stands as the cultural form most adept at recounting "the problem of woman" and, in particular, the discourse that developed in the field of American psychoanalytic psychiatry. According to Janet Walker, "two institutions, American psychoanalytic psychiatry and Hollywood cinema, at a certain point in history were absolutely central to the formation of feminine psychosexuality and women's life experience" between World War II and the mid-1960s. As a result, discourses and practices developed around female mental illness through a myriad of texts (films, manuals, journals, and magazines of various kinds) and contexts (organized psychiatry, psychiatric hospitals, and education).[12] Not all women's films, however, are about female mental illness and the doctor-patient relationship in a hospital context. In fact, there are relatively few cases in which a film's diegesis deals with female illness exclusively within the confines of a psychiatric institution.

In *The Snake Pit*, Olivia de Havilland's character is confined to a psychiatric hospital and made to undergo a series of treatments that ultimately appear successful. In *Possessed* (C. Bernhardt, 1947), the section set in the present always frames the protagonist (Joan Crawford) in a small hospital bed where she was brought at the beginning of the film, while long flashbacks show the causes of the woman's madness. The female mental illness/cure dynamic is also central in *The Three Faces of Eve* (N. Johnson, 1957). This film presents a case of multiple personality disorder, beautifully rendered by Joanne Woodward. But more importantly, it shows how the concerns of the 1940s woman's film melded with those of 1950s family melodrama. Such a process bears witness to a related but different historical convergence between text and context. In the 1950s, as we will see in chapter 5, the institution of the suburban family is such a dominant image that it necessarily marginalizes the representation of female autonomy that actually dominated the woman's film in the preceding decade. In other words, as female autonomy became less possible, it was therefore no longer represented. Nevertheless, *The Three Faces of Eve* is peculiar because it is closer to the woman's film ideology. Not only is it narrated from the female protagonist's point of view but is shot in black and white. While almost all family melodramas were shot in spectacular Technicolor, the choice of black and white here seems precisely to wink at the woman's film of the previous decade.

In other films, female mental illness constitutes a fundamental but not exclusive aspect of the diegesis. In fact, illness and cure are just two important phases in a more complex process of construction and/or transformation of the female subject beyond rigid parameters of marriage and family. In other words, the cure can be a viaticum for the radical change of woman's condition inasmuch as it opens never before considered possibilities. In *Now, Voyager* (I. Rapper, 1942), for example, protagonist Bette Davis first succeeds in freeing herself from her mother's strict authority in order to establish her own desire outside of marriage. But while she chooses a single life, she does not in fact give up on motherhood. In *Whirlpool* (O. Preminger, 1950), the woman's film and thriller are woven together. Protagonist Gene Tierney is a thief married to a famous psychoanalyst. Too interested in his own career, however, the husband does not realize that his wife has a problem. But a mysterious hypnotist does and he makes the protagonist believe that she can be cured through hypnosis. In reality, however, he uses this technique to make her take the blame for a murder he committed. Fortunately for her, the real killer is discovered by the end and Tierney is cleared of all charges. At this point, her husband understands that his wife needs help to overcome her criminal instincts. Paradoxically, the man's strong narcissism impeded him from seeing that the person closest to him needed some of the attention he usually reserves for patients. After falling victim to the wrong cure, the woman can now be healed thanks to her husband's therapeutic capacities. In *Johnny Belinda* (J. Negulesco, 1948), protagonist Jane Wyman is a deaf mute. The nature of her handicap requires a process of transformation closest to that of *Now, Voyager*, but one very different from the other films described up to now. Indeed, the adult female figures in the latter were caught in a liminal phase by rejecting traditional prescriptions of "normal femininity." These were all mature and married women whose mental illness in reality represented rejection of their condition and the emergence of a different female desire. But the deaf mute Belinda, just as Charlotte Vale in *Now, Voyager*, is a child who must become an adult. As such, she deals with the acceptance of sexuality and femininity, not rebellion. Thus, Belinda's trajectory is among the few to correctly follow Freud's hypothesis.[13]

Evidently, it is not necessary that a film deals with mental illness and the doctor-patient relationship to interpret it in relation to desire. For on the one hand, if films dealing with female mental illness constitute a fundamental corpus of the 1940s woman's film, in many others the analogous question of female desire does not develop within the confines of medical institutions. In these cases, psychoanalytic interpretation takes place in the relationship between the film's manifest and latent content and relies on techniques that allow us to catch sight of the unconscious in narration and mise-en-scène. In other words, the films require psychoanalysis of both character *and* text.

Before developing a typology of the genre, it is necessary to specify what we mean by psychoanalytic psychiatry and the relationship between the two disciplines in an American context. It has often been noted that the representation of psychoanalytic practices in Hollywood cinema is not only simplified, but patently false. For example, a psychoanalyst cannot prescribe medication or use electroshock therapy or even hypnosis as it very often happens in Hollywood films. Janet Walker has rightly noted that it would be wrong to consider these facts obvious errors on the part of incompetent screenwriters and directors. Such narrative choices represent not the letter, but at least the spirit of American psychoanalysis. For its key characteristic is its profound imbrication with organized psychiatry. Indeed, American psychiatry and psychoanalysis "grew up together and each strengthened the supremely authoritative status of the other." Thus, the popularization of these complex practices provoked a necessary simplification of each discipline and their relationship to one another. In the widely circulated magazines, as in cinema, there was a tendency to "conflate the various psychological disciplines without the careful specification of pertinent distinctions that would be underlined in the professional literature."[14] Among the films mentioned above, *The Snake Pit* is emblematic in this respect. The doctor subjects the protagonist to repeated sessions of electroshock therapy, but with the same determination and constancy he inquires into her past. Ultimately, she is made to recall past experiences that brought her to her present state.

In spite of the presence of heterogeneous techniques, however, here as in film noir it is psychoanalytic discourse more than psychiatry that explains the trajectories and forms of human desire. What drives the narrative logic of these films is the idea of a causal relationship between illness and a past event that took place in the familial environment, now settled into the unconscious and inaccessible to the conscious mind. Independently from the mixing of therapies, it is the abreaction of the traumatic event that determines the success of the cure. Thus, the kind of psychoanalysis to which these films refer is essentially derived from Breuer and Freud's *Studies on Hysteria* (1895).[15] In this early formulation Freud strongly believed in the possibility of recovery through analysis and abreaction. Subsequent Freudian skepticism that in reality "analysis is interminable," is not taken into consideration by the cinema of these years, despite the fact that such reflections are practically contemporary to the films discussed here. The preeminence of the psychoanalytic discourse over psychiatry is also linked, as in film noir, to the dominant narrative technique of flashback. In effect, the present is largely limited and at times insignificant—as in *Possessed*, for example, where we see the protagonist reclining on the couch for only brief instants, deprived of consciousness. Such moments barely interrupt long episodes of the past that are the film's real focus. Thus, even if the formula of crisis-therapy-cure represents a simplification of the real functioning of psychoanalysis, it is more useful to explore how such strategies might serve a purpose or ideological function, rather than simply declare them to be scarcely "realistic."

In his seminal study on 1940s cinema, Dana Polan puts the use of Freudian psychoanalysis in cinema in relation to contemporaneous beliefs in science as "rational humanism," as "the sense-filled journey through chaos to the stasis of an ending, the erection of a system."[16] Accordingly, Mary Ann Doane describes psychoanalysis as a way "to validate socially constructed modes of sexual difference which are already in place."[17] Thus, the woman's film adopted a model already refuted by Freud because it could integrate itself with extant narrative models, which were themselves products and producers of a patriarchal system. It did so because psychoanalytic discourse has "a form whose narrativity seems ready-made and thus allows the construction of suspense and climax. . . . Psychoanalysis serves precisely as a force of narrative resolution" fully consonant with Hollywood narrative device.[18] But different from film noir in which the protagonist often died, films on female mental illness had relatively positive resolutions in that the protagonist usually recovered. However, such an ending is at the antipodes of a classical solution because it fostered a *strategy of contradiction* characteristic of the woman's film and even 1940s cinema more generally. In fact, recovery was always a solution of compromise and showed that the woman's psychic crisis could be resolved only if she came to accept codified forms of desire under pain of social exclusion. But even in cases in which alternative solutions and new configurations of desire emerge, as in *Now, Voyager* and *The Three Faces of Eve*, the film's central device nevertheless focuses on the female subject's difficulties in affirming and realizing her own desire. Ultimately, the woman's film depicted femininity as a problem, Freud's famous "riddle of femininity," in a double connection with the subject's psychic structures and with sociomedial dynamics that aimed at the redefinition of femininity itself.

The key role of Freudian psychoanalysis explains first of all the centrality of oedipal scenarios and their function as narrative hinge points in all of the films analyzed here. Hollywood's plot structures required a high degree of conflict in intersubjective relationships while the use of psychoanalytic concepts needed to be tuned to the dramatic functioning of the text. For these reasons, Hollywood cinema always privileges one aspect of the oedipal triangle over another. There is even a clear divide between films that focus on the mother-daughter relationship as opposed to those that privilege father-daughter. Therefore one cannot really speak of an oedipal triangle since one of the parents is always absent from the scene. Thus, we have one of Hollywood's most evident "simplifications" of psychoanalytic theory. Such a simplification is a formal necessity: it is essential if one wishes to preserve the principles of dialectic and opposition, so central in Hollywood's narrative structure. Moreover, in the case of the mother-daughter relationship, the protagonist may alternately embody one role or the other depending on the circumstances set up within the film. Thus, our analysis aims to show how the 1940s woman's film suggests a complex discourse on femininity precisely because of the multiplicity of psychoanalytic dynamics activated in different films. Ultimately, female desire finds further confirmation in sociocultural practices and formal devices that consolidated over the course of the decade.

The imaginary of the 1940s woman's film is clearly incompatible with respect to 1930s cinema. Moreover, like film noir, the woman's film narrative technique and mise-en-scène also proved antithetical to those of classicism. The crux of this transition is a movement from objective to subjective narration. Such a transition engenders a whole spectrum of changes that radically alter the status of image and plot. For example, the main protagonist is often the same subject who narrates her own affairs in first person. Accordingly, the subject tells the story of constructing her own gender identity. And since the protagonist is also the narrator, this means that the act of narration is fused with the diegesis. Thus, the protagonist's subjectivity permeates the film at all levels. Moreover, the character-narrator is not a rational subject defined by action but a split subject ruled by her unconscious desires or trapped by the return of the repressed. Consequently, she is incapable of correctly overcoming the oedipal complex and accepting "normal femininity." The split between conscious and unconscious experience is inscribed within the text itself: instead of classical linearity, the story alternates between present and past events, between waking and oneiric-phantasmal states.

The story is likewise fragmented and discontinuous, presenting ambiguous situations and intersubjective relationships. Among the narrative techniques and shooting options employed to represent subjectivity and subjective states are: protagonist's voice-overs moderating transitions between present and past; close-ups on pensive female faces reflecting on the past just before a flashback; frequent recourse to superimpositions and dissolves in transition to a subjective past. Moreover, from a visual perspective the following formal devices are important: repeated use of contrast between light and shadow, particularly on the protagonist's face; unstable compositions and awkward camera angles; the use of subjective shots and of dissolves. And here, the visual rendering of subjective experience is masterly in its use of superimposition, even with respect to precedent. But in contrast to early 1930s cinema which linked superimposition and dissolve to the urban subject's excitation, in the 1940s woman's film it serves a psychic function. Indeed, scant legibility of the superimposed image makes the subject's psychic state manifest as she struggles to see and act rationally. Furthermore, her body often remains immobilized as she is subjugated by constant and unending psychic work. Thus, the question of the unconscious is really translated as *a problem of vision*. For as film noir (and earlier, *Citizen Kane*), the woman's film is concerned with questions linked to perspective and point of view. The image is consequently manipulated and deformed, alternating between the extreme legibility of depth of field and the confusion produced through obfuscated superimpositions. These visual parameters translate the subject's divided condition and are then inextricably linked to the spectator's perceptual experience. Conscious and unconscious states are materially registered on the filmstrip and neatly mark the duality of subjective experience proposed by psychoanalysis. Much like the early-twentieth-century modernist novel, the relevance of subjective experience and unconscious processes found in the most innovative 1940s Hollywood cinema bears the hallmark of modernity. And even though the woman's film retains a propensity for resolution, it does not depict the female subject's transformation in a corresponding linear fashion. Rather, it sketches out a number of oppositional modes of being, between illness and sanity, infancy and adulthood, and passivity and activity. Moreover, these oppositional modes of being and lifestyles make it clear that a healthy homeostasis is difficult to achieve. For one never really resolves one's psychic conflicts, but rather faces them constantly, much like the interminable analysis of psychoanalytic discourse itself.[19]

OEDIPUS I. DAUGHTER-MOTHER IN *NOW, VOYAGER*

The oedipal scenarios depicted in the woman's film reflect basic Freudian formulations. As is well known, Freud gave primacy to the oedipal phase and paternal role in a subject's formation over and above the pre-oedipal and maternal. In his first theory of femininity, Freud draws an analogous relationship between male and female childhood development: males initially desire their mothers while females, their fathers. Only later does Freud recognize the female child's equal desire for her mother.[20] But even recognizing this female specificity, for Silvia Vegetti Finzi, Freud "never contradicted his theories on womanhood and its inception in infantile monosexuality. He probably thought that female psychoanalysts would eventually bring about an integration to his theories and not, as did happen, a subversion."[21] According to the Freudian paradigm, the mother-daughter relationship is marked by conflict. Freud makes no mention of unconditional maternal love or the child's identification with the mother. Nor does he account for the possibility of more fluid relationships between women, often based on mutual compassion. All the same, we wish to set Freud's oblivion of the mother side by side with the obstinacy of several hysterical women who fought to "become subject of their own discourse, protagonists of their own lives."[22] For according to Vegetti Finzi, Anna O.'s case, Breuer's famous failure, rendered possible the passage "from a discourse on hysteria to a discourse of hysterics," and thus a real and autonomous form of female subjectivity. Anna O.'s story shows that hysteria has an emancipatory function since it liberates woman "from male authority and social conditioning of her subjectivity."[23] Indeed, Anna O.'s hysterical symptoms emerged against the backdrop of her father's illness. For months, the young girl lovingly cared for him. And during this time, Anna, aka Bertha Pappenheim, had her first contact with the naked male body. This commingling of sexuality, incest, and death probably sent her into shock and the trauma of the sexualized paternal body made her regress to a pre-oedipal maternal bond. But since the mother was absent, this lack symbolically manifested itself in Anna's loss of her native German tongue. Unable to identify with her mother, the young girl sank into an incurable repression. But Freud biographer Ernest Jones has shown that in her more mature years, Anna O. was able to cure herself through active involvement in the feminist movement and working with children from the pogroms. These activities clearly appear as "a sublimation of ancient phantasms of love and death." Thus, her refusal to get married and have children was replaced by intense activism with women and children and is interpretable "as a continuation of the unresolved parentage, as a mode of self-cure, of taking care of the phantasm of the child she never had."[24]

All of this bears remarkable similarity to the formative trajectory of Charlotte Vale in *Now, Voyager*. Thus, by drawing a parallel between Anna O. and Charlotte Vale, we aim to define the status and function of the woman's film in a dialectical mode. For as Charlotte refuses marriage but not motherhood, she replicates Anna O.'s search for autonomy from men. Furthermore, this choice inscribes itself in a broader range of genre-based action that clarifies the feminine voice in its difference with respect to discourses that would silence or marginalize it.[25]

Charlotte is the daughter of a Boston aristocrat—young, awkward, and hardly attractive. She lives in the solitude of her room, held prisoner by her mother who treats her like a servant. But thanks to her sister-in-law Lisa, who introduces her to a famous psychotherapist, Charlotte succeeds in freeing herself from her mother's clutches and building an independent life. Through treatment, she is able to become attractive and develop a sex life. Thus, the film narrates Charlotte's complete transformation from ugly duckling to beautiful swan, becoming beautiful, elegant, and very sophisticated after a period of cure far from home. Moreover, upon returning to Boston, Charlotte is able to resist her mother's order that she return to her earlier more sober demeanor. Truly on her own, she finally receives an acceptable marriage offer but has to refuse because she is in love with Jerry, a married man. The two began a relationship while Charlotte was away in treatment. Then, after her mother's death she becomes mistress of her family's substantial estate and decides to collaborate with the doctor who had cured her in his therapeutic practice. She even lets Jerry's daughter Tina come live with her. The two women also met at the clinic. And as it turns out, Tina, just like Charlotte, had psychological imbalances caused by a lack of maternal affection. Thus, in the contorted finale, Charlotte manages to retain her newfound autonomy by asking Jerry to sublimate his physical love for her and unite in common affection for Tina.

In sum, the film's core theme tackles desire and its role in the formation and transformation of the female subject's gender identity. Through a perfect administration of narrative and formal technique, plot dynamics fruitfully engage those of psychoanalysis. But while the presence of narrative and formal symmetries suggests fundamental elements of classical style, in Rapper's film the symmetries become real and true repetitions in service of the subject's abreaction and cure. As such, the protagonist's transformation is charged with a rather different tone than classical film. Far from narrating the process of reintegrating the subject in a social order typical of classicism, this film depicts the creation of an independent subjectivity in which the female self splits and adopts an ambiguous attitude toward established codes of femininity.

Formally, Charlotte's transformation involves a passage from invisibility to visibility, a passage particularly suited to film language. Before her cure, she is always alone, segregated in her room. After, she is always seen publicly, suddenly becoming the center of everyone's attention. Indeed, Charlotte represents something of a mystery since the beginning of the film with family and friends whispering about her before each of her three entry sequences. Woman as enigma is a common topos in the 1940s American cinematic imaginary, as well as in Freudian and Lacanian psychoanalytic theory and feminist theory. Such a dynamic is codified in the woman's film through careful articulations of point of view and on- and off-screen space.

At the beginning of *Now, Voyager* we learn from a conversation between mother, sister-in-law, and doctor that Charlotte Vale is an insecure young girl who never leaves the house. The protagonist's delayed entrance exploits an on/offscreen space dialectic. When the butler knocks on Charlotte's bedroom door, we see only her hands. The young woman is busy with some engraving work. She then quickly throws a cigarette butt in the waste basket and hides the ashtray in a drawer. Thus, the first shot of the protagonist, already foreshadowed by her mother's excessive austerity, underlines Charlotte's lack of freedom. She must hide certain behaviors from her mother as small children do. In the next shot, we see only the girl's feet coming down the stairs. The camera follows Charlotte's movements, emphasizing her tattered and graceless shoes while omitting her body and face. Already well-established as

Figure 18. Bette Davis, Ilka Chase, and Claude Rains in *Now, Voyager*, 1942.

Figure 19. Bette Davis in *Now, Voyager*, 1942.

Hollywood royalty, the spectator's anticipation for Bette Davis increases.[26] The mother's voice coming from offscreen then accompanies the image of the feet. Thus Charlotte hears her mother calling her the "ugly duckling" of the family. The next shot finally reveals the protagonist in full figure at the drawing room door. In a dark dress with homely florets, glasses, and the hairstyle of an old maid, Charlotte looks like a spinster. Bette Davis herself is barely recognizable.

A similar technique is employed when the transformed protagonist makes her public debut. After her time in Vermont at Dr. Jaquith's clinic, Charlotte is sent on a cruise so that she can learn to socialize again. But Charlotte never leaves her cabin, thus feeding into all the gossip circulating about her. She perpetuates it by boarding under the name of an acquaintance, Miss Beauchamp. But when she finally does dare to go out and visit one of the ports of call, Charlotte is introduced in a spectacular way. Her enigma is re-evoked once again through an effective use of offscreen space. The only one left to disembark, vacationers await Miss Beauchamp on the bridge below. They wonder who she is and what she might look like. At one point, someone claims to have caught a glimpse of her and reports that she seemed "interesting." The camera then cuts from the crowd of unnamed passengers as they direct their gaze on high to a shot of a *chic* pair of shoes. Charlotte's transformation is already evident, but it will be magisterially revealed with a beautiful dolly from low to high, running the length of her body and coming to rest on her face. This revelation is even more striking for the film's spectator, who has yet to see the "new Charlotte" in all her beauty. In fact, her makeover could not be more radical. Charlotte is now elegantly dressed, her figure sleek, and her face framed by a magnificent hat that keeps her hair gathered back. The same shock will hit Lisa and her daughter June—the niece who loved to make fun of her awkward aunt—when Charlotte returns home from her long cruise and disembarks in New York. If narrative event and visual form clearly resemble the two entrance sequences just described—i.e., Charlotte making her entrances descending staircases—in the New York episode the spectator instantly knows to whom the feet belong. Perhaps because we already "know," this time the camera does not exploit on- and offscreen dynamics as before. Thus, Charlotte and the spectator are empowered while Lisa and June, who do not even recognize her, are soon rendered speechless.

This passage from an invisible social marginality to visible centrality takes place by transforming Charlotte's body. In order for her to become an active subject, she must become the object of others' gazes. Moreover, she could only come out of obscurity in this way, taking her place on-camera as author of her own desires. For us this focus on the body is positive and far from dynamics traditionally denounced by Feminist Film Theory. For, while the protagonist's invisibility is linked to a sexless life and domineering mother—Charlotte once had a lover but was forced by her mother to give him up—her visibility implies her consequent desirability and rediscovery of active sexual drive. Indeed, sexual repression made Charlotte depressed, neurotic, homely, and insecure. And abreaction of the traumatic event renders her happy, stable, attractive, and confident. Thus, she is at once subject and object of desire, gaining autonomy through her desirability. Here, exhibition and spectacle of the female body do not represent woman's subordination, as Feminist Film Theory would have it, but the possibility of becoming an autonomous subject. Likewise, modern material culture—i.e., fashion, makeup, and beauty culture—are not shackles, but elements of gratification that lead to a process of female self-fashioning over and above male voyeurism and desire.[27]

But even if Charlotte is partially objectified by her aesthetic transformation, *Now, Voyager* also scrupulously avoids a diegetic male gaze in order to posit an ideal *female spectator*.[28] For example, in the first scene described there is no mediation between the camera's eye and the protagonist's ungraceful body. Later, in the ship episode when Charlotte appears transformed, the camera's dolly movement spectacularizes her body, creating another purely filmic perspective apart from the point of view of the vacationing onlookers. In this way, her figure moves beyond the diegetic world of the film and offers itself to the spectators in the movie theater. Again, while the vacationers watch from below, the camera moves on high. These diegetic glances are completely anonymous inasmuch as they come from subjects who play no particular role in the film. Thus, they cannot function as a link between the camera and the spectator. But if that is not enough, in the third episode described, the scene where Lisa and June greet Charlotte at the port explicitly inscribes a diegetic female gaze. This, in turn, activates a female reception of the film. Mother and daughter first look incredulously at the newly elegant Charlotte coming down the stairs of the ship. Then, after having greeted her, they look at each other in surprise, dumbstruck by this former ugly duckling now surrounded by attractive young men. The scene is constructed around a gaze that circulates between these three women. Lisa and June look knowingly, at first surprised but then happy. In their approval, mother and daughter also become accessories to Charlotte's move toward independence, encouraging her to confront her old mother. In fact, it was Lisa herself who set Charlotte on this path in the first place by introducing her to Dr. Jaquith.

The scene when Charlotte confronts her mother also centers on the relation between body and gaze. When her daughter returns home, Mrs. Vale does not approve of the girl's new look. Indeed, she orders Charlotte to present herself for closer inspection. Made to march up and down the room, Mrs. Vale then demands that the girl put her old clothes back on and retire to the room closest to hers. For an instant, we fear that Charlotte might accede and regress back into old habits, but that fear quickly vanishes as Charlotte goes to her old room instead of the new one appointed by her mother. Mrs. Vale then follows to reassert the orders she has just given, but Charlotte does not comply. Instead, facing up to her mother, she formally affirms her autonomy by moving offscreen behind a dressing-screen. Here, Mrs. Vale's outline occupies the right side of the frame while Charlotte is located behind the dressing-screen on the left. In a chiasmatic relationship with the film's beginning, when Charlotte had heard her mother calling her "ugly duckling," the daughter now claims her autonomy from offscreen while the mother is visible but rendered speechless. Thus, as Charlotte resolutely declares her intention to decide on her own, Mrs. Vale's disapproving gaze is denied access to her daughter's body. This absence of visual contact strikes a parallel with the film's earlier representation of the mother-daughter conflict. But now, by taking the two scenes together, one can readily understand Mrs. Vale's denied gaze as a loss of control over her daughter. At the scene's conclusion, Charlotte reemerges from offscreen in a new, long, low-cut black dress. She then pins on the camellias just sent by her lover Jerry. Again via the body, the film resignals the possibility of female autonomy. In this way, Charlotte definitively wins the argument by donning the dress she chose for herself rather than the one her mother prefers. Later that night, the "new Charlotte" seals the deal by presenting herself to the rest of the family, and everyone is astonished by her miraculous transformation.

Having come out from her mother's domineering shadow, Charlotte makes her way on the path toward "normal femininity" by getting engaged to a rich Bostonian. She initially met the man through her mother. Thus, after her great rebellion, she ironically seems to pursue acceptance of conventions. Indeed, for a woman of her social status, marriage was inevitable. Consequently, Charlotte seems to accept Livingstone's courtship despite the fact that she is not in love with him. But when the marriage appears imminent, Charlotte happens to see Jerry again and this rekindles her love for him. Unable to go through with the wedding, she and Livingstone agree to break off their engagement. Naturally, Mrs. Vale is against this decision, and the ensuing quarrel coupled with her declining health instigates her death. At this point

Charlotte leaves for Vermont. But upon reaching Jaquith's clinic, Charlotte meets Tina—Jerry's troubled daughter—and becomes very fond of her. Here begins the last part of the film, in which the path toward femininity develops in a twisted end. For Charlotte had already begun to identify with Tina after hearing about the child's unfulfilled need for motherly affection from Jerry during the cruise. Moved by the similarities to her own upbringing, Charlotte dedicates her affection to Tina, practically adopting her with an invitation for the girl to come live with her back in Boston. In the last scene, we then see Tina transformed as she comes down the stairs. In a *chic* dress with her hair pinned up, she goes to kiss her father who has just arrived at Charlotte's house. As Charlotte had been earlier, the girl is now almost unrecognizable. The cruise had allowed Charlotte to rediscover sexuality, thus completing her trajectory toward femininity. Such a trajectory had been arrested years before during a similar cruise when Mrs. Vale had discovered the young Charlotte flirting with a crew member. The mother had violently censored her daughter's behavior, initiating her life of loneliness in the big family mansion. At the end, Charlotte transforms herself once more, definitively adopting the role of motherhood. But rather than marry Tina's father, Charlotte chooses a single life and dedicates herself to the care of children just as Anna O. did. In fact, we see her discussing the project of a new clinic with Dr. Jacquith. Therefore, while Charlotte gives up on marriage, she does not give up on motherhood. Indeed, she ultimately calls Tina "our child," while at the same time reformulating Jerry's role in her life. Thus, their sexual relationship becomes a platonic one as their mutual love and affection is transmuted into a united effort toward Tina's welfare. In this way, in the name of absolute autonomy, Charlotte may now enter society on her own terms, free from the dominion of mother and husband alike.

In her reading of *Now, Voyager*, Elizabeth Cowie has argued that the film represents specific female fantasy scenarios. Drawing on Freud as well as Laplanche and Pontalis, Cowie explains that "fantasy is an imagined scene in which the subject is a protagonist, and which always represents the fulfillment of a wish albeit that its representation is distorted to a greater or lesser extent by defensive processes."[29] Fantasy has two fundamental elements: the mobility of the subject's position and the centrality of the scenario with respect to the object (of desire). On the one hand, the primal fantasy is "a scene in which the child is also present interchangeably with the other participants as onlooker, as one or other parent, or even as the person who will discover the child looking-on."[30] On the other hand, fantasy deals more with the mise-en-scène of desire than obtaining its object: "The pleasure of fantasy lies in the setting out, not in the having of the objects. Within the daydream and more especially in fictional stories, the demands of narrative may obscure this, for the typical ending will be a resolution of the problems, wars, feuds, and so on, bringing about the union in marriage of the hero and heroine." In other words, "the pleasure is in how to bring about the consummation, is in the happening . . . and not in the moment of having happened."[31] The first part of the film deals with the fantasy of obtaining the love of a man who had previously rejected Charlotte and the fantasy "for a secret love, passionate and fulfilling as 'reality' can never be." Besides the "banal wishes" of the first part, the film presents in the last part perverse scenarios. *Now, Voyager* recounts an incomplete female oedipal trajectory (or perverse according to Freud). By refusing Jerry, Charlotte excludes the father figure from the oedipal triangle, thereby choosing the mother-daughter relationship as the sole source of fulfillment and plenitude. Accordingly, Charlotte "sets herself up as the 'good' mother against Mrs. Vale's 'bad' mother." But she also clearly recognizes herself as a little girl in Tina. As a result, Charlotte becomes both "Mrs. Vale and Tina," simultaneously collapsing the roles of both mother and daughter unto herself. The female spectator, then, is left with a choice. If she identifies with Charlotte, the finale is disappointing because the woman gives up on the man she loves. If she identifies with the fantasy of the mother-daughter relationship, the ending is much more satisfying. In any case, the spectator is "the only place in which all the terms of the fantasy come to rest." Indeed the viewing experience consists in tracing the fantasy scenarios in the textual devices not in the character's psyche.[32]

OEDIPUS II. MOTHER-DAUGHTER IN *MILDRED PIERCE*

Mildred Pierce tackles the question of female desire through the tortuous experience of its eponymous protagonist played by Joan Crawford. First a devoted wife, then a single mother supporting two daughters, Mildred ultimately becomes a successful business woman only to lose the affections of those closest to her in the process. Based on a novel by James M. Cain, Curtiz's film was a key woman's film and vehicle for one of Crawford's best performances, landing her the Oscar that year. But *Mildred Pierce* also clarifies the generic affinities between the woman's film and film noir. As with many noirs, *Mildred Pierce* begins when the protagonist's destiny is already sealed and nothing remains but to recount it.

The film opens just after the murder of a man in a California coastal mansion. In the sequence immediately following, Joan Crawford walks despairingly in the vicinity of a dock. She is about to throw herself into the water, but a policeman suddenly arrives and prevents her suicide. With its homicide and femme fatale walking on wet streets at night, the beginning is typically noir. Then, from inside a noisy bar, a man recognizes Crawford and invites her for a drink. Mildred accepts the man's advances and brings him back to the house where the homicide took place. Hoping to pin the murder on him, she locks him inside and flees. He spies the murder victim, however, and manages to escape before the police arrive. Back at home, agents catch up with Mildred and ask her to follow them to the police station. The detective in charge of the investigation informs her that her second husband, Monty Baragon, is dead and that her first husband is the accused killer. Mildred does not believe the charges, but the detective seems rather sure. Still, Mildred insists and even claims that she made a mistake divorcing Bert. Then, seated in front of the detective, she begins to recount the last four years of her life.

Figure 20 and 21. Joan Crawford in *Mildred Pierce*, 1945.

Starting with her first marriage, Mildred describes her life as a housewife, baking cakes for her neighbors while Bert struggled to find work as a real-estate agent. He was also having an affair. But only after a fight over an expensive outfit purchased for their eldest daughter, Veda, does the couple separate. In fact, Mildred chases him out of the house, but she does not despair. She begins working as a waitress. Then, thanks to the help of Wally—Bert's ex–business partner who has always admired Mildred from afar—she manages to secure a loan, buy a house, and convert it into a restaurant. The seller, Monty Baragon, is an aristocrat fallen on hard times. As Mildred finally permits herself a moment of pleasure, he begins to court her. At the same time, the youngest daughter Kay catches pneumonia and dies. This misfortune pushes Mildred to rededicate herself to work, above all in order to satisfy the eldest daughter's expensive tastes.

The restaurant becomes successful and Bert finally grants Mildred a divorce. In a short time, the restaurant expands into a chain called *Mildred's*. Business proceeds marvelously thanks to Ida, indefatigable collaborator with whom Mildred also has a strong friendship. But with the success comes trouble. Not only does Veda disdain her mother "who smells too much of grease," she also begins to fancy Monty and his high-class lifestyle. On top of that, Monty begins to demand money to entertain himself as well as the girl. Mildred grows tired of this and decides to buy him off with a generous check. Then, after one offense too many, Mildred chases Veda away too. But upon reflection, Mildred regrets the act and asks Monty to marry her, hoping to win Veda back in the process. Monty accepts on the condition that he become co-owner of Mildred's business. Then one evening, after discovering one of her husband's countless schemes, Mildred goes to their coastal mansion to speak to him. There, she catches Monty and her daughter in an intimate embrace. Veda announces Monty's intention to divorce Mildred and marry her. Mildred leaves distraught. But when Monty negates Veda's claim and denies her subsequent advances, she kills him. Mildred promises to protect Veda, but is finally unable to prevent the police from discovering the truth. Crawford finally leaves the station at dawn, only to find that Bert had waited for her all night. In the end, perhaps they get back together.

In opposition to Mildred's projected autonomy, narrative structure and diegetic point of view suggest that female desire is either ultimately contained or tragically ended. Along these lines, dividing the narrative between past and present was a common, but particularly effective, technique for representing Mildred's two modes of behavior with respect to men. In reality, they represented two different worldviews expressed in two different visual styles. Accordingly, Pam Cook has observed that the brief sequences set in the present are shot in a film noir style, while that of the two long flashbacks is rather different. The latter sequences offer a more illuminated image and are devoid of oblique camera angles. Thus, the film is split "between melodrama and film noir, between 'Woman's Picture' and 'Man's Film,' a split which indicates the presence of two 'voices,' female and male."[33] Likewise, by studying the film's production history Thomas Schatz has also shown that this duality was born not only of the decision to use flashback as a means of getting by censors, but also to use two different screenplay writers.[34]

Despite the fact that the majority of the film is set in the past and told through a "feminine voice," the few instances set in the present carry a "male voice"—the police, the Law, the truth—and function as a frame, containing and annulling female autonomy. All of Mildred's success becomes a parenthesis in the past, already finished at the film's outset.

Mildred's guilt lies in her usurpation of male roles, regardless of Bert Pierce's inadequacies. As she recounts her story, she assures the detective that she practically lived in the kitchen during her first marriage. Indeed, the first flashback opens with images of her baking cakes. Bert, on the other hand, is a pitiful husband, father, and provider. He has a lover and is basically unemployed. As a result, Mildred thinks only of her children's desires, perhaps indulging them too much. This is especially true of Veda, whose character may even be taken as an implicit criticism of consumer culture. By comparison, Mildred is the only entirely positive character in the film. Moreover, her second husband is as weak as the first. Monty is an aristocrat fallen on hard times and disdains work. Along with Bert, these two models of weak masculinity are set against Mildred's activity and implicit masculinity. The film's only mutually complicit relationship is between Mildred and Ida, inseparable collaborator and hard worker. Unfortunately, this relationship is not enough to construct a "female genealogy" as in *Now, Voyager*, where Tina identifies with her symbolic mother Charlotte. And Veda, for her part, is not only unable to identify with Mildred, but she is also antagonistic. Indeed, Veda's hyperfemininity clashes with her mother's masculinity. While Mildred is an active businesswoman, Veda is interested only in becoming the male gaze's object of desire. Ironically, after paying for years of costly piano and singing lessons with the intention of making her an artist, Mildred's daughter will end by exhibiting herself in a cheap night-club, entertaining guests as a run-of-the-mill soubrette.

Typical in cinema's depiction of female autonomy at the time, Mildred's punishment for refusing a subaltern role in society represents a strong contradiction in the film. Despite the fact that she "left the kitchen" as a result of male weakness, however, her ultimate condemnation was in perfect harmony with the fear that seized a postwar sociomedial imaginary, i.e., that the American woman who "sacrificed" during the war did not want to leave her job and return to the domestic sphere.

Though never explicit about her "guilt" lest the pleasure of the text be destroyed, the film condemns Mildred through a variety of subtle, but nevertheless effective, narrative techniques. While she is innocent and never inculpated by detectives, the film's opening is constructed to make the spectator believe Mildred is the killer. First, we see the exterior of a house on the coast from two different angles. Then, we hear a round of gunfire that continues after the cut. In a third shot, we see the man who has taken the hit. Now inside the house, the man makes a half-turn toward the camera and falls. In the following shot, the man is on the ground and calls out "Mildred" while the killer throws the gun on him from offscreen. After another shot of the room, the camera returns outside and shows a car making a getaway. The next episode begins with a beautiful crane shot that slowly descends on a pier. A woman enters from the right, walking toward the end of the dock. She is seen only from behind. Then, finally, the camera swings around to reveal the protagonist's identity. It is Joan Crawford dressed in an elegant fur, her face frozen in an expression of shattered grief. She moves toward the railing of the pier. The adjacency of the two sequences cannot but implicate Mildred. In the first, the assassin's identity remains hidden, only showing the victim from an invisible shooter's perspective. In the second, Crawford appears to inhabit a space contiguous with that of the homicide. Both sequences have shots of the California coast and after the victim calls out her name, one cannot but take the woman for the killer. Thus, Mildred's transition from offscreen abstraction to onscreen assassin transposes the film's central question from "who killed Monty?" to "why did Mildred kill him?" Moreover, the woman's presumed guilt seems corroborated by her behavior toward Wally, having drawn him into the house so he could unwittingly take the blame. Film noir iconography does not help either, representing Mildred as a femme fatale—elegant, appearing mostly at night, surrounded by darkness with a well-lit face. Thus, despite the fact that the film begins with an enigma, narrative technique and visual style offer powerful suggestions in anticipation of the film's denouement. For even if Vera is rightly brought to justice in the end, Mildred's "false guilt" represents an implicit condemnation of her failure as a mother, that she was unable to raise her daughter properly and thus bears equal responsibility for Veda's actions.

OEDIPUS III. DAUGHTER-FATHER IN *NOTORIOUS*

As with every Hitchcock film, *Notorious* (1946) resists classification into discreet genres. Perhaps because of its more solid and institutionalized standing, however, most critics tend to discuss *Notorious* and Hitchcock's work in a noir context rather than that of the woman's film.[35] Nevertheless, the difference between the two genres is often only a matter of narrative perspective or point of view. Thus, we can discuss *Notorious* as a woman's film, inasmuch as the story belongs in large part to Alicia Huberman/Ingrid Bergman and is told from her point of view.

Behind the spy story line's MacGuffin uranium bottle, *Notorious* conceals a multiplicity of plots linking its three protagonists in a triangulation of desire and sexual identity. As in *Suspicion* (A. Hitchcock, 1941), the film depicts a female oedipal trajectory characterized by the protagonist's excessive love for the father and the absence of the mother. In Freudian terms, the lack of the maternal figure, that is, the figure with whom the daughter should identify, is one of the causes of Alicia's difficult oedipal trajectory.[36] But difficulty in reaching a correct heterosexuality also implicates the two male characters, whose gender identity is rather weak and potentially homoerotic.[37]

Alicia's psychic dynamics are doubly unresolved. Without a female role model or the ability to substitute her father's love for that of an appropriate life-partner, she precludes a key oedipal passage whereby parental love is transformed into a series of secondary identifications. For if such processes of identification are the basis for the imaginary construction of the self, their absence cannot but hamper the subject's development, directing it away from more stable norms of heterosexuality and monogamy. This is precisely what happens to Alicia as she takes the discovery of her father's illegal activities as a betrayal and becomes sexually promiscuous. "When I found out about him, I just went to pot. I didn't care what happened to me," she says to Devlin/Cary Grant. As in *Suspicion*, "the father's position with respect to the law decisively determines the daughter's (aberrant) sexuality."[38] Thus, in both films Cary Grant's character is the antithesis of the protagonist's father and can thereby logically stand in for him. In *Suspicion* he is totally irresponsible, while in *Notorious* he is an excessively severe representative of the law.[39] Through this father-Devlin dichotomy, the features of the feminine Oedipus complex are inscribed in the text right from the very beginning to set up the resolution. Alicia must fall in love with Devlin, so very different from her father, in order to go through the Oedipus complex and reach "normal femininity."

Alicia's role in the CIA investigation in Rio de Janeiro shows a precise transformation of behavior that alternates between phases of passivity and activity, which in turn confirm both Freudian (and Mulveyan) hypotheses. This transformation is cinematically executed according to a precise structural use of the point-of-view shot. Considering this rhetorical figure's articulation and the relation between subject and object of the gaze, the film can therefore be divided into three parts according to Alicia's alternation between object and subject of the gaze.[40] In the first part, she is object of the gaze for photographers and journalists hoping to fill their Miami gossip columns. At the same time, she is also an object for Secret Service agents attempting to use her as a means of discovering her Nazi-loving father's activities. In the central part, the roles reverse. Exploiting Alex Sebastian's fascination with her, Alicia infiltrates his organization and obtains useful information. Here, the female agent accomplishes what Devlin and his male colleagues failed to do. This activity is expressed through several memorable subjective shots in which gaze and camera movement render a powerful and elegant feeling of suspense, in particular the shots of the bottle and key. But while Alicia plays an active masculine role, she also runs the risk of becoming a heroine in distress, always on the brink of being discovered. With her help, Devlin is able to discover the uranium in the bottle, but unfortunately, Alicia is then discovered and slowly poisoned. Symmetrical to the film's opening, Alicia is rendered helpless, simultaneously becoming object of her compatriots' gaze and victim of her enemies. Ultimately, when Devlin saves her she becomes a shapeless body, carried away in his regretful arms. In the last episode, Alicia is the only character who cannot "look" as the poison has made her almost blind. Devlin can thus take control of the situation, becoming the definitive hero of the story. Here, Alicia finally accepts the limits of her agency, i.e., passivity, while Devlin takes back his capacity for action that Alicia usurped in the central part of the diegesis. Nevertheless, if *Notorious* ultimately confirms the Freudian paradigm, it also shows that exchanging of gendered roles is completely possible. Moreover, Hitchcock's *Notorious* also anticipates a tendency to be manifested more clearly in the 1950s, which illustrates the difference between *sex* and *gender*. Where the former can be understood as a biological fact, the latter must be seen as a performative construction of the subject, in turn revealing the discursive nature of the relation between gender and identity.[41]

THE WOMAN'S DESIRING GAZE IN *HUMORESQUE*

In *Humoresque* (J. Negulesco, 1946), Helen Wright's gaze is active, continuous, and insistent. Played by Joan Crawford, Helen is a mature New York society woman with an uncontrollable desire for the young, talented violinist named Paul Boray. Here, traditional male-female dynamics are completely reversed with respect to both a general cultural imaginary and the film's particular mode of mise-en-scène. Indeed, Wright's desire for Boray evolves by way of Paul's economic subordination to his mistress. She becomes Paul's patron, helping him obtain his first contract, showering him with gifts, and turning him into a sort of "kept man." As both musician and Helen's object of desire, Paul's performer status demands that their relationship be mediated through a spectacular and excessive orchestration of the gaze. Thus, the object of the gaze, arresting the narrative flow, is male while the subject is female. But Helen's agency is ultimately fatal to her because she is unable to completely obtain Paul's affections. Rather, he is and will always be primarily devoted to his music. As a result, Helen commits suicide one night by throwing herself into the sea while Paul plays in concert.

As in *Mildred Pierce*, Negulesco's film has a dual narrative structure based on a dialectic between female and male points of view. Curtiz's film not only reinvigorated Joan Crawford's career, but it also established Warner's mid-1940s studio style, so strongly attuned to noir.[42] In fact, *Mildred Pierce*, *Humoresque*, and even later *Possessed*—all of which feature Crawford—inflect the woman's film with noir and female desire with overtones of death.[43] In *Humoresque*, however, the imbrication of different genres is still more complex. At the beginning of the film, violinist Paul Boray is in crisis and his show is canceled. He is unhappy and laments nostalgically an entire childhood devoted to the violin. A flashback brings us back to 1920s New York before the Great Depression and recounts the more significant moments of Paul's life: his first violin; daily life in the distant suburbs; the family drugstore; his first audition with the city orchestra; the meeting with his maestro-friend that finally lands him a job. Thus, *Humoresque* is a typical biopic for more than a half hour, concentrating on Paul's personal and artistic development. The film changes narrative register and perspective only when he meets Helen Wright. From here, it becomes a woman's film, ceding Helen the lead role and adopting *her* narrative perspective.

Helen and Paul's first meeting takes place at a party in her house and defines the unusual terms of their relationship. Not only is the traditional subject-object relation reversed with respect to gendered norms, but several stylistic connotations carry significant weight. Having come on the advice of a friend in search of job contacts, Paul begins to play the piano instead. The sequence shows typical visual and formal traces of 1940s noir cinema. Open and elegant spaces are shot with a long depth of field and particular prominence is given to a wide mirror, reflecting guests and other objects together. Attracted by the music, Helen conspicuously puts on a pair of glasses in order to see the artist better. As she gets closer, she takes them off again. Their meeting is framed within the context of her strong gaze as he becomes an object, featured in the center of the screen as he performs. Thus, if a performer is by definition an object of spectators' gazes, the gesture of putting on glasses indicates Helen's particular desire to see and know more than the others. Even more significant is the repetition of this gesture, to the point of becoming a defining element of Helen's desire for Paul. Indeed, her glasses become an "expressive object." As Jim Naremore has argued, once expressive objects enter "into social relations and narrative actions, they are imbued with the same 'spirit' as the humans who touch them."[44] Under these circumstances, *Humoresque* shifts from biopic to woman's film, taking Helen's desire for Paul as its principal theme from here on out.

Mary Ann Doane has argued that the bespectacled woman is a trope indicating "a heavily marked condensation of motifs concerned with repressed sexuality, knowledge, visibility and vision, intellectuality, and desire. The woman with glasses signifies simultaneously intellectuality and undesirability; but the moment she removes her glasses (a moment which, it seems, must almost always be *shown* and which is itself linked with a certain sensual quality), she is transformed into spectacle, the very picture of desire."[45] Doane cites numerous examples, including Negulesco's film. But *Humoresque* seems to follow the path she describes up to a certain point, inasmuch as Helen never becomes a spectacle or desirable object. In fact, Helen remains

Figure 22. Joan Crawford in *Humoresque*, 1946.

an active subject right up to the very end of the film. So while it is true that Helen does take off her glasses, this gesture doesn't really conform to the circumstances described by Doane. Helen is always the spectator and never the object of the gaze. In fact, she appropriates the gaze too much and must therefore disappear from the scene—i.e., die—as she menaces an entire system of representation based on sexual difference. As such, the film confirms Doane's main argument on the genre. *Humoresque* shows that in the woman's film "the attempt to attribute the epistemological gaze to the woman results in the greatest degree of violence" (i.e., her death).[46]

The film visually executes Helen's exclusion, systematically elevating two other female figures in opposition. On the one hand, Paul's protective mother disapproves of her son's relationship with Helen, even after her divorce finally paves the way for a legitimate engagement. On the other, his pale study companion—Gina, the "girl next door" of his youth—waits patiently to be recognized.

At his debut, mother and Gina sit in orchestra seats while Helen attends with her husband in her private box. Just as before, Helen puts on glasses to better see her lover while her husband observes his wife in the act of gazing, demonstrating her desire for another man. As in other films of the period—*Laura*, *Gilda*, and *The Lady from Shanghai* (O. Welles, 1947)—there is a triangular relationship between two men and a woman, where the husband or official mate is older, immoral, ambiguous, or impotent. At this point, Helen retains primacy over the other two female figures inasmuch as she appears more often onscreen. However, the fact that mother and study companion also receive close-ups as they gaze at Paul on stage suggests their eventual parity with Helen and foreshadows the latter's decline. For instance, after Helen and Paul begin seeing each other, Helen arrives in glasses one day and is shot in half-light and shadow. This treatment signals the beginning of her decline, for in the subsequent concert sequence Helen is shot with a slowly approaching tracking shot that puts her more and more in shadow. Gina, on the other hand, aware of the lover's presence flees the hall in tears. Then, when Helen's husband finally grants her a divorce, Crawford runs to give Paul the news in the middle of an important rehearsal. Not wanting to interrupt, she sits in shadow in the orchestra seats, using her glasses to observe her lover from afar. Still unaware of her presence, she decides to send Paul a note to advise him of some important news. Unwilling to be disturbed, however, he casts her note aside, unaware that Helen is watching him. At this point, it becomes clear to Helen that her efforts to obtain a divorce were futile since Paul's priority is his career. And after having desperately sought Mrs. Boray's approval for so long, Helen decides to reflect on her relationship with Paul where it began, at her coastal mansion. Meanwhile, Paul is in the middle of giving another concert. Shots of the auditorium signal the distance between the two and the end of their relationship. Moreover, in Helen's absence, Paul's family now sits in the box that she once occupied. This substitution represents her definitive exit and condones the beginning of a new relationship between Paul and his study companion. No longer a spectator, Helen ultimately rescinds her agency of vision by listening to the concert on the radio and then killing herself.

5

EXCESS, SPECTACLE, SENSATION

Family Melodrama in the 1950s

FORMS OF MELODRAMA

In the Introduction chapter, we analyzed the function of melodrama in the theoretical debates concerning Hollywood cinema. Melodrama, or the melodramatic mode, is not simply another Hollywood film genre, but represents an alternative to the classical mode of representation. Melodrama is replete with its own aesthetic strategies that privilege the image's emotional and spectacular components and also undermines causal narrative logic based on motivated action. In this study we argue that the evolution of the filmic form in American cinema during its "classical" sound period can be understood in light of the shifting relationships between classic and melodramatic modes. While classicism dominated the second half of the 1930s, the melodramatic and attractional registers characterize the most innovative cinema of the 1940s and 1950s. This change is expressed through new modes of representation of the human subject, with renewed attention to the body and sexuality. In melodrama, the subject becomes a site of unfulfilled desire, of the split between conscious and unconscious desire, of the inability to act.

But what does it mean to characterize something as melodrama or melodramatic? Despite the fact that the term seems to refer to a fairly well-outlined object, in reality an analysis of the use and diffusion of the term reveals some ambiguity. In fact, its definition depends largely on the context and discourse in which it is found. In Anglo-American scholarship, there is a substantial difference between the use established and debated by Film Studies scholars during the 1970s and 1980s, and that of the film industry and professional print media since the 1910s. In the first case, starting with Thomas Elsaesser's "Tales of Sound and Fury" (1972), melodrama refers to several genres or subgenres in which the sentimental or emotive register springs from problems linked to family dynamics. These dynamics typically concern the relationship between parent and child, but there is also a maternal version of melodrama that focuses on the suffering and frequently unmarried mother. From a formal point of view then, family melodrama of the 1950s described in Elsaesser's essay shows a highly expressive style in which meaning is driven more by visual and auditory elements than by verbal or narrative ones. This aspect is particularly significant because it registers the genre's anticlassical status that will be elaborated in the following. Moreover, melodrama's visual excess and spectacle, achieved through the new technologies of the period such as Technicolor and panoramic formats, has been interpreted in light of psychoanalytic dynamics and processes. In this fashion, the study of melodrama has contributed in a decisive way to the development of a highly productive method of film analysis, born from the *convergence* of film aesthetics, semiotics, and psychoanalysis. The validity of this proposal is confirmed by a second equally important convergence since the hypothesis formulated by film scholars is very close to that advanced by Peter Brooks in his very influential study *The Melodramatic Imagination* (1976). But because of the far-reaching influence of Brooks's work in theater, literary, and even cinema studies, it bears repeating that these studies on family melodrama films developed their conceptual and methodological observations autonomously. For example, it is enough to think of Elsaesser's intervention, which in reality precedes Brooks's. But there is also the work of Brooks's contemporaries Geoffrey Nowell-Smith and Laura Mulvey, who directly explored the relation between film aesthetics and psychoanalysis.[1]

Later studies, particularly those by Steve Neale and Ben Singer, have expanded the field in both content and method. Neale's archival work has revealed that the film industry and professional print media reserved the term *melodrama* for films ruled not by emotion, but by action, violence, and suspense. His survey of industry periodicals between 1938 and 1960—*Variety*, *Film Daily*, *Hollywood Reporter*, *Motion Picture Herald*—has revealed that for professionals and public alike, the term melodrama did not refer to "pathos, romance and domesticity, but to action, adventure and excitement. It was not about 'feminine' genres or women's films, but war, adventure, horror and thrillers. Genres typically considered 'masculine.'"[2] The canonical family melodrama films of the 1950s such as *Written on the Wind*, were sometimes defined as melodrama. But this was only because they had "sensational" themes, and not for reasons underlined by 1970s criticism. Similarly, not even women's films were defined as melodrama. The most common term was simply "drama,"[3] while "blood and thunder melodramas" were basically what we now call film noir. In this sense, Neale observes that industry did nothing but reiterate the term as it had been used since the 1910s, when, for example, it was applied to serial adventure films. In *Melodrama and Modernity*, Ben Singer picks up on this phenomenon to join textual with contextual approaches in a very original fashion. Here, he examines film melodrama from the late 1900s to 1920, with respect to other forms of popular entertainment—principally theatrical melodrama and mass-market periodicals—and in relation to the period's processes of modernization and urbanization. Returning to theories formulated by Simmel, Benjamin, and Kracauer, Singer interprets early sensational melodrama as an expression of the physical intensity of the subject's daily experience in the modern metropolis. On the one hand, sensational melodrama was an updated version of Victorian theater melodrama. On the other, it was an aesthetic version of modernity, of its excessive sensorial stimulation. Through iconographic materials of the period, Singer then shows that the metropolis was predominately represented as a threat. From traffic, to electric tram, to automobile, metropolitan life was a continual assault against the individual's body. Thus, Singer argues that such context gave credibility to the sensationalism of film melodrama as well as popular entertainment more generally.[4] As it turns out, masculine, not feminine, traits dominated melodramatic films since 1907. Rather than emotions and psychological complexity, there was action and physical violence. Instead of the domestic environment's (false sense of) security, there was the dangerous metropolis. Using Tom Gunning's terminology, one has to observe that in these films the aesthetics of attractions dominates narration and this sets up an anticlassical foundation for melodrama. For there is, in fact, a propensity for lively sensations and for rapid and powerful impressions that tower above any interest in motivated or narrative causality. So much so, that recourse to an episodic structure, coincidence, or implausibility represented a challenge to the diegetic unity and logical development of the film's narrative action.[5]

In an effort toward compromise, however, Singer proposes conceiving of melodrama as a "cluster concept" such that one can speak of melodrama whenever an assorted grouping of its five constitutive elements is present in a text: pathos, overwrought emotion, moral polarization, nonclassical narrative structure, and sensationalism. So while Hollywood melodrama essentially activates the first two characteristics (excluding moral dichotomies), action melodrama often reverses the formula. Moreover, it actually seems to privilege moral polarization while excluding pathos.[6] For instance, the serial-queen melodramas of 1912–1920, which serve as the primary basis of Singer's analytic work, are an example of action melodrama. Different from Griffith's melodramas and the theatrical melodramas studied by Brooks, where the young female protagonist is typically a defenseless victim, here the heroine is strong, active, and gifted with masculine traits and abilities. Though not exclusively intended for a female audience, the genre reflects and nourishes the image of the emancipated woman of the period, a woman allowed to leave domestic space for the first time and autonomously venture out in public as a worker, consumer, and spectator.[7] Qualities of strength and courage made it impossible to feel pathos for such masculine heroines.

Thus, if conflict in action-oriented melodrama is external and characters risk their lives by encountering potentially dangerous spaces and objects, in emotional melodrama the conflict is completely inside the protagonist's body. In other words, the body, as in cases of hysteria, becomes the site in which meaning is inscribed. Brooks affirms that the melodramatic body transforms "the psychic affect into somatic meaning" and thus becomes a text to be deciphered.[8] And here, he finds one of the elements of melodrama's modernity. But beyond the differences underlined by Singer, I believe that one finds the essential trait of melodrama in the centrality of the body. Only in melodrama, through "an aesthetics of embodiment [are] the most important meanings . . . inscribed on and with the body," while in other fields the body is simply taken for granted.[9] Thus, the melodramatic component of film noir and women's films has to be seen in this sense, since the subject's experience is first and foremost corporeal.

According to Brooks, the emergence of a melodramatic aesthetic and rhetoric coincides with the French Revolution. Evidently, it is not about seeing the 1950s Hollywood family melodrama in direct relation with preceding melodramatic forms so much as reading the centrality of the body in this genre through a process of *historicization* and *reorientation* of these theories and forms.[10] This reading then moves melodrama into the modern era—not only in the sense that Brooks intended modernity but also that of Foucault, who insisted on the birth of modern man as an identification with control and submission of the human body.[11]

If representation of the body in serial-queen melodramas of the 1910s reflected the metropolitan subject's experience of danger, sensorial hyperstimulation, and ongoing physical activity, bodies in 1950s family melodramas are legible in light of sexual and psychological phenomena of their own period. First of all, the camera no longer privileges urban exteriors, but rather domestic interiors. These are the homes of the middle and upper-middle-class living in the rural and provincial areas of the Midwest and the South where protagonists seek to realize the postwar dream of a comfortable suburban life that was prevalent in the American cultural imaginary of the time. Action and movement in space are in fact limited as well as the physical dangers that the body encounters. And more than physical violence, the nucleus of melodrama seems to lie in *situations* where bodies are spatially trapped and where psychic-emotional conflicts explode. Here, the sensorial hyperstimulation of early-twentieth-century modernity described by Simmel and Benjamin gives way to repressed sexuality. Such repression can be linked to rigid male and female gender roles anticipated by the image of the suburban family. As we will see, the model of the suburban family envisages more traditional roles for its members, especially in relation to lifestyles and sexual practices that emerged with modernity. For example, the push to make women go back into the home is diametrically opposed to the New Woman straddling the early twentieth century. But this push is also opposed to the female worker who, in the early 1940s, took the place of her male counterpart in the factory as he went off to war. The gender dynamics of the suburban family also intertwine with the discussion of sexuality proposed by psychoanalysis in its popular Americanized form.

Freudian psychoanalysis swept over American society in the 1910s and in fact reached its apex in the 1940s and 1950s. As it has been documented, pop psychoanalysis is a specifically American phenomenon, which influenced the cultural imaginary at large. While in the first decades of the century open-minded doctors and psychologists had encouraged sexual expressivity, the discourse on sexuality in postwar America harked back to containment.[12] The image of woman as *homemaker*—devoted to educating her children and maintaining a large comfortable home—sent her back, if not to a Victorian model of femininity, to a status in which a separation of gendered space dominated according to traditional internal/external, public/private dichotomies. In family melodrama, female activities took place between the kitchen and the garden, as one sees in the respective beginnings of *Bigger than Life* (N. Ray, 1956) and *All that Heaven Allows* (D. Sirk, 1955). The only public space reserved for women was at the country club or during national holidays like Labor Day in *Picnic* (J. Logan, 1956). In rare cases of a working woman, her activity was incompatible with marriage or found to be debilitating to family. Beyond Lana Turner in *Imitation of Life* (D. Sirk, 1959), one can also think of Rosalind Russell in *Picnic*. Here, Russell plays a school teacher who pays for her career ambitions with spinsterhood until she pathetically succeeds in getting married through an involuntary stratagem.

In concert with theories of sexual expressivity such as the famous Kinsey reports on male and female sexuality, published in 1948 and 1953, family melodrama also shows that repression of the libido has devastating effects and that its free expression is vital to social order. The 1950s home is an unhealthy place, and the source of psychosexual pathologies that put the mental health and physical safety of household members at risk. A uniquely effective example is represented in *Bigger than Life*, where James Mason attempts to kill his little boy as a result of drug overdose. As we will see, in family melodrama female and male subjects often have similar pathologies. Such a condition is manifested through the spectacular representation of the body. *Picnic* stands as a model, where William Holden's character finds himself in a vast self-referential female world. Here, while each woman introduces a different psychosexual dynamic, Holden's character literally concentrates the fears and struggles of the postwar American male in his own body. And from here, we can see how the male-female/public-private dichotomies discussed in the Brooksian paradigm are reinforced in visible manifestations of the period's defining characteristics. Ultimately, these dynamics offer a version of melodramatic form where the relation between aesthetics and psychoanalysis remains central.

BODY/GENDER/CLASS: MALE IDENTITY IN THE 1950S

Despite rather marked differences, the body appears central in each theory of melodrama. Whether it is about the hyperstimulated masculinized female body of the modern metropolis described by Singer, the "suffering body" of the virtuous but victimized heroine discussed by Linda Williams,[13] or the hysterical body described by theorists of the 1970s, melodrama and its subgenres are by and large what Williams has called, in another influential essay, a "body genre."[14] In my opinion the gap between industrial and contemporary critical versions of melodrama is not as wide as Neale and Singer maintain if we primarily focus on Brooks's notion of body. The body becomes the locus in which identity—first and foremost the result of sexual and gendered practices—is inscribed. Be it male or female, the melodramatic body is a subject of desire that wants to freely express its drives and desires differently from dominant and codified models. Drives manifest themselves visually through spectacular corporeal attitudes and postures. Family melodrama thus implicitly recognizes that sexuality is a central component of human nature.[15] Therefore, the most melodramatic and formally excessive moments are realized in *situations* when the body materially becomes body-drive or is invested with the drives of another.

To find the origin of this modality, we can look to *The Outlaw* (H. Hughes/ H. Hawks, 1943) and above all, *Duel in the Sun*, where Perla's crawling body is alternately bandaged in red or black such that she becomes an increasingly shapeless, animal-like object and the victim of Lewt's fatal desires.[16]

In many ways, Vidor's film and Jennifer Jones's character then constitute the matrix of 1950s melodrama. It is enough to think about Marilyn Monroe's character in *Niagara* (H. Hathaway, 1953)—when she displays her full erotic charge dressed in red, dancing to a sensual melody in front of motel guests—or Dorothy Malone's character in *Written on the Wind*—when her father's heart attack and her wild dance episode occur at the same time. In fact, there are unquestionable similarities between the inscription of erotic drives on the three divas' bodies and their respective filmic images. On the one hand, the color red expresses each character's erotic desire through the most primitive and direct of codes. On the other, the camera privileges skewed angles and asymmetrical or out-of-focus framing to such an extent that the female body becomes an indistinct blotch of color, a pure dynamism. In the films of Vidor and Sirk, for example, there is a nonanthropomorphic shot where only the hem of the protagonist's dress occupies the visual field as she dances wildly. In such cases, there is an explicit recovery of sensationalism, of silent melodrama's most typical thrill. These episodes are saturated with primitive attractionalism and surrender themselves to brief and intense sensations. However, the recovery of these forms has to be historicized. Because if the serial-queen melodrama's aesthetic can be seen in relation to the New Woman's urban experience, I believe we can consider this inscription of sexual drives as a historical modality specific to the aesthetic of attractions of family melodrama. The *process of historicization* necessarily involves both the form or materiality of sensation and its function in the communicative act, i.e., the spectator's filmic experience. In this light I believe that Hitchcock's *Psycho* (1960) represents the final episode of the trajectory we are discussing. *Psycho* is the most radical development of film noir's approach to vision, and more broadly of the aesthetic of sensation developed since the 1940s in noir and later melodrama and the musical.[17]

Indeed, the aesthetic of sensation bears witness to a fundamental change in relation to classical cinema of the 1930s. Just as with film noir and the woman's film, melodrama of the 1950s constituted a mode of representation in which the visual dimension dominated both the verbal and the narrative registers. And not by chance, many of the period's technological advances facilitated this process. From Technicolor to Cinemascope, from stereophonic sound to extreme camera movements—as with shots taken from helicopters—image and music acquired new aspects. The image was suddenly more spectacular and the music evoked a purely emotional tone: together they made verbal language quite irrelevant.[18] The use of vivid colors, emphatic music, and bodily gestures then seem to bear out Brooks's theories. But beyond these, objects such as grids and mirrors, technical elements like filters and wide-angle lenses, as well as Cinemascope's excessively horizontal space also played a significant role in melodrama's preference for spectacle over dialogue. Indeed, Brooks affirms that melodrama's emphasis on visual codes showed "an effort to recover on the stage something like the mythical primal language, a language of presence, purity, immediacy. Implicit in this proposition of a dramaturgy of inarticulate cry and gesture is no doubt a deep suspicion of the existing sociolinguistic code . . . since the conventional language of social intercourse has become inadequate to express true emotional valence."[19]

But even though sexual and gender identity represent the most significant aspects, there are other categories of difference that define the relation between socially permissible and nonnormative desires. In fact, class difference is almost as discriminatory as gender difference, and this is yet another confirmation of the connection between the original melodramatic forms explored by Brooks, where the sex/class coupling characterized melodrama's most formative vice/virtue conflict. From the novels of Richardson to Lessing's *Emilia Galotti* (1772) and from Schiller's *Intrigue and Love* (1783) to Pixerécourt's melodramas, melodramatic plots centered on the clash between members of a declining aristocracy and the bourgeoisie. Typically, the villain was a libertine of corrupt sexual habits and morals that undermined the bourgeois heroine's virtue. She usually fought to defend her virginity, and her purity was a metaphor of the entire class's social virtue.[20] But 1950s melodramas were not so Manichaean. "Hollywood melodramas focused not on the battle between good and evil characters, but rather on the pathos of situations of moral antinomy in which two or more morally good (or at least nonvillainous) characters find that their interests are fundamentally incompatible."[21] However, this ambiguity did not mark the disappearance of class difference, which in fact remained an integral part of the genre. For class differences were still meaningful inasmuch as they could be connected to specific sexual practices.

But in film after film, family melodrama did not present a singular model for gender/class relations such that there was a precise correspondence between particular sexual and class identities. There were in fact varied combinations that reflected different social and cultural discourses of the time. Thus, if the suburban family model had the middle-class white person as its primary target, historical analysis has shown that "during the postwar years, there were no groups in the United States for whom these norms were irrelevant."[22] And this flexibility with which practices and behaviors passed from one subject to another, independently from their sex or social class, corroborates even Barbara Klinger's hypothesis that formal innovation is the "natural" procedure through which genres evolve.[23] For example, in the case of the male subject, excessive virility can characterize a rich property holder like Captain Wade/Robert Mitchum in *Home from the Hill* (V. Minnelli, 1960) or a man of popular extraction like William Holden's character in *Picnic*, who becomes the object of desire for many women in the film.

Picnic provides one of the best examples for assessing the body's status. Most significant is the similar visual treatment of male and female bodies. In the space of a few moments, the beautiful bodies of the two protagonists, William Holden and Kim Novak, are publicly exposed and looked upon as objects of desire. In the triumphal parade, Madge/Novak is seated on a throne consecrating her title as Labor Day Beauty Queen. She is exhibited to the whole community and forcibly reduced to an erotic object. Meanwhile, her younger sister, who has just won a college scholarship, is the classical tomboy and suffers because she is only considered intelligent. Madge, on the other hand, complains because she is only admired for her beauty. For example, in one of the first episodes, she looks at herself in the mirror and laments "I am getting tired of only being looked at." But a similar problem also afflicts Hal/Holden, whose arrival in a small Kansas town on Labor Day rouses the dormant and repressed urges of a small female community: Flo Owens, her two daughters Madge and Milly, and an elementary school teacher renting a room from Owens played by Rosalind Russell. Hal takes a room next door to the Owenses in exchange for some gardening work. Then after taking off his shirt to expose his well-defined torso, he attracts the gaze of the four women conversing in front of their house. Here, in a perfect inversion of Mulvey's paradigm, a point of view shot first shows us Rosalind Russell's gaze at the attractive male body. A second point of view shot frames the four women as they look at the stranger, attracted to his exceptional virility. And with this sequence, the film frames the male subject as an object of desire, just as the female had been long before him. Thus, this dynamic signaled a process of feminizing male characters that Steven

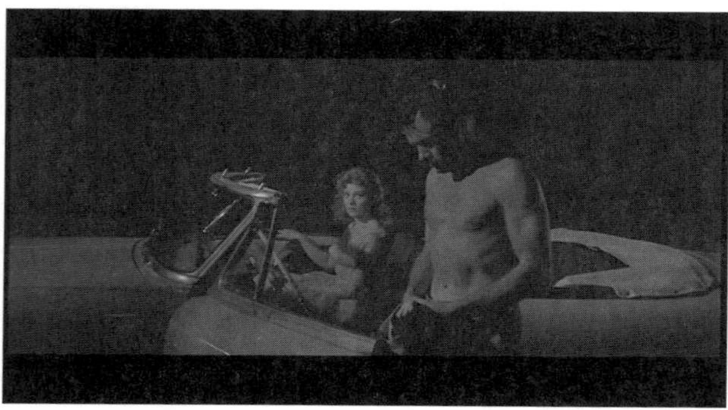

Figure 23. William Holden and Kim Novak in *Picnic*, 1956.

Cohan argues began at the end of the 1940s with Montgomery Clift's debut in *Red River*.[24]

Nevertheless, Holden's eroticized body functions through the modalities just described, but only if seen as a member of the "proletariat" or nonbourgeois class. Holden's sexuality is interwoven with his "gutter" identity, for which his rich and unattractive college classmate, Alan Benson, reproaches him as he pursues the beautiful Madge. Benson, in fact, comes from the family that controls local industry—like the Hadleys in *Written on the Wind*—and is destined to run the family business. He is also supposed to marry Madge—the poor yet attractive local beauty queen—and in his "gray flannel suit" he seems mature and ready to do so. But compared to his friend Hal, he is neither erotic nor exciting. Thus, for Alan, it is impossible to compete with Hal because the attraction between Novak and Holden is irresistible from the very start.

The opposition of Hal's sexuality and moral disorder compared to Alan's responsible yet boring behavior, represents two contrasting images of masculinity. These images dominated the sociomedial panorama of the time and may be found in any family melodrama. However, it is not always possible to spot a narrative mechanism in each film that literally reflects the period's tensions or narratively recoups its positive imagery. As a cultural text, a film genre has to negotiate contents and social desires through formal mechanisms inherited from its own history, which are partially independent from cultural norms. Nevertheless, family melodrama represents conflicting images of masculinity at the time in an exemplary way.

In the suburban family, the roles of men and women were divided in a more traditional way vis-à-vis the war period. While the husband, the *breadwinner*, provided economic sustenance for the family, the wife, the *homemaker*, occupied herself full time with family and householding. In her study of postwar masculinity, Barbara Ehrenreich shows how the construction of the breadwinner image resulted from the convergence of a series of discourses. Most important was psychoanalysis, which strove to validate this figure as "the only normal status for the adult male."[25] Doctors, sociologists, and thinkers of the time hypothesized that such conventional roles for both males and females had natural roots. And for behavioral psychologists in particular, the life cycle culminated in a maturity phase that implicated the male subject's acceptance of a series of tasks and responsibilities. He had to be mature at a young age—at this time the average American male married at twenty-three—and this meant choosing a partner, marrying, having a family, and assuming civic responsibilities.[26] The ideal breadwinner combined a capacity for social awareness in public and the work space with gifts of emotion and affection developed in private family space. Therefore, he not only had to provide economic sustenance for his wife and family, but also fulfill them with protective affection. The result was a new model of masculinity and marriage in which consumer culture played a primary role.

But fusing sensitivity and affection with a certain virility and decision-making capacity was no easy task. Perhaps as strong as the image of the breadwinner, was the image of man who rebels against this model, or the "gray flannel rebel" as Ehrenreich calls him. For example, many found it difficult to ensure the family's postwar mass consumerism standard of living. In this sense, *Bigger than Life* is exemplary. James Mason plays Ed Avery, a school teacher who lives in a beautiful house with wife and son. However, his salary is not enough. So unbeknownst to his family, he finds a second job in a taxi company. But the work wears him out and one evening he falls ill. At the hospital, the doctor prescribes him cortisone, which Ed soon begins to abuse. The drug renders him mentally unstable to the point where, in a moment of insanity, he tries to kill his son. But even though the doctor ultimately explains away Ed's insanity through casual abuse of the medication, Ray's film is a clear critique of suburban ideology, consumerism and the supposedly natural breadwinner role. In moments of crisis, Ed in fact allows himself to express his disgust for values he should hold dear. Permissiveness and emotional security—cornerstones of education at the time—become "petty domesticity" while Ed reasserts self-discipline, a sense of duty, and hard work in a discussion with the parents of some of his students, leaving them completely dumbfounded. In the end, Ed considers his life mediocre and banal, dreaming of heroic and important actions.[27] This dissatisfaction is an unequivocal sign of the failure of suburban ideology, which considered the very seriousness and responsibility of the breadwinner that Ed rejects to be heroic behaviors. For in fact, maturity was "a measured acceptance of the limits of one's private endeavors at a time when action on a broader political scale could only seem foolish—or suspect."[28]

Figure 24. James Mason and Christopher Olsen in *Bigger than Life*, 1956.

The breadwinner is typical of family melodrama, but his representation and narrative function vary markedly. In fact, the critique proposed by *Bigger than Life* was actually rather marginal and rare. It was more common that suburban ideology and the gender roles it envisioned were represented positively or as a source of lifestyle inspiration. Nevertheless, such films almost always privilege characters and dynamics marked out by an excessive and unrestrained desire through melodramatic techniques of mise-en-scène. This is done in clear contrast to the serious and responsible behavior of the suburban couple, typically represented in a sober visual style. Moreover, in many cases the original eighteenth-century form of melodrama actually survives since in many films members of the declining aristocracy acted as libertines and clashed with the emergent middle class over an irreproachable morality. Thus, *Written on the Wind* and *Home from the Hill* can be taken as paradigmatic examples. The former, Douglas Sirk's film, ends with Mitch/Rock Hudson and Lucy/Lauren Bacall leaving the Hadley property for marriage and a beautiful suburban home full of children and domestic appliances. This conclusion was motivated by a brief but important exchange between Kyle Hadley and Lucy at the beginning of the film. When Kyle asks, "What did the fortune teller tell you?" Lucy responds that "one day she would end up in a suburb, dressed in white with a husband, lots of debt and children." Nevertheless, it is undeniable that the film is more interested in the reckless pair of Hadley siblings, Kyle/Robert Stack and Marylee/Dorothy Malone. The former is an alcoholic and nearly impotent, the latter a nymphomaniac. Sirk called the two siblings "the secret owners of the picture." Indeed, through colors, music, and excessive camera angles, Sirk shaped their exuberant desires such that Kyle and Marylee become protagonists of the image, largely relegating Mitch and Lucy's involvement to narrative.[29]

And there is a similar dynamic in Minnelli's film *Home from the Hill*, where Captain Wade Hunnicut/Mitchum is the picture's undisputed protagonist. He is a great landowner used to having any woman he wants, while his wife in turn has long withheld intimacy as payback for marital infidelity. In addition to their son Theron, Wade also has an illegitimate son Rafe/George Peppard, who lives and works on the property although publicly unrecognized by his father. Rafe is a perfect breadwinner. He is affable, secure, and responsible. But he is also fond and protective of Libby, his future bride. Significantly, he proposes to her in a big supermarket, full of products clearly visible through depth of field. Just as Kyle Hadley in Sirk's film, Wade dies violently as payment for his faults. Purified from the presence of an outdated and excessive masculinity, the diegetic world legitimizes Rafe as representative of a new lifestyle as he invites his father's widow into his home. Hannah/Eleanor Parker will thus be able to help raise the coming grandchild. But even though mise-en-scène and camera work valorize the negative character by activating a certain degree of identification and empathy with him/her, it is also true that both films end by invoking the beginning of a new way of life. Family melodrama was thus irreparably split between two stylistic trajectories that returned to two very different lifestyles for the subject.[30]

The male figure, who then charged himself with validating a new familial and social model, also appeared to be a *redeemer* for all intents and purposes. He was a savior who not only eliminated the villain from the scheme, but also directed female sexuality into morally acceptable channels. Male purity could then set against female impurity, and in fact, before joining forces with the hero, both Libby and Lucy choose to bond with the villain of their own accord. It is only through Rafe and Mitch's intervention that they are saved from certain unhappiness. Rafe even assumes paternity for the child in Libby's womb out of compassion and thus doubly purifies the captain's world by rectifying Mitchum's bad behavior and failure to be a father.

Although a former victim of bullying and certain familial injustices himself, the redeemer is not psychologically torn in relation to his past and appears rather balanced. Under this profile, then, he is profoundly different from melodramatic characters with whom he interacts. They are totally enmeshed with their past and at the mercy of oedipal and regressive phases of desire. By virtue of his psychic equilibrium, the redeemer is therefore able to serve as moral guide for everyone, not only for the woman with whom he falls in love. This is the case of Michael Ross/Lee Phillips in *Peyton Place* (M. Robson, 1957). Michael is the new high school principal in Peyton Place, a rich town in New Hampshire. Not only does he want to introduce serious and responsible methods of instruction that strike a balance between innovation and tradition, but he also tries to attract the interest of Constance MacKenzie/Lana Turner. She is a single mother who dedicates herself exclusively to work and the care of her young daughter, Allison. Constance in fact seems to live in the memory of a dead husband, unknown to her daughter. But she does so to conceal a lie: Allison's father is not dead, and the girl is actually the fruit of an adulterous relationship. Much like Libby in *Home from the Hill*, Constance has to find a man that will rub out the stain of her past. But only after many refusals and vacillations, when Michael is about to leave Peyton Place, does she accept his love.[31]

In *Peyton Place* the male protagonist's role as moral guide is suggested right from the beginning through specific rhetorical devices. The beginning even recaptures several formal elements present in other melodramas of the period. For example, houses and local vegetation shot from a helicopter capture typical autumn colors that seem to quote the beginning of *All that Heaven Allows*. Then, a young woman's voice narrates over still shots depicting each of the four seasons. The voice announces the arrival of a "bittersweet time," a fifth season of love. The rarely used device of voice-over in family melodrama combined with the fictional quality of the still images gives the film a retro feeling. Then, the camera shows an automobile passing through toward the town. We see Peyton Place and the surrounding areas from the driver's perspective. Though we know nothing about him, the film underlines his subjective perspective and invites us to share his point of view. After passing the more outlying areas, the car arrives in a clean and perfect town, a seemingly undisguised reconstruction. Stopping to freshen up and ask directions at a diner, we can now see the protagonist up close. Like all the redeemers mentioned above, he is fully mature, physically pleasing, polite, and sure of himself. Michael Ross is the opposite of Hal in *Picnic*, who arrived by hitchhike and eventually had to run away. Here, rather, even the entrance to the school building presents itself under the aegis of propriety and moral irreproachability. Thus, when he goes to meet the eldest teacher—who was also considered for his position as principal—he is not only polite and affable, but eager to establish a collaborative rapport with her. Ross's most striking gift then is balance. On the one hand, he is antirepressive. On the other, he is not permissive and thinks that children must be educated responsibly. This does not mean that he is sexually inert, however. His erotic interest in Miss MacKenzie is clear from their very first encounter and he is in fact resolute despite her continual rejections. This bears resemblance to Hannah's situation in *Home from the Hill* since both women haven't been sexually active for years. Ultimately, the redeemer appears as an extension of the social image of the breadwinner. He is a mature and responsible man who, in a curious move with respect to early forms of melodrama, co-opts a sexual integrity that originally belonged to the female subject. Thus, he can eliminate the villain from the scene and morally save the woman.

STYLE, TECHNIQUE, IDENTITY

The era's dynamics of desire were realized not only in a specific story structure and through various types of characters, but also through style and mise-en-scène where new technological innovations played a leading role. As with the advent of sound, the impact and function of new technology did not stop at the stimuli that seem to have inspired them. As they came into contact with consolidated forms and styles, they contributed to their own transformation. The diffusion of panoramic formats, in particular Cinemascope, and the huge investment in Technicolor employed more extensively than in the 1940s after the introduction of Eastman Color Process, were due to the necessity of responding to the challenge laid down by television. Only by differentiating itself as much as possible from television could the film industry hope to compete in some measure with this new form of entertainment.[32] Indeed, as John Belton has argued in his study of 1950s wide-screen formats, these novelties spurred a new form of spectatorship based on visceral thrills and "a strong sense of physical participation."[33] The impressiveness of panoramic formats enhanced by the use of Technicolor set up a clear contrast with the black and white of the small screen. Likewise, the sensational and racy content of melodrama also marked another clear difference from the reassuring and domestic themes of television. This dynamic was formalized by the development of the "adult film," which was the result of a specific conjunction between production trends and new sociocultural values on sexuality that became visible in the years after World War II. While the adult film may intersect different genres, it finds itself most at home in family melodrama. As a whole series of theatrical dramas and popular novels of the period that often became cinematic adaptations,[34] family melodrama introduced narrative situations geared toward mature persons, offering an "impressive array of sensationalistic topics. Among these were psychological dysfunction, premarital intercourse, adultery, frigidity, homosexuality, nymphomania, sterility, illegitimate birth, alcoholism, family strife, violence, and drug abuse."[35]

If the emergence of spectacular technologies and sensational themes were both similarly, yet autonomously, explained in relation to the diffusion of television, it is possible to argue that their meeting produced a specific new style. Melodramatic style was born from the transformation of technique into form, from the refunctionalization of specific technologies in a formal model that was particularly adept at depicting 1950s social desires. But beyond the stylistic elements directly related to technological innovations and to general transformations within the film industry, there were also other formal devices that were involved in the revision of classic mise-en-scène that continued and enlarged the work already done by 1940s cinema. The transformation of the relation between space and characters was particularly important. Narrative and visual devices of 1950s family melodrama not only subordinated individual trajectories to those of the collective, but they also sanctioned a character's weak ability to control his/her surrounding space or to actively change it.

Compared to film noir, this condition did not occur in the urban space of big cities but in the small town's domestic and familial environment. The human figure now appeared to be controlled by the space surrounding it through strategies that *enclosed* or *bridled* the body. Cinemascope contributed to the first strategy: the effect of enlarging horizontal space while compressing vertical space was often intensified by the combined use of wide-angle lenses (and by depth of field). Clearly, the total effect of these choices depended on other factors as well, since the use of panoramic format was not in and of itself a sufficient condition for representing space that enclosed bodies. Nevertheless, the use of Cinemascope also involved the development of particular tendencies in shooting and editing. For example, with panoramic format the style of conversations became noticeably different from classical modes, with a particular effect on the representation of the human body. But the subject's lost autonomy was expressed in an even more significant way by visual work that tended to bridle the body, to put concrete obstacles in its way. In many episodes, the body was surrounded by a myriad of quotidian objects that seem to block its movement. Melodramatic framing is in fact characterized by an excessively dense screen. Depth of field was necessary to achieve this effect. But different from film noir, where it was often used in urban exteriors or the interior of bars and clubs, in family melodrama depth of field made the furnishings and decorations of bourgeois households completely visible.

Several objects had a more significant function than others. For example, "grids" formed by door and window frames were used in moments of profound detachment between characters, partially concealing their bodies. Particularly in Sirk, the grid was charged with stronger effects thanks to a combined use of chiaroscuro and colored filters. In *All that Heaven Allows*, for example, the moment in which Cary/Jane Wyman realizes that she must choose between her young lover and familial peace, the frame and particularly her face is flooded by blue and yellow colored filters. In *Written on the Wind*, Lucy is shot several times behind window mullions when her husband becomes drunk and violent after losing his battle with sobriety. In the beginning sequence, when Lucy's husband fights with Mitch—which in reality is the end point, given that the film is almost entirely a flashback—she is framed in half-shadow, behind the glass while looking outside. In another episode, she looks dispiritedly out the window after her husband inexplicably begins drinking again. The introspective gaze, or the act through which a character is shot near a window looking blankly into nothing or absorbed in thought, was rather pervasive in 1950s American cinema.[36] This figure, where the character is not looking, but

Figure 25. Robert Stack in *Written on the Wind*, 1956.

thinking or "listening" to his/her emotions, seems to suggest the emergence of thought in the Deleuzian sense.[37]

One last example of the grid in Sirk's cinema that bears mentioning is in *Imitation of Life*. At the end of the first half, Lora Meredith finally gets a much anticipated audition for a theatrical role, but her fiancé does not like her career choice and insists that she give it up. Lora, however, has no intention of doing so because acting is her raison d'être. The clash between the two is first suggested through a sort of split screen. On the right, Lora is illuminated by light, on the left Steve is immersed in shadow. Through the calibration of light and shadow, Sirk supplies stable empathic and emotional parameters in a clear and unambiguous way, in a gesture that is certainly comparable to Josef Von Sternberg's films with Marlene Dietrich.[38] And as the sequence ends, we reach the dramatic climax where irreconcilable positions force the two to leave one another. Here again, the shot is neatly divided in two. The right is occupied by a gridded front door through which Lora and Steve are visible as they follow one another down the stairs to leave. The left side of the screen, on the other hand, remains dark.

In the next episode after the breakup, we see Lora looking at herself in the mirror just as Cary did in *All that Heaven Allows*. But one finds similar episodes in all of Sirk's films. Perhaps even more than the grid, the mirror was of such importance to Sirk that it became a leitmotif. In *Written on the Wind*, he combines the insertion of particular objects into the diegesis through completely unique methods of camerawork, such as a particular approach to *mise en cadre* that seems to weave the intensely performative film together. In this sense, framing within a frame by means of a character's reflection in a mirror clearly suggests the subject's fragmentation. The use of the mirror was in fact part of a visual codification of excess inasmuch as there was a conscious directorial choice that the mirror and the image it reflected came perfectly positioned into the frame. For example, Kyle and Marylee both cast a reflection when they come back home after a night of excesses, the former carried on Mitch's back, the latter by the police. Not coincidentally, however, this happens just before the most important melodramatic scene of the film in which the father dies.

The character who looks at him or herself in the mirror in a moment of particularly dramatic emotional tension seems to experience a sort of "reverse mirror stage." In *Bigger than Life*, when James Mason looks at his reflection after having succumbed to drug addiction, his face is fragmented into many parts. This fragmentation was one of the most frequently deployed methods for representing a double, or the split between conscious and unconscious life. In family melodrama, this kind of image validated the unconscious side of the subject's personal experience. Thus, as was the case for the eroticization of the body, here too was a symmetrical treatment of male and female.

SENSATION AND SITUATION: *PICNIC* AND *WRITTEN ON THE WIND*

Melodramatic style and the aesthetic of sensation became paradigmatically manifest in the *situation*, a foundational aspect of melodrama. In these episodes, the formal elements and the genre's imaginary discussed earlier were forcefully expressed, particularly in relation to treatment of the human figure. An analysis of two critical moments in *Written on the Wind* and *Picnic* will also demonstrate how male and female bodies were equally eroticized.

The scene in which Marylee undresses while dancing wildly to a jazz tune picks up on many issues raised to this point. The character's body is *bridled* by her possessions, the rhythm of the dance is excessively fast, the color red dominates. The camera later privileges angled, out-of-focus, and uncentered shots through a perspectival and visual manipulation of the body. These devices proceed to such an extent that at certain moments, Marylee's body becomes an indistinct and shapeless red object.[39] And here begins the recovery of sensationalism that culminates in her father's tumble down the stairs. This is the same thrill typical of silent melodrama and popular theater, saturated in a primitive attractionalism that gave way to brief and intense sensations. But this particular episode must also be seen in relation to the notion of *situation* as explored by Lea Jacobs, who posits a duality between *situation* and *action*. She argues that in a situation, narrative action slows down while characters are introduced to new circumstances. During

Figure 26. Dorothy Malone's wild dance in *Written on the Wind*, 1956.

such moments, the audience experiences a stronger dramatic tension. In a cinematic situation, which is sort of a theatrical tableau, a sudden articulation of events leaves characters at an impasse or in a dilemma that requires prompt action.[40] This idea can be expanded further because the situation is a scene of particular intensity in which contrasting impulses and desires become proximate *only by chance*, without narrative causality. The lack of classical motivation renders the conflict unresolvable, precisely because it is unmotivated. For these reasons, the situation is antithetical to classical action. Thus, in these moments bodies are spatially compressed almost to the point of bursting, making the strength of drive and sensation clearer, but also rendering these moments more spectacular.

The main quality of *situationalism* in the father's death scene is partially concealed by crosscutting between the father and daughter in different spaces. The editing brings two characters who have been avoiding one another for most of the film closer together. The relation is purely formal, but such a move increases the emotional intensity because it makes it look as though Marylee's wild dance causes her father's death. This sensation is essentially created by nonnarrative elements. The rhythm of the editing increases frenetically, almost mimicking the rhythm of her dance. At the same time, the volume of the music is so loud that it invades the entire home—and every shot of the sequence for that matter. As a result, however, it is almost impossible for the spectator to *hear* the father falling as he rolls down the stairs. This produces a significant effect on spectatorship. For while Mitch and Lucy run to the father's rescue after *hearing* the fall (they could not possibly have *seen* it), the music volume prevents Marylee from *hearing* and thus noticing the accident. Moreover, the music is so loud that spectators do not hear Mr. Hadley's fall either. They only *see* it. So from here, the film invites spectators to partially identify with Marylee—hearing what she hears, that is, the music—while at the same time preventing them from identifying with Mitch and Lucy who do not hear the music but only the father's fall. Thus, if the spectator's sensorial experience is both audio and visual, and therefore superior to that of any single character, it is revealing that one can only (partially) identify with Marylee and not the other protagonists. Ultimately, in this case, identification then deals with the sensation that both music and dance cause in Marylee's body, and not with the reading of narrative action.

In *Picnic*, the most melodramatic situation concerns Hal as the film attempts to feminize his body. During the long Labor Day episode, the protagonists get together seemingly by chance, stealing away from the festivities. Rosalind Russell pathetically asks Hal to dance, but he declines. Hal is restless and indecisive because he is attracted to Madge but does not want to hurt his friend Alan Benson, her fiancé. Meanwhile Russell insists repeatedly to the point where she accidentally tears off Hal's shirt. Hal's muscular and sexy chest is exposed just as it was at the beginning of the film. The image is excessive and rather affected. From the moment Hal's shirt is torn off he is motionless, almost like in a freeze frame, and incapable of uttering a single word. He occupies the center of the screen and his demeanor seems like that of a pantomime. The framing is a literal return to the "text of muteness" of the theatrical *tableau* discussed by Brooks.[41] Mute and immobile, Hal sees the world around him collapsing. But Russell, in a particularly noteworthy performance, explodes and shouts that he's a loser and should stop pretending. Milly, Madge's younger sister, is also drunk and shouts that she hates her sister and is tired of always being thought of as the smart girl. Thus, without a particular motive, the conflict explodes as the melodrama reaches its emotional apex. Just like in Sirk's film where Marylee's body was symbolically the cause of her father's death, here Hal's body causes other characters to react hysterically. From now on, nothing will be as before. Hal and Madge will decide to leave town in order to try and live their own story. And in both films, the visual dimension means more than the verbal one. Technicolor, panoramic format, music, and acting become autonomous from plot. Thus, in a renewed skepticism for the spoken word, the erotic body communicates that which language is incapable of expressing.

DOUBLE STYLE AND MODERNITY: *HOME FROM THE HILL*

Family melodrama clearly surpasses classicism within evolving modes of representation, particularly with respect to transparency and invisibility. Melodramatic style is not only excessive and narratively unmotivated, but meaning is driven more by the visuals than by plot. A constitutive element of the genre of melodrama, then, is an alternation in the film between two different styles of shooting and directing. On one hand, the melodramatic register is characterized by chromatic, photographic, musical, and narrative excesses. On the other, at certain points the film resorts to a more sober, i.e., classical, style lacking all melodramatic elements. This paradox brings transparency and the power of narrative device into question. And *Home from the Hill* exploits this problem in exemplary fashion, reading it through the different modes of masculinity represented in the film. The three male characters, Captain Wade Hunnicutt and his two sons, Theron and Rafe, are each gendered through the spatial connotations of their private rooms.

Wade's sexual exuberance is omnipresent in the film. However, there is a particular moment in which this quality is also linked to Theron's tragic destiny. It is the episode in which Wade decides "to make a man of his son" by teaching him about hunting and, implicitly, sex. And it is here that the gap between story and style is accentuated. For although the scene is an important lead-up to Theron's destiny—because it is at this moment that his destiny is decided—it is not he, but his father, that dominates the scene.

Disdainful of his son, Theron is convinced by his father's sharecropper to remain in the woods all night waiting for prey that everyone knows to be diurnal. Later, his father finds him whistling and waiting, still unaware of the joke, and takes him back home. Theron is shaken by the event and asks his father to teach him "the rules of the game." Thus, Theron's *Bildung* begins that same night in his father's room, when he takes up a rifle and fires a single shot. The scene between father and son is divided in two parts, the first set in the son's room, the second in the father's. And just like the parallel scene that will draw Rafe into his own room, this episode is fundamentally laid out to understand character through the choice of objects that adorn his private space. In fact, here objects are used symbolically and charged with important connotations that invoke specific lifestyles and cultural values. In sum, they personify the protagonists.

In the scene between father and son, the dichotomies of nature/culture and instinct/knowledge are clear. This is the film's most essential sequence because it allows a specific stylistic articulation to go well beyond the text's primary narrative, which it had privileged up to that point. The visual codes and their relation with dialogue refer back to an ideological and cultural heritage that is not made explicit through story but by the scene's stylistic excess. While Wade and Theron speak, the camera does not privilege their conversation (as in classic cinema). With short tracking and pan shots, the camera intently follows Wade sneaking into his son's room. He behaves as if it were his first time there, looking at and touching various objects:

a world map, a rock from Theron's collection, even the telescope in the center of the room that we saw in the very first shot. Pointing the telescope toward the parquet in reference to what happened in the woods, the father affirms: "I think you need to learn a few things." At this point, a tracking shot pulls back and allows both characters to share the field of vision. The camera fixes on father and son in the last part of the dialogue. Though close, visually they appear separated by the telescope. After having observed the room once more, Wade leaves and reinforces this interpersonal distance by saying: "This is a boy's room. I'll make you see how a man lives."

The impact of this scene stems from the contrast between verbal and visual language, which in turn produces a gap between the spectator's experience and that of the character. Against Wade's preoccupation with his son's virility (or lack of), culture as a system of knowledge and civic values emerges through Theron's scientific interests. Here, we see a codified discourse, but one that Wade perceives as a lack of direct experience of an impulsive reality beyond any convention or social law. It is a dichotomy between *nature* and *culture*, visually expressed from one room to the other. So in the next scene, Theron follows his father to see "how a man lives" as the camera moves to the Captain's room.

The camera combines tracking and pan shots by following the Captain into his private space. In all its grandeur we instantaneously compare it to Theron's. The differences are immediately apparent, especially the chromatic tones: the armchair's red color and the vividly rendered Technicolor browns are in stark contrast with the much softer and unfiltered tones of Theron's room. Beyond this, however, the quality of objects in each space also varies. The Captain's walls are covered in an *excess* of rifles, taxidermy, and hunting trophies, and a larger wide-angle lens also exaggerates the dimensions of the room. When the Captain sits in his red armchair, the room appears enormous and the planes of action more numerous. This makes the distance between Wade and his son appear noticeably out of proportion. In effect, with the dogs at his feet, the Captain seems like a king at court and his son's presence offers the opportunity for an external perspective in alignment with the camera. In reality, it is the spectator, not the character (Theron), who sees the grandeur of the Captain's realm and notes his dominion over it through a consistent frontal view. In the preceding scene, in Theron's room, the Captain was always shot from behind and did not dominate the space. Here, everything appears stylistically enlarged and textually overloaded in relation to the rest of the film. There is an excess of rifles, prey, chromatic flourish, and depth of field in the style of Orson Welles. As one critic has observed, style is a symptom of the Captain's excessive sexual appetites.[42]

Figure 27. Robert Mitchum and George Hamilton in *Home from the Hill*, 1960.

Thus, one can conclude that style functions in a manner that contradicts plot: Wade dominates the image, but he is doomed to die before long. In fact, the camera "aestheticizes" him exclusively, setting the tension in this sequence apart from the rest of film. We see his room numerous times through expressive camera movement only partially motivated by character mobility. The camera frames characters in long or American shot so that to include as much space as possible. Only in the last part of the episode, during the conversation between Wade and his wife do we shift to medium-cut shot/reverse shots that privilege conversation over vision. Here, we note how Wade's wife is filmed from a slightly closer perspective than Wade himself. But her entrance only partially reduces the tension between Theron and his father, because subsequent scenes dedicated to the son's education allow Wade to continually dominate the screen.

If Theron's room was shot in the nonmelodramatic style, a melodramatic mode of representation becomes even more clear if we compare the camera's visual treatment of the Captain and Rafe's spaces. In particular, thanks to classical cinema's stricter and more durable rules, symmetry and repetition, it is possible to confront Wade and Rafe through a set of narrative and stylistic similarities and differences.[43] In contrast to the excessive melodramatic style reserved for the Captain, certain features used to represent Rafe, like color, appear more sober and in fact very similar to the ones used to represent Theron. Here, I refer to the sequence in which the illegitimate son is portrayed in his modest room, a perfect parallel to the analogous sequences shot in the Captain and Theron's rooms just described.

This is the episode in which Theron seeks out his brother. The choice of setting invites us to compare Rafe and Wade. Here, Rafe is presented in his kingdom, just as the Captain was before. The similarities go too far, however, to be coincidental. Rafe has dogs, but they are not as submissive as those of the Captain. Instead, the sequence opens with a dog thrashing about as

Rafe tries to wash him. A tracking shot then pulls back when Theron opens the door and this offers a glimpse of the whole room. It is a dignified room, *normal* and without decorative excess. The camera's movements are likewise free of excess. Depth of field is not visually intrusive and coloring tends more toward the muted browns of Theron's room than the vivid reds we saw in the Captain's. The space and Rafe's relation to it are more denotative than connotative because the film is more interested in constructing a character than the surrounding space. The initial reframing movements are followed by a slow tracking forward shot toward Rafe as he finally becomes the film's narrative focus. At last the illegitimate son gets the opportunity to speak about himself and reveal his suffering. The forward movement constructs and legitimizes Rafe's character and stylistically anticipates the story's ending when his name will appear next to Theron's on the Captain's tomb.

At this point, the film invites the spectator to identify with Rafe and what he represents, a masculinity founded on middle-class family values. Different from feudal or aristocratic masculinities in which the male sexually and economically possesses everyone around him, here he partners with a wife to create a nuclear family. Together, they recognize their values in a community of peers and private affection. With respect to setting then, the supermarket sequence where Rafe sees Libby and proposes marriage is fairly inconsistent with the rest of the film. The image of the supermarket is part of a social reality concurrent with the film's production, i.e., the postwar middle American family and its new fascination with consumption, and not the film's general setting. Even the dialogue is clearly situated in a 1950s social context. So as Libby suggests to Rafe that he find himself a wife who will take care of the house and spend his money, she defines the roles of breadwinner and homemaker of the suburban family.

We see the Captain's excessive space only one other time in the film, when he is killed immediately following the conversation with his wife. The two decide to reconcile for the sake of their son and the Captain, now visibly satisfied, proceeds toward his room, the *melodramatic space par excellence*, in a transition accentuated by the camera. In terms of point of view, the episode is nearly identical to the one described above. The Captain performs the same action, setting off toward the refrigerator for a beer. The camera follows him with a panning shot that pivots from left to right and then right to left just as before. The Captain will die amid his objects of desire, struck by Libby's father, who wrongly takes him as the father of his daughter's baby. The space, once so majestic and full of sensuality, becomes more of a trap than a kingdom as Wade is entangled by the excessive quantity of objects and strong colors.

But even the film's contradictions are not totally resolved as its dichotomy of styles can effectively be traced back to the last shot. It is as if the copresence of two separate and distinct registers could be ascribed to the film's narrative resolution. As soon as the Captain's wife, Hannah, reaches her husband's grave, she sees Rafe. This is the first time that she has left the house after weeks of mourning. Rafe proposes that she come and live with him and Libby. But before leaving the cemetery, Hannah asks Rafe to look at the gravestone. We note its unique dimensions and color, a large block of red reminiscent of the Captain's room. The gravestone is noticeably present during their dialogue, but only significantly so in a few shots. However, when the two walk off, the camera does not follow them. Instead, it makes small deliberate movements until the left part of the screen is completely filled by the red gravestone. At this point, the camera remains fixed while on the right side of the screen we see Rafe and Hannah turn back for one last look. The last frame is a kind of split screen that divides oppositional material. Though dead, the Captain does not disappear from the screen and his red gravestone cannot but remind us of his red room. The chromatic dichotomy of the two halves thus recalls and grounds the film's two visual styles. It therefore seems to indicate the genetic presence of the old in the new, of the past in the present. It is as if the film, though having legitimated the new through Rafe, does not want to cast off the old. After all, as with *Written on the Wind* with the Hadleys, *Home from the Hill* has saved its visual flamboyance and emotional force for the Captain's illicit desire and lifestyle.

6

PERFORMATIVE BODIES AND NON-REFERENTIAL IMAGES

Excesses of the Musical

The most innovative 1950s cinema deals explicitly in the visionary and spectacular. In family melodrama, these characteristics stem from the convergence of new forms of subjectivity, technological innovation, and melodramatic tradition. The cinematic image's spectacularity, however, may also be a vehicle for a different kind of reflection. Near the end of Hollywood's Golden Age, American cinema had a tendency to combine spectacle, particularly in the musical, with theoretical reflection on the image and its capacity to represent the relation between fiction and reality. Not simply a question of films about the cinema, however, some films dramatized the philosophical status of the image itself. Rather than a neat division between fiction and reality, such films denied the possibility of representing reality altogether, insisting that only different levels of fiction were possible. Here, *Singin' in the Rain* is emblematic. Stanley Donen and Gene Kelly's film suggests that we have entered the realm of the image and simulacrum and that reality can be evoked, but not represented. In fact, the film's theoretical project is quite in tune with the discourse on the postmodern. Donen and Kelly's film is the most radical in this regard and this also explains why we conclude the chapter and the volume with the analysis of this film.

Beyond key reflections on the image, however, *Singin' in the Rain* also probes the relationship between art and entertainment—in particular, the conflict between theater and cinema and the supposed hierarchy between them. This strategy fits into a wider tendency in musicals of the period as they confronted the relationship between cinema and other arts. The relation with painting in *An American in Paris* (V. Minnelli, 1951) immediately springs to mind, as well as the opposition between classical and popular music in *Silk Stockings* (R. Mamoulian, 1957).

The investigation on the relation between fiction and reality does not simply concern the image, but also affects the mise-en-scène of the subject who undergoes similar processes. This is not the modern split subject of film noir or the woman's film. Subjectivity is not grounded in an idea of the ego's outward expression of an internal self. Nor is the truth of the ego to be found in the unconscious. Rather, in 1950s cinema one's identity is the product of performative acts or socially recognized gestures and actions. Sense and meaning can be born only through such discursive practices, while every form of biological determinism loses value. For example, gender inversion, or reversibility of the masculine and feminine becomes more and more frequent. In addition, questioning traditional modes of being is no longer masked but rendered more explicit, and in some cases such questioning is even endorsed. One need only compare *Only Angels Have Wings* (1939) with *Red River* (1948) to see how, in the same author, masculine camaraderie shifts from virile friendship to an explicitly homoerotic relationship in the space of ten short years. Or we can confront *Sylvia Scarlett* and *Some Like It Hot* (B. Wilder, 1959) for an explicit radicalization of transvestitism and gender inversion.

This chapter analyzes *The Harvey Girls* (G. Sidney, 1945) and *Gentlemen Prefer Blondes* (1953) as exemplars of the subject's performative construction. By reworking the musical genre's conventions, Judy Garland and Marilyn Monroe redraw the map of the feminine, giving life to characters of more fluid identity. Just like the non-referential image, the concept of *performative subjectivity* is skeptical of notions of reality, nature, and essence, as well as of the body as a direct expression of the psyche. Marilyn, in particular, represents the apogee of this skepticism and manifests a radical break that Andy Warhol would ingeniously harness with his silk-screen prints, transforming the diva into pure image.

Film historians have long agreed that technological innovations introduced in 1950s cinema were primarily a result of the film industry's need to compete with television. Mass exodus from large urban centers to suburbs gave rise to lifestyles very different from the modern ethos of the previous decades when cinema had been the dominant mode of urban amusement. Now the home became the locus of individual happiness and comfort and television the principal form of entertainment. Thus, the presence of the "small screen" was palpable in the 1950s cinematic imaginary. Moreover, it is significant that television's textual function conformed to the same genre-based values of the film. For example, in family melodrama, television contributes to the family's disintegration by emotionally separating its individual members. In the beginning of *Bigger than Life*, protagonist Ed Avery arrives home tired after a long day's work and finds his son in front of the television. He criticizes the boy for wasting his time watching annoying and repetitive programs. In *All that Heaven Allows* the protagonist's children, in opposition to their widowed mother's relationship with a younger man, give her a television for Christmas to combat her loneliness.

Cinema testifies to the pervasiveness of television in American life at the time. In *An Affair to Remember* (1957), a remake of *Love Affair* (1939), both directed by Leo McCarey, television assumes a secondary narrative role. However, in its relatively few appearances, television unequivocally implied falsehood and lying, just as cinema had often been seen as fictional and fake by proponents of theater. As we will see, *Singin' in the Rain* is a case in point. In films like *It's Always Fair Weather* (S. Donen/G. Kelly, 1955) and *A Face in the Crowd* (E. Kazan, 1957), moreover, cinema represented television as a medium strongly tainted by commercialism. This was so much the case that according to Chris Anderson the television image "seems more a product of the Frankfurt School than of Tinsel Town."[1] Thus, unlike radio, which cinema usually portrayed in a positive light, television was always criticized.

Over the course of these introductory remarks, one might speculate that the advent of the television image, both similar and different from the filmic image, contributed to the loss of a reliable notion of reality and the real in the cinematic image itself. If we look at the film and television image side by side, we are led to think that there has been a paradigm shift vis-à-vis the relation between image and reality. Perhaps television, like cinema, does not have a direct relationship with reality but is only one of many possible (and infinite) representations. We therefore move in the realm of postmodern indeterminacy, most radically defined in Baudrillard's notion of simulacrum.[2] Though this is not the context in which to confront such a thorny and complex question, I nevertheless argue that the image's loss of referentiality in 1950s American cinema was obvious. This was particularly the case in MGM musicals by the Arthur Freed Unit. In fact, the musical is unique in the context of classicism inasmuch as it seems to contradict the idea that classic film depends on the preeminence of narrative, causality, and transparency, as we have already seen in the works of Busby Berkeley discussed earlier. In this chapter, I attempt to account for such diversity from both historical and aesthetic perspectives by putting the musical's unique status into relief against evolving modes of representation in American cinema.

THE MUSICAL FORM: CLASSIC FILM VERSUS GENRE FILM

The musical, in many ways a unique genre, holds an *ambiguous place* in the critical-theoretical panorama of classical cinema. Its status moves between two contradictory poles. On the one hand, it has always been considered a kind of synonym for classic Hollywood production itself, especially by producers and nonacademic critics. Indeed, musicals embody the notion of spectacle, of Hollywood as a dream factory; "the epitome of mass-produced, mass-consumed entertainment."[3] On the other hand, as film scholars started to study the musical in a more scientific way, it became obvious that the musical appears to be at odds with classical cinema, calling some of its key formal mechanisms into question. Thus, the musical can be considered either the essence of American cinema's Golden Age or a significant exception. These claims will undergo clarification below, as they corroborate a nonprescriptive interpretation of American cinema.

The musical's peculiarity with respect to other genres has to do with narrative structure, or the relationship between *story* and *spectacle*. Ideological interpretations of the 1970s and 1980s, as well as Bordwell's cognitive theories claim that classical cinema is a narrative system that represents subjects who act purposefully in order to reach very specific goals. Even though these two strains ultimately diverge on the nature of the spectator's experience,[4] they share in an idea of classicism that recognizes the same operation in every kind of film while scarcely mentioning generic differences. Moreover, at bottom, such theories are grounded in an "economic determinism" that reveals uniformity over difference, forgetting that strategies of differentiation were important to production. The primary victim of such oversight is the genre itself. Such a notion of classicism undervalues all genre specificities. *Syntactic* specificities are given little room, and *semantic* specificities are believed to be without impact. As Rick Altman argues, an ideological approach considers "each individual genre as a specific type of lie, an untruth whose most characteristic feature is its ability to masquerade as truth."[5] In effect, both ideological and cognitivist interpretations are unified by another element: they construct their discourse on the formal and linguistic macrosystem of classical narrative film, without considering the specific genre codes or the cinematic imaginary. Thus, in an attempt to liberate itself from content-based criticism and construct formal methods founded on "cinematic specificity," such theories passed over other fundamental traits. Ultimately, in those years only Feminist Film Theory succeeded in fusing the analysis of cinematic structures and devices with that of the cultural imaginary.

Under these circumstances, Rick Altman's argument is crucial in that he does not put genre in ancillary relation to classicism. Rather, he problematizes every universalizing position on classic film. In evaluating the available critical panorama, Altman emphasizes that literary and cinematic genre theories emerged in the wake of structuralism essentially fall into two categories: semantic and syntactic. The first looks to genre for a "list of common traits, attitudes, characters, shots, locations, sets, and the like" while the second is interested in the relationship between these elements. "The semantic approach thus stresses the genre's building blocks, while the syntactic view privileges the structures into which they are arranged."[6] But even more important are the different *qualities* of these two approaches. Semantic studies apply themselves to a vast number of films and do not have any "explanatory power" insofar as they appear interested only in recognizing genre films and compiling lists. On the other hand, syntactic approaches propose interpreting the film genre itself. They "surrender broad applicability in return for the ability to isolate a genre's specific meaning-bearing structures."[7] Altman's proposal combines these two approaches or unites them in application to a vast corpus of films with the capacity to interpret the corpus itself, thereby fusing the aims of *film history* with those of *film theory*. For Altman, genres are born in one of two ways: "either a relatively stable set of semantic givens is developed through syntactic experimentation into a coherent and durable syntax, or an already existing syntax adopts a new set of semantic elements."[8] For example, early sound musicals (1927–1930) attempted to create melodramatic syntax with the semantics of the backstage musical to reflect the pain of death or parting. After the genre's crisis period in 1931–1932, the musical took a different direction. Though "maintaining substantially the same semantic materials, the genre increasingly related the energy of music-making to the joy of coupling, the strength of the community and the pleasure of entertainment."[9]

Altman's approach overcomes deficiencies of methods that subordinate the "genre text" to the "classic text." Not only does it highlight a film's relevant semantic elements, but through the combination of semantic and syntax it also accounts for the uniqueness of each genre, relegating a discussion of elements common among different genres to a more general, secondary level. Nevertheless, in order to better define our discursive field, it is necessary to clarify the relationship between genre and classic text in connection to the musical. We have already underscored the error of giving primacy to story or narrative when defining the musical, especially when the importance of spectacle is so obvious. Dancing and singing numbers, in fact, mark a suspension of the story and present themselves as moments of pure entertainment. Here, then, the spectator's experience is clearly defined by *pleasure* more than *knowledge*, thus undoing the primacy of narrative.

But there are multiple ways of articulating the relationship between story and spectacle. Here, as a point of departure, one can construct a typology leading to a discussion of the musical genre, both in historical and theoretical terms. The musical revue, the oldest form, lies at one extreme: like its original theatrical form it strings together a series of autonomous musical numbers in a manner almost entirely devoid of narrative structure.[10] But with the exception of this radical form, the registers of story and spectacle alternate over the course of a single film. The nature of this alternation, however, varies significantly from the 1930s to the 1950s. It is essential to detail this changing dynamic if one wants to understand the musical's unique attributes vis-à-vis classicism. As Richard Dyer contends, because "entertainment is a common-sense, 'obvious' idea, what is really meant and implied by it never gets discussed."[11] Thus, since the musical thematizes the question of entertainment—which other genres mask via their own semantic—it is uniquely suited to a theoretical discourse on the nature of cinema and image in relation to other media. In the changing mediascape of the 1950s, the musical could reflect on the status of Hollywood cinema better than any other genre. Indeed, MGM musicals sang the swan song of grand old Hollywood in a transitional moment, that is, the moment when cinema was no longer the dominant form of popular entertainment but had not yet been definitively eclipsed either.

Despite the vast number of films and subgenres produced, three kinds of musical were particularly influential and problematic, both from formal and interpretative perspectives. In chronological order, they are Busby Berkeley's films for Warner Brothers, Fred Astaire/Ginger Rogers musicals for RKO, and the films produced by the Arthur Freed Unit at MGM. Besides the constantly evolving story-spectacle dynamic, the opposition between *show-* and *integrated*-musical represents a second interpretive key. In fact, every musical film in all three of these series falls into one of these two categories: either the show-musical concerning the preparation of a Broadway show, where numbers alternate with scenes of the protagonists' lives outside the theater, or the integrated musical where the numbers and story are part of the same narrative world. Here, an implicit (and unconscious) propensity to valorize the story has led scholars—much like cinema itself—to consider the history of the musical as a slow conquest of narrative and of integration.

But if Berkeley's films are the most radical example separating show and spectacle, the films of Astaire and Rogers constitute a different form of musical, or an early example of integration in which the polarity between the two registers is attenuated. Martin Rubin, for example, has emphasized that the spaces of diegesis and spectacle are not distinct, but in fact one and the same. In Astaire/Rogers musicals the space of performance "is not confined to a separate, compartmentalized domain such as a theatrical stage. Instead, any place becomes a potential performance space." Other strategies contribute to the rapprochement of the two registers. On the one hand, the world of the performance appears "more natural and restrained," less excessive than in Berkeley, while on the other, the world of the narrative is "more artificial and stylized" with respect to the Warner Brothers musicals. The overall effect of these choices drastically reduces the gap between story and spectacle.[12] Moreover, the integration of story and musical numbers is due also to the fact that moments of spectacle are in part motivated by the events of the story, to the degree that musical numbers featuring the couple "are a story" unto themselves.[13] Here, even the style of shooting tends toward uniformity. For though dance numbers are often filmed with continuous shots, following the two dancers' movements in medium or long shots, the style is entirely classical and in tune with the period. Furthermore, Astaire/Rogers musicals filmed between 1933 and 1939 share many traits with the sophisticated comedy, the classic genre par excellence.

But if the musical's history can be taken "as a progression from the primitiveness of aggregation to the maturity of integration,"[14] this trajectory reaches its conclusion in the MGM Arthur Freed Unit's musical productions.[15] Here, critics have said, the insertion of a musical number is motivated by narrative so that the artificiality of the integrated musical, in which any person may suddenly burst into joyous song and dance, is attenuated. This notion is problematic, however, because it betrays the desire to subordinate spectacle to story. For if Altman had recognized a critique in claiming that the very notion of integration "itself champions a standard of realism which I believe antithetical to the spirit of the genre as a whole,"[16] in more recent times queer studies has advanced Altman's critique even further through the notion of *camp*.

Beginning with Susan Sontag's initial formulation in the 1960s, the notion of camp has been continually developed, most notably by Richard Dyer in his article on Judy Garland. This perspective has been particularly amenable to the study of American cinema insofar as it melds questions of aesthetics with those of identity, recognizing camp as the inscription of a nonnormative subjectivity. Camp may be either a style or a spectatorial attitude, i.e., a particular mode of relating to the film. At its core, however, camp is an ironic attitude toward the rigid division of gender into masculine and feminine. From this perspective, the excessive and artificial style of MGM musicals—and of the musical numbers in particular—can be perceived as a critical commentary of the romantic plot thread dominating the story. Therefore, one has to question this supposed tendency toward integration, according to which the spectacle's excesses are motivated and finalized by narrative, i.e., the formation of a couple. The visual and spectacular excesses take a parodic stance in relation to action, creating—much like in family melodrama—a fissure between story and style. According to this line of investigation, the dialectic between these two textual levels is as important as ever and must therefore be maintained, not neutralized. But at the same time, camp is born at the moment of reception, i.e., it is in the eye of the beholder more than in the film. Moreover, camp has historically been the reading and interpretative practice employed by gay culture in the United States regarding products of mass entertainment. This phenomenon is especially relevant when we consider that the musical has been decidedly out of fashion for some time now, yet it maintains a cult following in the homosexual community in America and beyond. Indeed, the parodic status of camp is understood as an overturning of the rules. Thus, camp became the style of gay self-reflexivity during a period of sexual censorship, when gays had to pass as heterosexual while at the same time wanting to acknowledge each other in a proverbial wink.[17]

Camp has also transformed some female Hollywood stars into gay icons. And such cults, according to Cohan, have even acquired new life via the Internet. But here, Judy Garland's legendary appeal in the gay community is both paradigmatic and particular. Dyer has explored the reasons for the actress' adulation in gay culture. Beyond the androgyny of her characters, as in *The Pirate* (V. Minnelli, 1949), for example, he argues her appeal is due to the copresence in her image of "ordinariness" and "difference," making Garland a person who challenged codified sexual norms and roles. Thus, rather than mere image produced by a camp interpretation, she is a star who expresses the mechanisms of camp itself.[18]

From these presuppositions, Matthew Tinkcom has underscored how the Freed Unit's creation of camp style is owed to "gay labor," understood not only materially as the creative work of its numerous gay artists and professionals, but also as an effective influence on the style or look of the image. "Gay labor" renders the story of heterosexual love problematic by fusing "straight romance" and "gay inflected visual codes," resulting in the musical's excessive visual look.[19] Moreover, camp style allows the film to "pass" as innocuous entertainment, just as gays had to mask their homosexual tendencies and pass as heterosexual in everyday life.

The parodic distance evoked by camp can be seen in the context of the new status of image and subjectivity in cinema. The idea that camp offers an alternative reading to the dominant model should be seen in this sense, that it proposes the musical genre as a mode of identity deconstruction over and above a flatter notion of the musical as pure entertainment. However, the idea that meaning is created in partly autonomous fashion from the film itself also confirms the cinematic image's loss of referentiality. Furthermore, such strategies are important precisely because they invest in the status of the subject and gender identity. The artificiality of the musical numbers, while integrated into the story in some measure, may put the artificial and performative element of every human action into relief, thereby exhibiting the constructed or social nature of gender. Thus, the MGM musical is more radical than family melodrama, dedicated to criticizing codified forms of gender identity but stopping short of declaring the discursive nature of gender itself as the musical finally does.

When defining the musical in relation to questions of referentiality and performance, however, one should consider motivation more than concepts of integration as they are not such interchangeable notions as they might seem. Since motivation is the hinge point of action in classic cinema, reading the musical in terms of classicism depends on the degree of motivation linking musical numbers to the story. If we consider the three main forms of musical delineated above, there is a progressive diminution of motivation. In the Busby Berkeley films, musical numbers are entirely motivated insofar as the story deals with preparations of a Broadway musical. Thus, every event regarding the spectacle is narratively motivated. But if we consider the films of Astaire/Rogers from this perspective, we should ask ourselves whether dance numbers are also narratively motivated. In other words, do they occur in the codified spaces of spectacle and exhibition? In reality, Fred Astaire, whether solo or coupled with Ginger Rogers, tends to dance anywhere he pleases, transforming every space he encounters into a sort of stage. In fact, it is more convenient that he dance in an everyday or liminal space like that of a hotel lobby, rather than that of a nightclub or theater. Even so, with the exclusion of *Carefree* (M. Sandrich, 1938), motivation is always present since it stems from the fact that Astaire is a professional dancer. It does not make a difference whether he dances in a Venetian luxury hotel instead of a theater as in *Top Hat* (M. Sandrich, 1935) or directs and sings with a troop of marines after his fiancée and dance partner has refused to marry him, as in *Follow the Fleet* (M. Sandrich, 1936). Astaire's character is defined by his artistic qualities, by his being a professional dancer. This element motivates the dances and renders them verisimilar. In other words, motivation assures the plausibility of the story. Moreover, when Astaire/Rogers dances do not occur in spaces specifically dedicated to performance, they do not emit a feeling of artificiality but are simply the demonstration of their professional abilities. In fact, narrative motivation bears an inverse relation to the excesses of spectacle defined by pure visual pleasure. Thus, in motivating musical numbers, narrative checks and partially deactivates visual excess. This operation is even more successful in Astaire/Rogers films, since spectacularization of the image, so central in Busby Berkeley's work, is missing.

In Freed Unit's films, the relationship between the story and musical number is the opposite. In most cases there is no motivation for the characters to start singing. They are not artists, singers, or dancers, and usually the typical official performance spaces are absent. Yet characters sing and dance, transforming everyday spaces into fantastical ones. Thus, only here does the dichotomy between story and spectacle begin to break down while spectacle and fiction invade the whole film. Show and entertainment are no longer the story's object. It's the image itself that becomes pure spectacle. The effect is particularly strong when the main character is a common person and not a professional artist, like Judy Garland in *Meet Me in St. Louis* (V. Minnelli, 1944) and *The Harvey Girls*. In the former, she plays a high-school girl in early-twentieth-century St. Louis; in the latter, she is a waitress in a Harvey's restaurant in Santa Fe.

Freed Unit's musicals gather together various kinds of excesses. The use of Technicolor and wide camera movements make the image both spectacular and artificial, while normal everyday activities are continually interrupted by songs and dances that often involve the whole community. But if Berkeley's films implicitly valorized the community according to the New Deal's spirit of cooperation, Astaire's musicals are the exact opposite inasmuch as he "is too skilled as an individual performer to be a suitable vehicle for an ethic of collective effort and cooperation."[20] MGM musicals therefore reassessed the value of the collective, but the scenario is quite the opposite of Warner musicals of the early 1930s. Energy, abundance, intensity, transparency, and community values now characterized the everyday and extended throughout the whole world of the film, not just the musical numbers.[21]

Dyer maintains that the musical's escapism is indicative of the genre's utopian project. The categories enumerated above are utopian categories inasmuch as they represent the solution to social tensions or inadequacies that are always partly "real." The relation between social problem and utopian solution is staged through the formal conflict between story and musical number, for which Dyer proposes three models. In *On the Town* (S. Donen/G. Kelly, 1949), for example, "the distinction between narrative and numbers" is dissolved, "thus implying that the world of the narrative is also (already) utopian."[22] To achieve such an end, one would usually avoid anchoring the film in any precise time and space. Rather, the preference would be for geographically distant places, or for turn-of-the-century America, or choosing communities that were different from those of the standard urban white audience, i.e., the countryside or African American community. In this way, the choice of setting would make an urban white American audience believe that "song and dance are 'in the air'" in a still integral world of the past. The narrative would then be introduced later, representing a temporary threat to utopia. Thus, the model employed by *On the Town* overturns the other musical models "where the narrative predominates and numbers function as temporary escapes from it."[23]

Dyer's argument is particularly useful here. Though he seems to believe that the utopian model is a rare one, it seems to me rather apposite for defining the Freed Unit's musicals. The utopian model is definitely the most exploited during the postwar period. Indeed, almost all the best MGM musicals are dominated by a utopian impulse: both *Meet Me in St. Louis* and *The Harvey Girls* of course, but also *The Pirate*, *Yolanda and the Thief* (V. Minnelli, 1945), *Brigadoon* (V. Minnelli, 1954), *Gigi* (V. Minnelli, 1958), and many others.[24] Likewise, it is evident that the utopian register and its attendant lack of verisimilitude are specific traits of the image's loss of referentiality. Spectacle and performance become the hegemonic form of the film, and the spectator must accept this "genre pact" establishing the musical's unreal mode of representation. Thus, if the goal of the musical is to entertain—that is, to produce pure pleasure only barely implicated in the process of signification—at the same time, experiencing the genre's pleasure requires an implicit cognitive operation, inasmuch as the spectator must understand and accept the pact that what he or she sees is free of referential data.

ARTIFICE AND SUBJECTIVITY I: *THE HARVEY GIRLS*

The Harvey Girls is a "typical" MGM musical of the mid-1940s. From production to stylistic elements, from structures of the imaginary to the actor's presence, recitation, and singing techniques, the film is a quintessential example of the studio style. The creative and productive recipe is so successful that one might even think that the director was Minnelli himself, the Freed

Unit's principle auteur, and not George Sidney. If we think about the beginning, we cannot help but notice its similarity to the opening scene of *Meet Me in St. Louis*. After establishing shots depict a train bound for Sandrock where Susan/Judy Garland meets the Harvey girls, the town is introduced with a spectacular passed-along song, or a collectively sung motif, which is literally passed from one character to the next in connected segments. This musical trajectory is accompanied by spatial movements, with the camera following the characters' displacements with broad travelings. Unlike the solos and duets that are linked to the romantic plot and formation of a couple, the passed-along song is linked to community, simultaneously constructing and evoking its unity. Rick Altman has noted that "as we move from one contented citizen to another we recognize the extent to which their common interests have synchronized their every movement," while Jane Feuer has remarked that "paralleling the making of the couple with the making of a stable community is one sure sign of the folk sub-genre."[25] In *The Harvey Girls*, the construction of community is more important than in other folk musicals because of its strong western component. Better, the film can best be defined as a musical-western hybrid.

Editing is crucial to the passed-along song. The film's recurrent melody, "On the Atchison, Topeka, and the Santa Fe," begins inside a saloon, the western setting par excellence. Intoned by the black assistant chef, he crosses the whole space of the saloon right up to the exit in a typical "nonchoreographed" step of the folk musical, closer to a strut than dance.[26] At this point, the song passes on to other members of the community and we return to the train car through a sound bridge, with the image of train wheels in movement. The song continues to pass from character to character, with the Harvey girls facing their car windows, singing until the train reaches its destination. Now an aerial shot frames both the train and the town's main street. Thus, the two spaces are first shown separately, then drawn metaphorically closer through the same song, and finally fused in the same space. The train stops to let Susan and the Harvey girls off. The young women are welcomed by cowboys in search of wives. The girls will work in the Harvey restaurant chain's new location opening in Sandrock, while Susan has left a small town in Ohio to come and get married after having responded to a marriage ad. If from a narrative perspective the initial episodes present us with characters and their motivations, from a formal point of view the passed-along song anticipates the construction of a community, or even better, the transformation of Sandrock into a more advanced stage of civilization.

The plot deploys core aspects of the western. It is not just that the story takes place in the West, but it is a confrontation between *wilderness* and *civilization*, here articulated in the dichotomy between the saloon and Harvey's family restaurant.[27] The two locales represent two different kinds of amusement: a "wild time" and a "good time," as the local reverend will put it, offered and embodied by two kinds of women: the prostitutes of the saloon managed by Angela Lansbury and the waitresses of the restaurant guided by the energetic Judy Garland. But here, the idea of community anticipated at the beginning of the film will be more difficult to attain in comparison to the folk musical. This is because the western's ideological values sit in direct opposition to those of the musical.

The film, in fact, had been conceived as a western with Clark Gable, but after months of preproduction nothing was resolved and MGM decided, according to Sidney, "to give it to the Freed Unit" so that they might turn it into a musical.[28] The film's unusual production history had a positive outcome, however, and the hybridization of the two genres' formal and ideological structures produced a successful result, no less interesting than the much more acclaimed *Mildred Pierce* released that same year at Warner Brothers. But if Sidney's film is in harmony with the MGM folk musical, its unique discourse on feminine sexuality—often absent from the genre—may be explained by this notion of hybridization. For our purposes, it should be underscored that the fusion of the two genres results in the negation of any supposed feminine essence. Rather, the film invites us to entertain the idea that gender identity is the product of performances, that it is a discursive practice more than expression of the subject's interiority.

Sandrock prepares for the opening of the Fred Harvey Company's restaurant, the newest link in its chain of locations providing refreshment and lodging along the Atchison, Topeka, and Santa Fe Railway around the year 1870. As may be read today on its Web site, Harvey's restaurants were not only intended to bring good food to the Southwest, but also "civilization, community, and industry to the Wild West" thanks also to the employment of an almost exclusively female staff. Furthermore, Harvey's hired women at a time when most working women were either schoolteachers or domestic servants and, in doing so, contributed to the widening of female employment options.[29] The film explicitly puts this dynamic on display as Susan cancels her engagement after meeting her betrothed. Rather than return to Ohio, she takes a job in the new establishment. As was the case for other girls who also arrived from various back-country parts of the Midwest, the trip and employment at Harvey's represented a unique opportunity for social and economic emancipation. Susan's empty lunch bag is a sign of her poverty, making her prearranged marriage first and foremost an economic opportunity.

The new restaurant's opening worries Ned Trent, the owner of the saloon. As the only entertainment spot in town, the saloon fears new competition directly across the street. The duality between wilderness and civilization is expressed through the saloon's managers' attempts to sabotage the immediately successful restaurant. First they steal its meat supplies (the famous Harvey's steak). Then they scare the Harvey girls by shooting at their rooms during the night. Then they put a snake in one of their bedrooms. Finally, they burn down the restaurant itself. With the exception of the first episode where Ned Trent is involved, however, the intimidations are organized by the saloon's manager autonomously behind the owner's back. Having by this point fallen in love with Susan, Trent desists from any illegal activity, even if in the end the restaurant puts the saloon out of business. Then, after Harvey's successful party where the men of Sandrock are discovered to prefer dancing with the waitresses to gambling and amusing themselves with the saloon girls, Trent decides to transfer his business to Flagstaff. In the end, the saloon's old premises are taken over by the restaurant, whose previous location lay in ashes. But while Susan joins the saloon girls and boards the train for Flagstaff in secret, in order to remain with Trent, he decides to leave his shady business and stay in Sandrock with Susan. Upon realizing their unintentional separation, he then follows the train on horseback to retrieve his beloved and bring her back to town.

The fusion of western and musical is particularly productive because the two genres belong to opposite orders. Taking up Thomas Schatz's congenial formula, the western is, like the gangster movie and the noir, a "genre of order" inasmuch as it foresees "the elimination of some threat to the social order" carried out by the hero. On the other hand the musical, like the screwball comedy and melodrama, is a "genre of integration," set in an already civilized social space and traces "the integration of the central characters into the community."[30] Indeed, the fusion of two opposite genres is much more interesting than would be two of the same "system." Mixing oppositional semantic elements provides the occasion for a kind of unmasking of the cultural values supported by each genre, because each inputs that which its opposite normally represses.

In *The Harvey Girls*, there is no typical western hero, but neither is there the typical romantic couple of the musical, usually presented and constructed by a series of formal and visual "parallelisms."[31] Thus, on the one hand, the western cedes the hero function to the musical and Judy Garland. On the other, the plot reflects a conflict close to that of the typical western in open contrast to the dramaturgic structure of the folk musical, which slows narrative to make space for musical numbers, rendering narrative conflict more or less nonexistent. If we think of *Meet Me in St. Louis*, for example, the father's decision to move his family to New York meets with disfavor from every one of its members. However, this threat is not only introduced rather late in the film, but it also seems unreal and pales in comparison to the film's strong utopian component. In Sidney's film, on the other hand, the conflict is much more tangible, well-constructed, and present throughout the whole film. Moreover, rather than basing its narrative on the principle of parallelism typical of musical, the plot centers on the dialectic between the two female characters, Angela Lansbury and Judy Garland.

Most of the important action unfolds in the areas around the main street, a straight thoroughfare alongside of which line up all of the community's commerce and entertainment. As in a shot/reverse shot sequence, the diegesis concentrates on two different spaces facing each other, populated by two groups of women who display opposite lifestyles. On the one side are the prostitutes of the saloon, the *vice* of the West still free from the iron rule of law. On the other, the modest waitresses of the restaurant, the civilizing *virtue* of the East. This typical western conflict remains up until the end, despite the effective absence of violence or death, which can be attributed to the influence of the musical.[32] Yet, conflict development can happen only when the initial separation of the two spaces is broken and they begin to contaminate each other as well as their corresponding value systems.

The Harvey Girls does not simply insert western iconography into a musical story but melds the cultural and countercultural values of both genres. Thus, we have a double "dual-focus text,"[33] in which the narrative solutions and values deployed are the product of the two intersecting genres. The depiction of female sexuality is extremely significant under these circumstances, for the film presents two opposed and ostensibly irreconcilable female ontologies: one allied with the western, the other with the musical. However, narrative development evinces various moments of intersection and overlapping between the two modes.

The first significant episode of confrontation between the two women is a "parallelism at a distance" that underscores their different styles of singing. If parallelism is normally a formal mechanism of the musical, here it is revised in harmony with the western, confronting not the two subjects of a future couple, but two women representing opposing cultural codes. In the film's first scene, Judy Garland is secluded in the back of a train, singing a sad song while we see the Monument Valley in rear-projection and slightly out of focus. This solo expresses her suffering and is directed at the public in the movie theater: it is the only number in which there is no diegetic audience.[34] It is a long take where the dolly-supported camera approaches and pulls back from the character until finally moving in for a definitive close-up. The use of rear-projection has the effect of setting the protagonist's focused face apart from the surrounding background, and the scene presents Garland's singing performance as having no narrative function. It is followed by a long episode inside the train during which Susan meets the Harvey girls. Then, the diegesis moves to Sandrock inside the saloon where Angela Lansbury is singing accompanied by a piano. Here, the mise-en-scène lies at the opposite end of the spectrum in relation to Susan's scene. The woman's scarce talent for singing is obvious, especially in comparison to Garland's performance. Moreover, depth of field sharply renders all the surrounding objects and furnishings of the locale, decentralizing the human subject. In fact, Lansbury is positioned on the right side of the frame, not in the center, and shot from above. Garland's suffering and singing face stands in opposition to the space of the saloon, while Lansbury appears of little more consequence than any of the other inanimate profilmic elements. The second episode of confrontation between the two feminine models is collective and composed of two scenes. The first shows Harvey's maître d' teaching the waitresses about the rules and ways of serving. The second scene is a mirror episode inside the saloon in which the girls practice the can-can. From their clothing—the former in long skirts and aprons, the latter in sexy revealing outfits—to coloristic and visual parameters, the two scenes oppose modesty and sexual exhibition.

The spaces of the restaurant and saloon remain separate for the first part of the film without any cross-pollination. The virginal Harvey girls dressed in their long black-and-white outfits are the first attracted to the space of the other. They become curious about the easy and uncouth saloon women. Moreover, even though Trent's attraction to Susan is obvious from the beginning, he does nothing to start a relationship with her. It is Susan who approaches him for the first time and is therefore responsible for initiating their relationship. But the decisive clash between the two groups and spaces happens during the restaurant's party. Here, the Harvey girls no longer limit themselves to offering good food but begin to entertain the local men with dancing. As a result, the saloon finds itself empty. So Lansbury's girls then go to the restaurant, intrigued by the goings-on. But the men do not follow them back to the saloon, now seeming to prefer a "good time" to a "wild time." Ultimately, the saloon will have to close its doors and start over in a new place, where civilization has yet to arrive.

After Trent's girls are forced to leave, the restorative Harvey's girls—having moved into the old saloon after the fire—metaphorically absorb a residual element of the women who preceded them there. Furthermore, the final sequence of the saloon girls on the train for Flagstaff is symmetrical to the initial scene featuring the future waitresses on their way to Sandrock. Susan is present in both, first on the side of one group, and later on the side of the other, representing a crucial link joining the two different groups and feminine modes. Ultimately, Susan decides to become a saloon girl out of love for Trent, noting no great difference between the two kinds of girls. After all, she says, they only wear a different kind of dress. This declaration makes the narrative mechanism of the film explicit and exemplifies Dyer's camp reading through Garland's duplicity and ambiguity. Susan puts socially sanctioned modes of being into question and moves between opposing sexual identities. But if the distance between virgin and prostitute is not unbridgeable, then gender and identity more broadly are the fruit of performances and acts, not expressions of an essence. In contrast to the "pure musical" that tends to eliminate sexual discourse, the musical's fusion with the western is a transgressive operation that undermines the typical strategies of containment of classical cinema.

ARTIFICE AND SUBJECTIVITY II:
GENTLEMEN PREFER BLONDES

Gentlemen Prefer Blondes rewrites female dynamics by merging Hawks's auteurial style—defined, first of all, by ambiguous gender relationships—with Monroe and Russell's divistic attributes.[35] In Monroe's filmography, *Gentlemen Prefer Blondes* and *How to Marry a Millionaire* (J. Negulesco, 1953) are films where female complicity is most central. But there is a considerable difference between these two films. While in Negulesco's film female complicity is the means through which three friends ensnare eligible men, in Hawks's the friendship between Lorelei/Marilyn Monroe and Dorothy/Jane Russell is a conflict-inducing alternative to the standard heterosexual couple. Repeating the general scheme of *Red River*, Hawks shows that homoerotic friendship—female in this case, male in the preceding western—cannot coexist alongside heterosexual relationships. With Hawks, friendship is always of a sexual nature and it explicitly configures the mechanisms of desire that undermine more traditional ones.

The strength of Lorelei and Dorothy's relationship in *Gentlemen Prefer Blondes* is evident and has already been thoroughly analyzed elsewhere.[36] Of particular interest here, though, is an articulation of the male-female relationship through an original use of the musical's narrative topoi and formal devices. As is the case with many of his films, Hawks's involvement with genre is clearly auteurial as he operates both inside and outside the genre conventions. He does not transgress its essential features, and yet in observing them with a highly critical eye he succeeds in creating an unexpectedly personal vision. Thus, reflection on gender is fundamental here. For in Hawks's hands, genres restore a representation of the human subject and its desire that is not fixed, but performative. Indeed, here Hawks constructs the masculine/feminine dynamic by reworking narrative structure, coupled with a tendentious reuse of the relationship between story and musical numbers.

The narrative mechanism of the musical introduces peculiarities that distinguish it from the standard classic structure. Constitution of the heterosexual couple, i.e., narrative and ideological center of the genre, is determined by rhetorical strategies such as the continual parallelisms between the two protagonists at the level of "set and situations, costumes and movement, even dialogue and shots."[37] In place of psychological motivation and causal relation, in the musical "the sequence of scenes is determined not out of plot necessity, but in response to a more fundamental need: the spectator must sense the eventual lovers as a couple even when they are not together, even before they have met."[38] Thus, such parallelisms bring the two together, *formally* uniting them before their diegetic meeting. From this perspective, it is obvious that no heterosexual couple embodies this definition in *Gentlemen Prefer Blondes*. In fact, the only couple present throughout the whole film is that of Lorelei and Dorothy. So if anything, the film may be described as an attempt to divide the showgirl couple and set them on their way to normal marriages. Indeed, the film concludes with a double wedding. Nevertheless, the camera's final movement throws this into question, closing in on the two female protagonists and pushing the two grooms offscreen. With a typically *progressive* strategy,[39] whereby the visual register undermines plot, Hawks overturns the normal heterosexual couple by suggesting a female-female union.

The film begins with Lorelei and Dorothy performing a duet at a nightclub. With the exception of Dorothy's brief exit, she and Marilyn are constantly filmed in two-shots. This is the first in a series of duets through which the friends demonstrate their perfect and harmonious partnership. But the film also suggests that the two have opposite and complementary characteristics, just as a male-female couple might. Dorothy is a brunette, Lorelei blond. One is tall, the other more petite. These contrasting elements—later, we will also see difference through the color of their clothing—give the idea of a complete and self-sufficient couple (as was the case with many couples in comedies, especially American ones).

Figure 28 and 29. Marilyn Monroe and Jane Russell in *Gentlemen Prefer Blondes*, 1953.

In the next episode, Gus, Lorelei's stupid and rich fiancé—whom we saw in the audience—runs backstage to the women's dressing room with an engagement ring for Marilyn. The man's entrance appears as an outright intrusion, momentarily separating the two women. But Dorothy does not let it pass without some plainly jealous jokes. As such, the matrix of the film's narrative project lies in these oppositional movements. Indeed, the two friends are alternately united and separated and this process is often mirrored by an alternation between musical numbers and story. In other words, female friendship seems possible only in the realm of performance, of spectacle, and by extension, of fiction, while reality (story) is dominated by attempts to unite man and woman. According to this itinerary, we can also locate the articulation of the various gazes directed at Marilyn, for she is the object of both traditional masculine gazes and of that of her female friend.

But on top of this, Lorelei and Dorothy's moments of union and complicity are also stylistically more elaborate. In these episodes, representational techniques become visible and highlight the importance of narrative events. This expressive strategy—in harmony with typical 1950s cinema—is systematic and also applies to the last shot described above. On the other hand, there are no stylistic excesses in episodes where the protagonists are committed to male characters, i.e., Gus, detective Malone, or the elderly millionaire attracted to Lorelei. In these cases, the mise-en-scène is more sober and disinclined to excess.

Female friendship is thus uniquely developed in the realm of performance and spectacle. Though most directly applicable to musical numbers, this dimension also concerns moments in which the two women's appearance is transformed into spectacle. The film's first and third scene (when the couple arrives at the port in New York) respectively represents the first example of these two cases. Indeed, it is a curious reversal that female autonomy should be represented through spectacularization of the female body. For Hawks's film suggests that when objects of the masculine gaze are two women, complicit in and conscious of the role attributed to them, their canonical subordination may be subverted. This dynamic is repeated twice and is reworked a third time in the film's finale.

After the initial performance and Lorelei's official engagement, the two friends embark on a cruise taking them to Europe where Marilyn is supposed to marry Gus. The two women's arrival at port is presented with typical classic rhetoric. We see some well-dressed youths, gymnasts for the American Olympic team, hypnotically staring offscreen. In the next shot we see their objects of interest: Lorelei and Dorothy walking toward the ship, elegantly dressed and made up. Then a tracking shot follows them walking between two lines of men who continue watching them. Their entrance is choreographed as if it were a ballet or military parade. Though a normal diegetic event and not a musical number, their appearance is nevertheless transformed into spectacle. The same strategies are employed later when the two enter the ship's dining room for the first time. In this case, their arrival, followed by a similar camera movement to the one in the earlier boarding scene, activates the scopic desire of an elderly millionaire who stares incredulously. Even the band is distracted by the women's beauty, so much so that they begin to make mistakes.

The opposition between friendship and love is *formally* evinced by the way in which musical numbers are inserted into the story. The first of these episodes takes place as the ship is about to set sail, with passengers bidding their friends and loved ones farewell. Having moved into her stateroom, Dorothy has some fun with the gymnasts and their girlfriends. While singing the now famous song *Bye, Bye, Baby*, everybody dances and sings the chorus. In the next room, Lorelei is saying goodbye to Gus in a moment of private intimacy. But suddenly, Marilyn begins singing the song, too. Though the song's addressee would seem to be her fiancé—i.e., the lyrics are certainly motivated by the ship's diegetic departure—it is hard not to connect Lorelei and Dorothy via their musical performances, especially considering the relevance of parallelism in the genre. Perhaps the women are saying a mutual goodbye. The trip is, after all, the last occasion for them to be together before Lorelei's wedding. But this parallelism might also be connected to triangular desire, i.e., Dorothy is singing to Lorelei, who is in turn singing to Gus. This second hypothesis finds confirmation in the following scene where Dorothy is at Lorelei's door, desirously watching the heterosexual couple. She then knocks on the door as if to remind them of the time. Gus and Lorelei's intimacy is then broken, and everybody enters the room while Lorelei immediately responds to her friend's call. At this point the group continues the performance begun earlier in Dorothy's room and the spectacle becomes pure entertainment. Thus, female friendship is linked not only to performance, spectacle and fiction, but also fun. And we sense that the male-female couple's relationship is linked to oppositional modalities, i.e., boredom. Gus's temporary exit from the scene reunites the two friends, putting their separation off yet again.

The force of female friendship is also strengthened by the weakness of the male characters. And as Laura Mulvey has highlighted, in this film, "the male gaze itself becomes a site of impotence." For example, the members of the Olympic team are first shown voyeuristically watching the two women, but later in the pool "they perform a chorus dance of physical fitness that is more a homoerotic display than a heterosexual celebration."[40]

Alternation between moments of union and separation continue throughout the film and their comprehensive analysis confirms the paradigm discussed up to this point. Thus, the film's finale seems to be a logical conclusion in light of Hawks's formal politics, for if exclusion of the two men from the final shot indicates a preference for female friendship, the wedding nevertheless takes place. From this standpoint, the film narrates a prolonged process of maturation and acceptance of the Law while advancing homoerotic friendship as a privileged phase of human experience. As such, one could say that *Gentlemen Prefer Blondes* is the female version of *Red River*. For if the herd's long journey in the latter suspended man's union with woman, permitting the unfolding of a free male friendship,[41] the cruise to Europe in the former performs the same function. But the difficulty with which certain narrative solutions take shape is also evidence of a potentially different sexual imaginary. In both *Gentlemen Prefer Blondes* and *The Harvey Girls*, classic formal and narrative techniques are broken. In the latter, this happens through the fusion of two antithetical genres, and in the former, through the rewriting of genre conventions, especially parallelism. This allows for the reformulation of traditional notions of identity, suggesting that the subject is a construction just like the filmic text. Because it is a staging of materials and practices, new forms of desire and lifestyles can substitute for, or appear alongside, conservative or worn-out models.[42]

THE NON-REFERENTIAL IMAGE: *SINGIN' IN THE RAIN*

Singin' in the Rain is one of the most beloved films by public, critics, and academy alike because it wondrously sets notions of entertainment and pure pleasure alongside theoretical reflection on the nature of the image.[43] An explicit homage to Hollywood and the musical genre,[44] the film calls into question a strict dichotomy between reality and fiction, the dramaturgic linchpin of movies about the cinema. More specifically, in the same way that the significance of an image emerges in confrontation with other images, subjectivity no longer depends on the ego's expression or mere translation of interiority into actions and words. Alternatively, the ego is generated by performative and discursive strategies. These levels of discourse add up with a more obvious, but certainly not insignificant, point that deals with the film's metalinguism, or the fact that the film shows and narrates the dynamics of filmmaking in the transition to sound and the relationship between audience and film.

Unlike the 1970s musicals, such as Fosse's, *New York, New York* (M. Scorsese, 1977) and *Nashville* (R. Altman, 1975), *Singin' in the Rain*'s metalinguistic structure does not diminish the musical's primary entertainment function. In fact, the spectator's delight reaches its apex when the image's construction is revealed. Just think of the problems with sound and positioning of the microphone during takes in the studio, or the audience's laughter during *The Dueling Cavalier* when difficulties of synchronization between sound and image occur, or the final sequence when the diegetic audience discovers that Lina Lamont's cinematic voice is actually Kathy Selden's. Although the metalinguistic function is pervasive in *Singin' in the Rain*—as well as in other notable examples of the period[45]—it does not compromise the genre's primary function. Moreover, the spectator's laughter in the theater does not diminish when it is mediated by that of the diegetic public.

Discourse on self-reflexivity and metalinguism dominates the entire film, even if it develops according to various reference points. In many cases, it is interwoven with reflections on sound and the sound/image relationship. The first significant episode of this takes place when a festive audience welcomes Gene Kelly outside the theater before a screening of *The Royal Rascal*. This scene is an excellent development of the film's discourse on the cinema and its relation with the other arts and popular entertainment forms. At the request of an interviewer, Don recounts the beginnings of his career with Cosmo. His verbal commentary overlaps a series of brief sequences featuring the two friends during their early days. However, there is a sharp contrast between Don's description of his show business experiences and the actual images shown. While he recounts the development of their career according to high artistic practices (classic theater, the conservatory, dramatic arts academy, dance, sophisticated roles in silent film), the images instead show Don and Cosmo on the stage of popular theater (nightclubs, vaudeville, tip-tap, and roles as stuntmen). The protagonist's story then concludes with the image of Simpson, the man in charge of Monumental Studios, offering Don his first role in a film with Lina Lamont.

This episode solicits a series of observations. First, it recognizes the musical's reworking of conventions and devices of older forms of popular entertainment.[46] The editing also establishes a kind of obligatory chronology, similar to that of Gene Kelly's own biography (and many other artists of the time), indicating that Hollywood was the goal of many performers. However, the sequence primarily reflects on the cinema's status as an art. Should it be considered low as the images show or as high as Don's commentary suggests? Or better still, is there a low cinema in the flashbacks and a high cinema in the sword-and-cape drama about to premiere? Finally, where does the film *Singin' in the Rain* inscribe itself? Perhaps the episode's parodic style provides us with an answer. Though not sufficient unto itself, parody does turn the question into a false one, setting the whole issue of high and low on the level of play. Thus, the opening is a parody of the cinema as an apparatus, especially the relation between star and audience.[47] However, its metalinguistic strategy is not enough to produce a true criticism. Later on, the question of cinema's legitimacy is formulated according to different parameters.

No longer a question of aesthetic canons, the cinema's legitimacy becomes a question of public taste and Kathy's character is used thusly. When Don is assaulted by fans and seeks refuge in her car, she does not recognize him, claiming that she seldom goes to the cinema. But she herself has ambitions of becoming an actress in the theater, which she holds in higher esteem because "only theater actors really act," while "cinema actors merely pantomime." Accordingly, the cinema uses codified stories for the sole purpose of entertaining the masses. But Kathy's assertions are negated in the following episode when she emerges scantily clad from an enormous cake at the studio party for the film's premiere, initiating a musical number in the style of the Ziegfeld Follies. And later (before declaring her love for Don), Kathy admits to having seen all of Don Lockwood's films, and to having even read gossip about him in fan magazines, contradicting her earlier claims. In sum, Kathy suddenly changes her mind about the cinema and the film exploits this about-face to legitimate cinema, and in turn, the musical.

The use of musical motifs also contributes to the film's self-reflexive strategy as *Singin' in the Rain* pays homage to the history of the musical, especially that of MGM. There are very few songs composed specifically for the film. Most were written by the film's producer Arthur Freed (lyrics) and Nacio Herb Brown (music) and recycled from the studio's other musicals. In fact, motifs like that of "Singin' in the Rain," "Broadway Rhythm," and "Broadway Melody" had been used repeatedly since the studio's first musicals from the late 1920s.[48]

According to Christian Metz's terminology, the film's metalinguistic strategy is supported by a dialectic between *discourse* and *story*. *Singin' in the Rain* alternately exploits each of these.[49] Under these circumstances, however, it should be clarified whether the story contains discourse or conserves verisimilitude, or whether discourse exceeds the story to reveal the constructive process involved in producing the cinematic image and the story itself.

The story/discourse dichotomy is developed through others like sound/image and true/false. Indeed, the story unfolds on two separate but related levels. On the one hand, in the making of the film, *The Dueling Cavalier* becomes *The Dancing Cavalier* when it is remade into a talkie. This is the level of fiction and deceit. Everything concerning cinema as an apparatus or the public role that the actors must periodically assume is shown to be false. For example, the supposed romantic connection between Don Lockwood and Lina Lamont is only a marketing strategy. Don himself lies to the audience in the first sequence, and Lina must remain mute in public because her grating voice would contrast too much with her sophisticated silent film image. Later, when Monumental Studios decides to transform *The Dueling Cavalier* into a musical, they solve Lina's problem by dubbing her over with Kathy Selden's voice. Here, the film shows how dubbing produces a "reality effect," artificially uniting body and voice, which on the contrary stem from two separate entities. It is evident, however, that if such a manipulation is revealed to the viewing public of *Singin' in the Rain*, then the diegetic public also requires a diegetic unveiling in the theater. In short, it is as if the aesthetic of the verisimilar is confused with reality. The construction of fiction must be diegetically unveiled for the audience to realize it, as well as to demonstrate cinema's capability of infinite layers of fiction.

But if everything in cinema is false—from its very images to the behavior of the stars—what happens off-set is in effect true. The characters' sentiments that develop far away from the set are most true, so that actors can become "real *people*." As such, fiction and reality are visualized by two different styles of acting. Don is not a braggart but rather extremely insecure of himself. Moreover, he does not lie to Kathy and Cosmo as he does to the public and to Lina. With them, rather, he can be himself and these are the moments in the film that count most. Likewise, Don's feelings for Kathy are real.

Looking back then, in the first part of the film there is a neat separation between true and false, with few moments of cross-contamination. On the one side, we have the story of the film that needs to be made and dominated by discourse. On the other, we have the off-set events, presented as story. And as the film proceeds we are witness to a process of double contamination, i.e., discourse invades story and story invades discourse.

We can thus begin with the romantic plot between Don and Kathy. Up until now we have spoken of their love as *true love*. The beginning of the

Figure 30 and 31. Gene Kelly and Debbie Reynolds in *Singin' in the Rain*, 1952.

episode ending with Don's love declaration confirms this. He and Kathy exit from what appears to be a dressing room for a break. Their dialogue is conducted in intimate tones and accompanied by an objectifying use of camera. Cinematic manipulation is reduced to a minimum. It is a long take with tracking movement that follows the moving characters at a constant medium distance. It is day outside with natural lighting. But if one watches closely, it is possible to deduce the presence of a wind machine making Kathy's scarf flutter. The main mode of choreography, however, stems from the two characters' movement around a pole placed at the center of the frame. It is a thoroughly thought-out episode trying to pass itself off as entirely natural, or unconstructed.

In the next scene, the procedure is reversed. Although the dialogue foreshadows Don's imminent declaration of love for Kathy, it is not verbalized right away because it requires the "proper setting." Don leads Kathy to a bare set that he then prepares for just this moment. He positions her on a step, turns on the lights so that she will be illuminated in soft focus, turns on the wind machine so that her hair becomes lightly ruffled, and finally, rather than simply declaring his love for her, he sings it. The camera's movements are added to the profilmic manipulation. It moves alternately closer and further from the action and then again on high—and so too with the editing. The story is then contaminated by discourse, and the relationship of reciprocal exclusion between the two is thus overturned. For if Don and Kathy's emotional involvement is presented as real and evinced by the scene's initial unobtrusive style, then the second and more elaborate part of the episode shows that emotional expression can happen only through preexisting codes. Thus, the sequence has a double function. On the one hand, it indicates that the film's initial support for an easy separation of fiction and reality, actor and person, can no longer be maintained. On the other, it allows us to go beyond this film and recognize that every love scene is consciously codified. In other words, this episode deconstructs the classic Hollywood love story.

But the relationship between true and false is also developed through the Lina/Kathy dichotomy. As noted earlier, Lina has an unpleasant voice over which Kathy must dub. In other words, Lina has a voice not her own, and by the same token Kathy a body not her own. The final recognition scene then unveils this fiction, reasserting reality by recomposing the unity of body and voice for both characters. But upon closer inspection, the love declaration scene described above problematizes the idea that Kathy's body can be real, if *real* in this case means natural. Indeed, Kathy is artificially beautified and transformed from a simple girl into a star, and thus she undergoes the same transformation already completed by Lina in that Kathy gets a more beautiful body just as Lina got a more beautiful voice.[50]

Singin' in the Rain then seems to suggest that the love story, presented to us as a true romance, is actually no less constructed than the movie being filmed. This is confirmed in the film's final scene, where just as the love declaration could only have happened on a set, the recognition of this love can only happen in another scenic space: in the theater and in front of a public. But there is also a stylistic similarity between the two scenes in their profilmic makeup and camera work. In fact, in both scenes there is diffused light, construction on the axis of shot/reverse shot, close-ups, and long shots. Thus, the two scenes that ought to be categorized on the level of story and truth are precisely those filmed on stage according to discourse and cinematic romance conventions. As a result, *Singin' in the Rain* not only reveals the construction of the relationship between image and sound (the film within the film), but also the constructions deployed on the level of story. In sum, in this film, we are constantly attempting to distinguish between its various levels of construction.

Yet the film also operates in a manner contrary to that described above, with the story invading discourse. The image/sound relationship is in fact constructed at Lina Lamont's expense, and unveiling the construction of image/sound unity is not an end in itself. That is to say, it does not have a merely metalinguistic function. Rather, it is used from the very beginning for narrative ends and is freighted with moral implications. For if the image's construction is in itself neutral, Lina—the beneficiary of such a construction—is actually an evil character, and her wickedness a true component of the story. Indeed, she has Kathy fired, the girl's name taken from the title credits, and tries to control the studio's decisions. It is certainly still a musical though, in the sense that the villain of a musical is never too dangerous. But it is also necessary to narrativize her trajectory so that *Singin in the Rain*'s story can find resolution.

Furthermore, it is indispensable that story balance discourse, and the film's final shots seem to serve this purpose. A giant billboard for *Singin' in the Rain* with the portraits of its two main actors, Don Lockwood and Kathy Selden, occupies the whole screen. Then it covers only a part of the frame, while a dolly pulls the camera back to reveal the two actors in flesh and blood, dressed in everyday clothing. For an instant we are made to believe that the meadow outside is a real space, far from any set. But it becomes evident soon that we are still on the premises of Monumental Studios and that the flesh and blood actors are only slightly more real than the image advertising their film. Thus, in *Singin' in the Rain*, the fictional level definitively incorporates that of story and the final frames reveal every image to be a palimpsest of different levels of fiction over and above a mere imitation of reality. With *Singin' in the Rain*, Hollywood cinema has entered into the realm of postmodern aesthetic.

NOTES

INTRODUCTION

1. On the concept of discursive formation, see Foucault, *The Archeology of Knowledge*, which defines an epistemological framework for the study of culture. Additionally, all the research developed in this book on the circuit of desire between subjectivity and imaginary formations draws on Foucault's reflections on sexuality and discourse in Foucault, *The History of Sexuality*.

2. For a comparison of Bellour and Bordwell's theoretical paradigms, see Elsaesser, "Classical/Post-classical Narrative."

3. For a clear and concise elaboration of Bellour's theoretical framework, see his opening essay "A Bit of History" in Bellour, *The Analysis of Film*, 1–20, especially 10–16.

4. All theoretical and methodological modes of textual film analysis that were proposed since the early 1970s, and even more recent interpretive ones that integrate textual and contextual analysis through categories of spectatorship or historical audience, emerged broadly speaking through the study of classical American cinema. For a survey on the role of American cinema in the development of film analysis, before the "turn to historical research," see Bellour, *Le cinéma américain*; Nichols, *Movies and Methods*, vol. 1, 2; Aumont and Marie, *L'analyse des films*.

5. Whenever used, the term *mise-en-scène* is a synonym of direction. It refers to the organization of all the technical and linguistic components used in filmmaking. For Italian semiotician Gianfranco Bettetini, mise-en-scène is "choice/coordination/signifying organization/'poetic' composition of all the elements present during the projection of the film: including those explicitly absent or hidden." Bettetini, *Produzione del senso*, 137. Therefore I do not rely on the common American usage of the term that refers to the elements placed in front of the camera and appearing in the film frame. In their influential textbook, David Bordwell and Kristin Thompson state that "mise-en-scène includes those aspects of film that overlap with the art of the theater: setting, lighting, costume, and the behavior of the figures. In controlling the mise-en-scène, the director *stages the event* for the camera." See Bordwell and

Thompson, *Film Art*, 145. Without being polemical, I think this use is misleading since the French themselves use the term *mise-en-scène* precisely for film direction. The most elaborate contribution on the topic is Aumont, *Le cinéma et la mise-en-scène*.

6. Cf. Baudry, "Ideological Effects"; Baudry, "The Apparatus"; Metz, *The Imaginary Signifier*; MacCabe, "Realism and the Cinema"; Bordwell, "The Classical Hollywood Style, 1917–60"; Bordwell, *Narration in the Fiction Film*. For a helpful analysis of 1970s psychoanalytic film theory, see Allen, *Projecting Illusions*.

7. Morin, "Author's Preface," 224–225.

8. Cf. Oudart, "Cinema and Suture"; Dayan, "The Tutor-Code of Classical Cinema"; Heath, "On Suture."

9. Bertetto, "L'immaginario cinematografico," 62–64.

10. Greenblatt, *Shakespearean Negotiations*, 6.

11. Ibid., 14.

12. Ibid., 19.

13. For a discussion of the notion of lifestyle in relation to identity and consumption, see Bell and Hollows, "Towards a History of Lifestyle."

14. Scott, "Gender," 39.

15. In this regard, cf. also Elsaesser, *The Persistence of Hollywood*, 13–28.

16. Altman, *Film/Genre*.

17. Looking at recent Feminist Film Studies, Doane has stated: "there is a great deal happening within Feminist Film Studies. . . . Yet what seems to be lost in the flurry of this activity are some basic questions and . . . a desire that often goes by the name of *theory*. . . . Current film feminisms often ally themselves with the logic of the local and its corresponding suspicion of abstraction. . . . The solution is not to valorize the local but to theorize historically." Doane, "Aesthetics and Politics," 1230–1234.

18. Petro, "Reflections on Feminist Film Studies," 1272.

19. R. Williams, *Marxism and Literature*, 121–135.

20. See Ray, *A Certain Tendency*, 25–125.

21. For noir, see Kaplan's very influential anthology *Women in Film Noir*; Polan, *Power and Paranoia*; Doane, *Femmes Fatales*; Naremore, *More than Night*; Dimendberg, *Film Noir*. For the woman's film, see Doane, *The Desire to Desire*. For melodrama, see Gledhill's anthology, *Home Is Where the Heart Is*; Kaplan, *Motherhood and Representation*; Singer, *Melodrama and Modernity*; L. Williams, *Playing the Race Card*. All these works will be discussed in the following chapters.

22. Peiss, *Cheap Amusements*, especially 36–40. I develop this topic more at length in chapter 1 and in Pravadelli, "Cinema and the Modern Woman."

23. Hansen, *Babel & Babylon*, 245–294.

24. Scholarship in this area is rapidly growing. See, at least, L. Rabinovitz, *For the Love of Pleasure*; Stamp, *Movie-Struck Girls*; Bean and Negra, *A Feminist Reader*; Mahar, *Women Filmmakers*; Hastie, *Cupboards of Curiosity*; Garrett Cooper, *Universal Women*; Callahan, *Reclaiming the Archive*; and Gaines, Vatsal, and Dall'Asta, *Women Film Pioneer Project*.

25. In one of her most recent pieces, Laura Mulvey has interestingly pointed out that, starting with Miriam Hansen's work on Valentino, historical research done by feminists has allowed them to modify and open up her earlier notion of gendered voyeurism and make the representation of gender in cinema more complex. In relation to the 1920s flapper film, in particular Clara Bow's famous vehicle *It*, Mulvey states: "Unlike the passive femininity that gave rise to theories of a 'masculinised' cinematic gaze in 1970s feminist film theory, the flapper star could control the look of desire and drive the narrative (for what it was worth) forward." And later: "For feminist film theory, the flapper films offer a glimpse into a regime of cinematic desire in which the supremacy of the male protagonist is displaced." See Mulvey, "Thoughts on the Young Modern Woman," 214 and 216.

26. Bergstrom and Doane, "The Female Spectator," 7; Mayne, *The Woman at the Keyhole*, 20.

27. Rodowick, *The Crisis of Political Modernism*, 75. For an in-depth analysis of the debate on the progressive text, see ibid., 67–110. See also Klinger, "'Cinema/Ideology/Criticism' Revisited."

28. Comolli and Narboni, "Cinema/Ideology/Criticism."

29. See *Cahiers du Cinéma*, "John Ford's *Young Mr. Lincoln*"; *Cahiers du Cinéma*, "Morocco de Josef von Sternberg."

30. Elsaesser, "Tales of Sound and Fury," 48.

31. The most relevant contributions on family melodrama in that vein appeared in Gledhill's *Home Is Where the Heart Is* and in Landy, *Imitation of Life*. For a discussion of the role of family melodrama in film theory, see also Mulvey, "'It Will Be a Magnificent Obsession.'"

32. Johnston, "Women's Cinema as Counter-Cinema," 140.

33. Cook, "Approaching the Work of Dorothy Arzner," 47.

34. The expression *dramatistic approach* is used by Peter Burke in discussing the work of anthropologists, such as Clifford Geertz, that have contributed to the "cultural turn" in the Humanities and the Social Sciences. See Burke, *What Is Cultural History?* 38.

35. Janet Bergstrom showed the weakness of symptomatic feminist readings, such as Johnston's, by arguing that it was necessary "to take the narrative movement as a whole into consideration." See Bergstrom, "Rereading the Work of Claire Johnston," 86. A similar critique to symptomatic readings is proposed by Bill Nichols in "Form Wars."

36. In the mid-1980s, *Stella Dallas* spurred a very animated debate among feminists. The main focus of the discussion concerned spectatorship and the kind of identification the film elicited for female viewers. The debate was inaugurated by Kaplan's "The Case of the Missing Mother." It continued in *Cinema Journal*, first with L. Williams's "Something Else besides a Mother" and then with Kaplan's response (*Cinema Journal*, vol. 24.2). The debate continued in later issues. For Kaplan's final assessment on Vidor's film, see *Motherhood and Representation*, 169–173.

37. From a methodological perspective, this important piece of scholarship was a response to the psychoanalytic, ideological, and feminist approaches to Hollywood

cinema of the previous 15 years. While *The Classical Hollywood Cinema* is primarily a historical investigation of Hollywood's mode of production and its relation to the film form, it also proposes a cognitivist approach to spectatorship antithetical to psychoanalytically based approaches. Bordwell has discussed this issue, among others, in Bordwell, "Contemporary Film Studies."

38. When I discuss specifically the question of representation and style, I refer only to David Bordwell, as he is the author of that part of the book.

39. Gunning, "The Classical Hollywood Cinema," 77.

40. Pye, "Bordwell and Hollywood," 47 and 51. In a similar vein, R. Barton Palmer states that the major problem with Bordwell's neoformalist approach is that it "lacks a semantic component, one that would speak to questions of 'meaning.'" Barton Palmer, "The Classical Hollywood Cinema," 91. Another important assessment on the pitfalls of Bordwell's approach is contained in Nichols's "Form Wars." Overall most reviews have a similar structure: after stressing the volume's novelties—historical research and massive data—they all similarly go into its weakness. A strenuous defense of Bordwell's method is done by Eitzen in "Evolution, Functionalism."

41. Ray, "The Bordwell Regime," 62.

42. In contrast to most scholars of American contemporary cinema, Bordwell recognizes the persistence of the classical model within American cinema from 1960 onward. Contemporary cinema is still marked by the continuity system which is "intensified" via specific technical-formal devices: faster editing, extreme lenses, pyrotechnic camera movements, and closer shots. See Bordwell, *The Way Hollywood Tells It*.

43. The case of Feminist Film Theory is emblematic. At the end of the 1980s, we witness the publication of key works in the field, from Doane's study of the 1940s woman's film (1987) to Modleski's work on Hitchcock (1988) and Studlar's analysis of the Von Sternberg/Marlene Dietrich collaboration (1988). However, while the semiotic-psychoanalytic approach reaches its apogee, the *Camera Obscura*'s issue on *The Spectatrix* (1989) represents a foundational episode in the transition to a new paradigm in Feminist Film Studies, based on cultural and historical approaches. For an overview of Feminist Film Studies at that transitional moment, see the editors' opening remarks in Bergstrom and Doane, "The Female Spectator."

44. Altman, "Dickens, Griffith, and Film Theory Today," 323.

45. Ibid., 337–338.

46. Ibid., 326–327.

47. Ibid., 338–339.

48. Gunning, "The Cinema of Attractions," 58. André Gaudreault's idea that early cinema is ruled by the principle of "monstration" has clear affinities with Gunning's perspective. See Gaudreault, "Film, Narrative, Narration." For Benjamin's theory of shock, see Benjamin, *The Theory of Art*.

49. Gunning, "An Aesthetic of Astonishment," 743. For a more recent reconsideration of Gunning's thoughts on cinema and modernity, also in relation to Bordwell's criticism, see Gunning, "Modernity and Cinema."

50. Gunning, "The Cinema of Attractions," 57.

51. Hansen's first essay on Valentino appeared in 1986. See Hansen, "Pleasure, Ambivalence, Identification." For her earliest assessment of Benjamin's film theory, see Hansen, "Benjamin, Cinema and Experience."

52. Hansen, "The Mass Production of the Senses," 334.

53. Ibid., 343.

54. Naremore, *More than Night*, 45.

55. Singer, *Melodrama and Modernity*; Dimendberg, *Film Noir*; Casetti, *The Eye of the Century*.

56. On criteria of the sample's formation, see Bordwell, Staiger, and Thompson, *The Classical Hollywood Cinema*, 388–396.

57. According to Kathryn Fuller, in provincial towns one could essentially see the same films that came out in first-run theaters in large urban centers. The difference is that films came to the luxurious picture palaces of large cities first and visual quality was better. See Fuller, "'You Can Have the Strand.'"

58. For production information, see Steinberg, *Film Facts*. Cf. also Taves, "The B Film."

CHAPTER 1. THE EARLY THIRTIES

1. Brasillach and Bardèche, *Histoire du cinéma*, cited in Bordwell, *On the History of Film Style*, 47.

2. Sklar, *Movie-Made America*, 175–194.

3. Cott, *The Grounding of Modern Feminism*, 147. See also Freedman, "The New Woman"; Cott, "The Modern Woman of the 1920s"; Patterson, *The American New Woman Revisited*. On the relation between women and leisure time, see Kathy Peiss's seminal *Cheap Amusements*. On the specific role of cinema in relation to the New Woman, see Hansen, *Babel & Babylon*.

4. Stokes, "Female Audiences," 43–44.

5. Women scriptwriters had a tremendous impact in Hollywood, especially from the mid-1910s to the mid-1930s. Of the 25,000 screenplays copyrighted between 1911 and 1925 half were written by women. And it is fair to say that without the contribution of screenwriters such as Frances Marion, Anita Loos, June Mathis, Jeanie Macpherson, and others, Hollywood's imaginary would have been quite different. Cf. Francke, *Script Girls*; Casella, "Feminism and the Female Author."

6. Balio, *Grand Design*, 237.

7. Stokes, "Female Audiences." The box-office rankings of stars compiled according to movie theater exhibitors is very telling in this sense. See Steinberg, *Film Facts*, 57–59. On the star system in the 1930s, see Balio, *Grand Design*, 143–177; and McLean, *Glamour in a Golden Age*.

8. While the flapper was a pivotal figure in all areas of American culture, from literature to fashion, from the popular press to advertising, in cinema her status was assured by the genre of the "flapper film," which developed roughly from 1922 to 1929, when Clara Bow played her last flapper role in Dorothy Arzner's *The Wild Party*. On the "flapper film," see Ross, "Banking the Flames of Youth." On the flapper and

American culture, see Zeitz, *Flapper*. On Clara Bow and modernity, see Pravadelli, *Le donne del cinema*, 55–60.

9. Ryan, "The Projection of a New Womanhood," 369–370.

10. On these issues in American silent cinema, see Higashi, *Virgins, Vamps, and Flappers*.

11. Welter, "The Cult of True Womanhood."

12. The exciting freedom enjoyed by young women in the modern metropolis is, of course, the subject not only of many films, but also of women's biographies and diaries, sociological studies, and so forth. In relation to Hollywood and the American film context I would like to refer the reader to two very different works, Louise Brooks's famous memoir *Lulu in Hollywood*, and Cari Beauchamp's *Adventures of a Hollywood Secretary*. Beauchamp collects the letters of Valeria Belletti, an Italian girl from New Jersey who moves to Los Angeles in 1924 to become the secretary of Sam Goldwyn. While Valeria's letters to her friend Irma contain countless episodes regarding all aspects of the film industry, they also provide a detailed account of the life of a young working woman living far from home and family. Of particular interest is the narration of Valeria's leisure time and her relation to her female friends.

13. According to the American Film Institute Catalogue, 4 films were produced between 1921 and 1930 with working-class female characters and 46 with household maids. Almost all of these were minor roles. Whereas there were 49 films with saleswomen, 28 with stenographers and 114 with secretaries. Ryan, "The Projection of a New Womanhood," 374–375.

14. Cf. Singer, *Melodrama and Modernity*, 101–102.

15. Ibid.

16. Ibid., 221. On serial-queen melodrama, see also Stamp, *Movie-Struck Girls*; Mahar, *Women Filmmakers*; Dall'Asta, *Trame spezzate*.

17. On this fundamental aspect of modernity, see the following classical works: Simmel, "The Metropolis"; Kracauer, "Cult of Distraction"; Benjamin, "On Some Motifs"; Benjamin, *The Theory of Art*.

18. For a comprehensive account of the debate around the concept of attraction, see Strauven, *The Cinema of Attractions Reloaded*.

19. Gunning, "The Cinema of Attractions," 58.

20. Quoted in Crafton, *The Talkies*, 334.

21. Mizejewski, *Ziegfeld Girl*, 148.

22. Casetti, *Eye of the Century*, 130–135.

23. For information on 1930s female employment, see Milkman, "Women's Work."

24. Mizejewski, *Ziegfeld Girl*, 148.

25. See Berry, *Screen Style*, 24–30.

26. On the fallen woman film, cf. Jacobs, *The Wages of Sin*.

27. The film employs numerous other visual devices of great interest, which are far from classical canons and much closer to Josef Von Sternberg's sensual style. One finds other examples of Milestone's visual bravura in *All Quiet on the Western Front* (1930).

28. Gunning, "The Cinema of Attractions," 58–59.

29. On *Rain*, cf. also Lawrence, "Constructing a Woman's Speech."

30. Gaines, "Introduction: Fabricating the Female Body," 5.

31. Foucault, *The History of Sexuality*, 17.

32. D'Emilio and Freedman, *Intimate Matters*, 223.

33. Ibid., 224–226. On the relation between Freud and Ellis, see also Mitchell, *Psychoanalysis and Feminism.*

34. D'Emilio and Freedman, *Intimate Matters*, 225–226.

35. For a panoramic view on the different images of femininity in 1930s cinema, see Dooley, *From Scarface to Scarlett.*

36. Kaplan, *Women and Film*, 54–56.

37. Ibid., 50.

38. Beyond those works already directly cited, I found particularly useful: Nichols, "*Blonde Venus*"; Weiss, "'A Queer Feeling'"; Petro, "The Hottentot"; Mayne, "Marlene"; Kuzniar, "'It's Not Often.'"

39. Studlar, *In the Realm of Pleasure.*

40. Jacobs, *The Wages of Sin*, 88–93. Jacobs mentions three versions of the screenplay and at least two different endings.

41. On this issue, see Weiss, "'A Queer Feeling'"; and Gregg, "Cary Grant in *Who's a Fairy*."

42. Mulvey, "Visual Pleasure."

43. On Hollywood in the transition era, see Doherty, *Pre-Code Hollywood.*

44. Patrice Petro has stated that Gunning "says very little about the way in which the female body functions as a main 'attraction' in the cinema of attractions." In this chapter, I offer a gendered reading of Gunning's notion of attraction by historicizing both the concept itself and Hollywood's film style. Cf. Petro, "Film Feminism and Nostalgia," 171.

45. On the relationship between Busby Berkeley and Hollywood, see Schatz, *The Genius of the System*; and Mordden, *The Hollywood Studios.*

46. On the crotch-shot and gender politics in Berkeley's musicals for Warner Brothers, see Willis, "'110 Per Cent Woman.'"

47. On the impossible perspective in Berkeley musicals, cf. also Rubin, "Busby Berkeley."

48. On the ritual of courtship in the musical, see Altman, *The American Film Musical.*

49. For an interesting analysis of the collective's function in Warner musicals, see Roth, "Some Warner Musicals."

CHAPTER 2. NORMATIVE DESIRES AND VISUAL SOBRIETY

1. Aristotle, *Poetics*, 349.

2. Ibid., 350.

3. Ibid., 352–353.

4. Bordwell, "The Classical Hollywood Style," 3–4.

5. Bazin, "La Politique des auteurs," 135–136.

6. Bazin, "The Evolution of the Language of Cinema," 28–32.

7. Bordwell, "Film Style and Technology," 339.

8. de Lauretis, *Alice Doesn't*, 106.

9. On the "comedy of remarriage," see, of course, Cavell's *Pursuits of Happiness*.

10. Steinberg, *Film Facts*.

11. For a comparison of the different musical genres, see Rubin, "Busby Berkeley"; and the classic Altman, *The American Film Musical*.

12. Cf. Doss, "Images of American Women." On Bette Davis' star persona in the 1930s, see Fisher, "Bette Davis."

13. For a reconstruction of the film's censorship case, see Jacobs, *The Wages of Sin*.

14. Along with other scenes and dialogue, these sentences would be cut in the theatrical release. For a comparison of the original version and the censored released version, see the DVD *Forbidden Hollywood* (vol. 2) released by TMC Archive, 2006.

15. For a more detailed analysis of *Baby Face*, see Pravadelli, *Le donne del cinema*, 61–65.

16. Kaplan, *Motherhood and Representation*, 173.

17. On these arguments, see the volume edited by Robert Sklar and Vito Zagarrio, *Frank Capra*, especially essays by Schatz, Sklar, Taves, and Buscombe.

18. Bordwell, "The Classical Hollywood Style."

19. Bellour, *The Analysis of Film*; Heath, "Film and System: Part I" and "Part II."

20. I borrow the expression *genres of integration* from Thomas Schatz. See Schatz, *Hollywood Genres*.

21. In thinking about the film's opening I have been influenced by Marc Vernet's thoughts on film noir's beginning. Vernet argues that noir is peculiarly structured around the opposition between two "movements." Noir usually begins by juxtaposing heterogeneous elements by contrasting "the set-up," where everything seems in place, to "the enigma," where "the nearly perfect accord of the first movement now falls into chaos." Cf. Vernet, "The Filmic Transaction," 6.

22. Morris Dickstein has stated that "some of the little character bits on the bus are fine examples of Capra's common touch and sense of community. . . . These touches showing ordinary people amusing themselves provide a good background for the humbling of the two proud central figures. In a surprising twist, at one low point they too find themselves hungry, foraging for vegetables in the fields, as if stripped down to their unaccommodated selves." Dickstein, *Dancing in the Dark*, 397–398.

23. On the relationship between Capra's films and the New Deal, see Muscio, "Roosevelt, Arnold, and Capra."

24. Simmons, "Modern sexuality."

25. On the New Deal for women, see Wiesen Cook, *Eleanor Roosevelt*.

26. Simmons, "Modern Sexuality," 27.

27. Ibid., 30.

28. Ibid., 31–32.

29. Ibid., 24–27.

30. Simmons, *Making Marriage Modern*, 138.

31. Cited in Todd, *The 'New Woman' Revised*, 147. I refer the reader to this study for its exemplary analysis of the relationship between the 14th Street New York School iconography of the New Woman during the 1930s and the dynamics of gender connected to modernity.

32. LaSalle, *Dangerous Men*, 66. On Gable's "extreme masculinity," and more generally his 1930s star persona, see also Becker, "Clark Gable."

33. Schatz, "La 'screwball comedy,'" 68.

34. Lévi-Strauss, *The Elementary Structures of Kinship*.

35. Schatz, *The Genius of the System*, 199–227.

36. I take Jacobs's quote from Robé, "Taking Hollywood Back," 77.

37. Ibid., 78. Robé has further developed his thesis, also advancing a gender reading of 1930s film theory, in Robé, *Left of Hollywood*.

38. On the relationship between director and studio, see Elsaesser, "Film History as Social History."

39. Altman, *Film/Genre*, 42.

40. Speaking of Muni in *The Story of Louis Pasteur*, Thomas Schatz observes that the actor "was given to histrionic excess, long-winded tirades, and an inflated sense of his own status as an artist and social crusader." We can also extend this observation to the character of Zola. See Schatz, *The Genius of the System*, 208.

41. Thomas Elsaesser has claimed that "the historically vanished intertext of the bio-pic might be live radio broadcasting, and the relevant intertext to Muni's acting or Dieterle's direction something like Roosevelt's fireside chats, going straight to the nation, bypassing the press, and straight into the homes, bypassing government bureaucracies, or political parties." Elsaesser, "Film History as Social History," 30.

42. Ray, *A Certain Tendency*, 59.

43. At the beginning of his famous analysis of a sequence of Hawks's *The Big Sleep* (1946) Bellour recalls Rivette's statement that "obviousness is the mark of Howard Hawks' genius." See Bellour, "The Obvious and the Code," 72; and Rivette, "The Genius of Howard Hawks." Cf. also Sarris, "Howard Hawks," 104.

44. Wollen, "The Auteur Theory," 91.

45. Hawks's films have played a fundamental role in the elaboration of auteurial theories, which we can only begin to acknowledge. According to Claire Johnston, clearly influenced by Wollen, "for Hawks, there is only the male and the non-male: in order to be accepted into the male universe, the woman must *become* a man." While Wollen considers Hawks a less complex auteur than Ford, Johnston states that a Hawks woman "is a traumatic presence that must be negated." On the other hand, in Ford's universe she "plays a pivotal role" inasmuch as she represents culture and civilization. See Johnston, "Women's Cinema as Counter-Cinema," 138. More recently, always with an eye toward gender analysis, Elizabeth Cowie has proposed a radically different thesis, observing that "what is striking about Hawks's films is the lack of fixity of the conventional characteristics of masculine and feminine; not only do women act like men, but men act like women, and this is true of the adventure film as well as the comedies." See Cowie, "Feminist Arguments," 30.

46. Cited in Ray, *A Certain Tendency*, 99.

47. Cf. Deleuze, "How Do We Recognize Structuralism?" 173.

48. Useful sources for a structural analysis of the film can be found in A. Williams, "Narrative Patterns."

49. Wollen, "The Auteur Theory," 82–91.

50. Laura Mulvey has said in a private conversation that the original idea for her essay came out of this episode when Rita Hayworth arrives at the bar where the male group hangs out.

51. Trimberger, "Feminism, Men and Modern Love," 136.

52. Cott, *The Grounding of Modern Feminism*, 156–157.

53. Doane, *The Desire to Desire*, 105.

CHAPTER 3. THE MALE SUBJECT OF NOIR AND THE MODERN GAZE

1. Pye, "Bordwell and Hollywood," 50.

2. Barton Palmer, "The Classical Hollywood Cinema," 91. For a reception of *The Classical Hollywood Cinema*, see the Introduction.

3. Turim, *Flashbacks in Film*, 182.

4. Krutnik, *In a Lonely Street*, 164.

5. Walker, *Couching Resistance*, 164.

6. Belton, *Cinema Stylists*, 329.

7. Vegetti Finzi, "Introduzione," xiv.

8. There is iconographic resemblance here to the space and locations of *The Maltese Falcon* (J. Huston, 1941): the shot of the exterior of the detective's office displays the reversed name printed on the window glass, just as in Huston's film. The office furthermore appears to be elevated and near the train station, just as Sam Spade's seemed to be at the height of the Golden Gate bridge, shown at the beginning of the film.

9. Naremore, *More than Night*, 89.

10. For an in-depth analysis of the film, see Naremore's classic *The Magic World of Orson Welles*, 52–83. For a recent reassessment of *Citizen Kane*'s style, see Naremore, "The Magician."

11. Bordwell, *On the History of Film Style*, 225.

12. The function of speech in 1930s classical cinema can probably be interpreted also in relation to radio's essential role in the mediascape of the decade. Cf. Hilmes, *Radio Voices*.

13. This comparison has been analyzed in various ways by scholars. Particularly influential in the seventies and eighties was MacCabe's "Realism and the Cinema."

14. Polan, *Power and Paranoia*, 194.

15. For an analysis of the two models, see also Winston Dixon, *American Cinema of the 1940s*.

16. See Reid and Walker, "Strange Pursuit," 61.

17. Renov, *Hollywood's Wartime Women*, 47.

18. Silverman, "Historical Trauma," 114. Reid and Walker argue that in discussions of noir and the "crises of masculinity," it is often forgotten that it was the Depression, more so than the war and the postwar period, which first brought about the "extraordinarily harsh blows to the 'phallic' cult of aggressiveness, individualism and self-reliance." See Reid and Walker, "Strange Pursuit," 63. These trends are also treated in McElvaine, *The Great Depression*.

19. Heath, "Narrative Space," 30.

20. Ibid., 32. Cf. also Jay, "The Camera as Memento Mori."

21. Heath's thesis falls into line with those of Baudry and Metz. On this aspect, see the Introduction.

22. Crary, *Techniques of the Observer*, 14.

23. Ibid., 16–17.

24. Ibid., 20.

25. Ibid., 24.

26. This subgenre is a category already established by Borde and Chaumeton in the early 1950s. See Borde and Chaumeton, *A Panorama of American Film Noir*.

27. For a useful analysis of the subgenres of noir, see Krutnik, *In a Lonely Street*, 188–226.

28. See, for example, the device of the montage sequence devised at the beginning of the 1930s, which was at once narratively functional, expressive, and economical. On this aspect, see Schatz, *The Genius of the System*, 145–147.

29. On this question, see the excellent essay by Meisel, "Scattered Chiaroscuro."

30. Telotte, *Voices in the Dark*, 121. On the dynamics of the gaze in the film, see also Casetti, *Eye of the Century*, 62–66.

31. Dimendberg, *Film Noir*, 21–23. See also Georg Simmel's seminal "The Metropolis and Mental Life."

32. Jules Dassin's *The Naked City* (1948) is among the films making the best use of real locations in New York.

33. On Bogart and Bacall's star personae in 1940s cinema, see Worland, "Humphrey Bogart and Lauren Bacall."

34. The function of the glass and the techniques of reflection and mise-en-scène share elements with a similar sequence in *The Woman in the Window* (F. Lang, 1944), Lang's noir released in the same year, in which Prof. Wanley/Edward G. Robinson sees reflected in a shop window a woman whose portrait he is looking at in that very window. Although the complexity of Lang's scene is greater, thanks to the presence of the female figure, it seems to me that the visual dynamics at work in *Murder My Sweet*, and the seductive impact upon the spectator, are similar to those in Lang's episode. For an analysis of this scene, in part applicable to Dmytryk's film as well, see Bertetto, *Lo specchio e il simulacro*, 37–41.

35. Jay, *Downcast Eyes*, 186–209.

36. Blumenberg, "Light as a Metaphor for Truth," 46.

37. These are 2 of the 5 films that inspired French critics to coin the term "film noir" after their postwar release in Paris. On this important episode in the history of criticism, see Naremore, *More than Night*, 11–17.

38. On this fundamental aspect of film noir, see Kaplan, *Women in Film Noir*; and Doane, *Femmes Fatales*.

39. Naremore, *More than Night*, 90.

40. For a psychoanalytic reading of the film, see Johnston, "*Double Indemnity*."

41. For a very convincing interpretation of this aspect as well as of the whole film, see Naremore, *More than Night*, 81–95.

42. Bazin, "The Evolution of the Western."

43. Bazin, "The Virtues and Limitations"; Bazin, "William Wyler"; Comolli, "Technique and Ideology"; Bordwell, *On the History of Film Style*.

44. Bordwell, *On the History of Film Style*, 163.

45. Ibid., 163 and following.

46. P. Rabinowitz, *Black & White & Noir*, 25–59.

47. Dimendberg, *Film Noir*, 67–68.

48. Polan, *Power and Paranoia*, 193–196.

49. Place, "Women in Film Noir," 41.

50. *Rear Window* (A. Hitchcock, 1954) was doubtless influenced by noir iconography, despite the fact that it was shot entirely in Paramount studios. The building that L. B. Jefferies sees from his window is a tenement house, a lower-class dwelling similar to those that appear in many noirs, as in *Where the Sidewalk Ends* and *The Dark Corner*. Even more important, however, is the iconographic and narrative motif of a character who accidentally witnesses a murder or a clue from his window, such as someone furtively leaving the building, as occurs in the two aforementioned films as well as in *The Window* (T. Tatzlaff, 1949). Finally, as in many noirs, Hitchcock's film makes use of the opposition between rich and poor neighborhoods, in this case between James Stewart's Greenwich Village and Grace Kelly's Upper East Side. On this and other matters regarding New York in Hollywood cinema, see Sanders, *Celluloid Skyline*.

51. In her study of Preminger's visual style, Mary Ann Doane has argued that in his cinema "it is the space within the frame that matters." For Preminger the frame is a "container" and not a "window" (in the Bazinian sense) as the filmmaker "is skeptical about what cannot be seen." Therefore he tends to "repress" offscreen space. See Doane, "Vicinanza, distanza e scala," 33–36.

52. Besides *Where the Sidewalk Ends*, another characteristic example of this model is the relationship between Van Heflin and Lizabeth Scott in *The Strange Love of Martha Ivers* (L. Milestone, 1946), a film of rare hopelessness in which, however, the couple finds some peace.

CHAPTER 4. (DIS)ADVENTURES OF FEMALE DESIRE IN THE 1940S WOMAN'S FILM

1. On the discursive construction of *Rosie the Riveter*'s image, see Dabakis, "Gendered Labor."

2. See Wiesen Cook, "ER's New Deal for Women."

3. Roosevelt, "Woman's Place."

4. See Schneider, "1942. Movies and the March to War," 89. On Greer Garson's character in *Mrs. Miniver* and her other wartime hits, see Hamad, "Greer Garson."

5. On the impact of war on gender relations and Hollywood's contribution to such a scenario, see Cott, *Public Vows*, especially 185–191.

6. Lugowski, "Claudette Colbert," 105.

7. Basinger, *A Woman's View*, 20.

8. Ibid., 7.

9. Here, I refer to Doane, *The Desire to Desire.*

10. The concept of "female genealogy" has been a key element in feminist theory (especially in the French and the Italian contexts). See, among others, Muraro, "Female Genealogies."

11. On pop psychoanalysis in America, cf. Ehrenreich, *The Hearts of Men*; D'Emilio and Freedman, *Intimate Matters*; Zaretsky, *Secrets of the Soul.*

12. Walker, *Couching Resistance*, xiii–xiv.

13. The film is an interesting hybridization of the woman's film and family melodrama. As such, it is possible to explain the protagonist's mastery of a traditional (maternal) role within the family in place of the more typical rebellion against conventions in the woman's film. The film has most of the major components of the family melodrama: setting in a small town, repressive social climate, generally excessive hypocrisy of town inhabitants.

14. Walker, *Couching Resistance*, 6.

15. Breuer and Freud, *Studies on Hysteria.*

16. Polan, *Power and Paranoia*, 164.

17. Doane, *The Desire to Desire*, 46.

18. Polan, *Power and Paranoia*, 164. See also Walker, *Couching Resistance.*

19. Freud, "Analysis Terminable and Interminable."

20. On Freud's theories of femininity, see Brennan, *The Interpretation of the Flesh.* Freud's essays on femininity are collected in Young-Bruehl, *Freud and Women.*

21. Vegetti Finzi, "Introduzione," xii.

22. Vegetti Finzi, "Le isteriche o la parola corporea," 23. Here, one finds exposition and interpretation on the famous case of Anna O. Anna O.'s case history is published in Breuer and Freud, *Studies on Hysteria*, 21–47.

23. Vegetti Finzi, "Le isteriche o la parola corporea," 25.

24. Ibid., 24–25.

25. Therefore, the film's strategies aimed at contradicting and subverting patriarchal discourse are consonant with the operation at work in the films of Dorothy Arzner and Ida Lupino, as noted by Claire Johnston and Pam Cook. The seminal essays on Arzner (and Lupino) were: Johnston, "Women's Cinema"; Johnston, "Dorothy Arzner"; Cook, "Approaching the work of Dorothy Arzner."

26. When shooting *Now, Voyager*, Bette Davis had already won two Oscars as best actress for her roles in *Dangerous* (A. Green, 1935) and *Jezebel* (W. Wyler, 1938).

27. On this important aspect see Gaines and Herzog, *Fabrications*; Berry, *Screen Style.*

28. Teresa de Lauretis tackles the question of the female spectator in relation to this film in de Lauretis, *The Practice of Love*, 130–139. As with *Blonde Venus*, *Mildred Pierce*, and a few others, *Now, Voyager* is one of the films most analyzed by scholars, especially feminists. Beyond the interventions already cited, see Jacobs, "'Now Voyager'"; Barton Palmer, "The Successful Failure"; LaPlace, "Producing and Consuming"; Kaplan, *Motherhood and Representation*, 110–115; White, *Uninvited*, 124–129.

29. Cowie, "Fantasia," 127.

30. Ibid., 131.

31. Ibid., 133.

32. Ibid., 146–150. For a critique of Cowie, see White, *Uninvited*, 127–129.

33. Cook, "Duplicity in *Mildred Pierce*," 71.

34. The film's producer, Jerry Wald, worked with obstinate perseverance to overcome difficulties of a long production phase. Much of the film's success is owed to him. After having come to an agreement with Joseph Breen of PCA, Wald hired Catherine Turney to write the film. She was the principal melodrama screenwriter at Warner Brothers. At that point, "Wald found that his flashback structure created two very different types of stories, a domestic melodrama and a murder mystery, which required different styles—and ultimately different writers." As such, while Turner developed the woman's film, Albert Maltz developed the noir plot. He was a specialist in masculine action films. See Schatz, *The Genius of the System*, 416.

35. On Hitchcock and the noir, see Naremore, "Hitchcock at the Margins of Noir."

36. Cf. Freud, "The Dissolution of the Oedipus Complex" and "Some Psychical Consequences."

37. Regarding triangular relationships between two presumed heterosexual males and one woman, who is desired by both, Eve Sedgwick has argued that this dynamic masks one man's homoerotic desire for the other. In this scenario, the woman acts as the medium through which each man gives shape to his desire for a member of the same sex. See Kosofsky Sedgwick, *Between Men*.

38. Modleski, *The Women Who*, 58.

39. In her famous essay, Mulvey underscored the significance of Hitchcock heroes as "exemplary of the symbolic order and the law," which in turn served as a precondition for woman's subordination to man in male/female relationships. See Mulvey, "Visual Pleasure," 23.

40. For a more detailed analysis of the film, see Pravadelli, *Alfred Hitchcock*. See also Renov, "From Identification to Ideology"; Flitterman-Lewis, "To See and Not to Be."

41. On the relation between sex and gender, cf. Judith Butler's seminal text *Gender Trouble*.

42. See Schatz, *The Genius of the System*.

43. On Joan Crawford as melodrama actress, see Bourget, "Faces of the American Melodrama."

44. Naremore, *Acting in the Cinema*, 87.

45. Doane, "Film and the Masquerade," 27.

46. Doane, *The Desire to Desire*, 179.

CHAPTER 5. EXCESS, SPECTACLE, SENSATION

1. See Nowell-Smith, "Minnelli and Melodrama"; and Mulvey, "Notes on Sirk." Christine Gledhill's anthology *Home Is Where the Heart Is*, which provides a very good survey of noteworthy studies on melodrama up to the mid-1980s, rightly places Nowell-Smith and Mulvey's pieces after Elsaesser's "Tales of Sound and Fury" in the opening section "Starting Out."

2. Neale, "Melo Talk," 69. Reprinted in Neale, *Genre and Hollywood*.

3. Neale, "Melo Talk," 73–74.

4. Singer, *Melodrama and Modernity*, 59–99.

5. Ibid., 46–49.

6. Ibid., 44–55.

7. There are many significant scholarly contributions on this phenomenon. Beyond those already cited, see Peiss, *Cheap Amusements*. For film-based studies on the same topic, see L. Rabinovitz, *For the Love of Pleasure*; Stamp, *Movie-Struck Girls*; and Mahar, *Women Filmmakers*.

8. P. Brooks, "Melodrama, Body, Revolution," 21.

9. Ibid., 17.

10. This has also been suggested by Tom Gunning in "The Horror of Opacity," 51.

11. We refer in particular to Foucault's *Discipline and Punish*.

12. See D'Emilio and Freedman, *Intimate Matters*.

13. In a volume dedicated to American melodrama in its various forms, Williams proposes at least two arguments worth noting: on the one hand, virtue in suffering is specific to American melodrama because it is through these operations that "American democratic culture has most powerfully articulated the moral structure of feeling animating its goal of justice"; on the other hand, melodrama is neither a tendency nor a tradition of American cinema, but rather, its dominant mode of being. See L. Williams, *Playing the Race Card*, 26 and 22–23.

14. L. Williams, "Film Bodies."

15. Haskell, *From Reverence to Rape*, 251.

16. On this film, see Mulvey, "Afterthoughts."

17. Linda Williams takes a similar position in "Discipline and fun." As always, Williams offers many valid arguments, even if she establishes an extremely direct and perhaps underhistoricized relation between Hitchcock's film and primitive attractions.

18. For a theoretical perspective on the relation between spectacle and vision, see Costa, *Il cinema e le arti visive*.

19. P. Brooks, *The Melodramatic Imagination*, 66.

20. For a survey of the development of melodrama in its various forms, see Gledhill, "The Melodramatic Field."

21. Singer, *Melodrama and Modernity*, 54.

22. Tyler May, *Homeward* Bound, 13. Refer to this study for an analysis of the social and political implications of this question.

23. Klinger, "'Cinema/Ideology/Criticism' Revisited."

24. Cf. Cohan, *Masked Men*. Cohan reconstructs the male image of the 1950s through such stars as Montgomery Clift, William Holden, Cary Grant, Humphrey Bogart, Marlon Brando, Rock Hudson, etc.

25. Ehrenreich, *The Hearts of Men*, 15.

26. Ibid., 15–19.

27. In her study of James Mason's 1950s star persona, Amy Lawrence has similarly argued that in "deconstructing one male authority figure after another (husbands, fathers, teachers), Mason also subverts the illusions of masculinity as the foundation of patriarchal dominance by exposing the agony at the heart of it." Lawrence, "James Mason," 87.

28. Ehrenreich, *The Hearts of Men*, 17.

29. Sirk's comment can be found in Halliday, *Sirk on Sirk*, 98.

30. For more analysis on these films, see Elsaesser, "Tales of Sound and Fury"; Nowell-Smith, "Minnelli and Melodrama"; Rodowick, "Madness, Authority and Ideology."

31. For a broader analysis of the film's sexual and "moral" dynamics, beyond the figures of Michael Ross and Constance MacKenzie, see Pomerance, "1957. Movies and the Search for Proportion," 179–185.

32. After some initial experiments in the 1930s, thanks in particular to David O. Selznick who produced *A Star Is Born* (W. Wellman, 1937), *Nothing Sacred* (W. Wellman, 1937), *The Adventures of Tom Sawyer* (N. Taurog, 1938), and above all *Gone with the Wind* (V. Fleming, 1939), around twenty Technicolor films per year came out during the 1940s. During the 1950s, color films accounted for about half of all production. For an in-depth analysis of these issues, see Neale, *Cinema and Technology*.

33. Belton, *Widescreen Cinema*, 194.

34. For example, *Picnic* by William Inge, *Tea and Sympathy* by Robert Anderson, and *Peyton Place* by Grace Metalious.

35. Klinger, "'Local' Genres," 138.

36. One can find useful analysis of *Written on the Wind* in Elsaesser, "Tales of Sound and Fury"; and Mulvey, "Notes on Sirk and Melodrama." The most in-depth analysis of the film is in Klinger, *Melodrama and Meaning*.

37. Deleuze, *Cinema 2*.

38. In his analysis of *Blonde Venus*, Bill Nichols shows how lighting is used in opposition to narrative and dialogue. "The shifting degree of shadow upon their faces sets up an ironic counterpoint to the coincidence of dialogue with social mores: at the very moment Ned is socially vindicated in casting Helen out for blackening her-

his name, the lighting vindicates her and criticizes him." Nichols, "*Blonde Venus*," 115–117.

39. On Marylee's function in the total economy of the film, see Orr, "Closure and Containment."

40. Jacobs, "The Woman's Picture."

41. P. Brooks, *The Melodramatic Imagination*, 56–80. For an analysis of Holden's character, see Cohan, *Masked Men*, 164–200.

42. Cf. Klinger, "'Cinema/Ideology/Criticism' Revisited," 84.

43. On symmetry and repetition, cf. both Bellour and Bordwell's analysis in, respectively, *The Analysis of Film* and "The Classical Hollywood Style."

CHAPTER 6. PERFORMATIVE BODIES AND NON-REFERENTIAL IMAGES

1. Anderson, *HollywoodTV*, 17.

2. Though not the only philosopher to have theorized the simulacrum, we owe Baudrillard for the most "systematic" elaboration. See in particular Baudrillard, *Simulations*. See also Deleuze, "The Simulacrum"; Jameson, "Postmodernism." For an analysis of the question in relation to film theory, cf. Bertetto, *Lo specchio e il simulacro*.

3. Cohan, "Introduction. Musicals of the Studio Era," 1.

4. According to Bordwell, the viewing process is a consciously guided operation. In the case of the classic film the spectator desires to understand the story, its junctions, and its motivations. Ideological analysis sees the story as a means for masking the values endorsed by the narration. Thus in the attempt to follow and understand the narrative, the spectator would be unconsciously led to accept its values. On this, see the Introduction.

5. Altman, "A Semantic/Syntactic Approach," 219.

6. Ibid.

7. Ibid., 220.

8. Ibid., 221–222.

9. Altman, 222. For a more in-depth analysis of these questions, see Altman, *The American Film Musical*.

10. It is a subgenre "limited mainly to the anything-goes, music-crazy period of the conversion to sound." Rubin, "Busby Berkeley," 54.

11. Dyer, "Entertainment and Utopia," 19. Dyer's article constitutes the foundational essay for musical's serious analysis, just as Thomas Elsaesser's "Tales of Sound and Fury" a few years earlier had initiated a sophisticated way to study melodrama.

12. Rubin, "Busby Berkeley," 59.

13. Altman, *The American Film Musical*, 167.

14. Cohan, *Incongruous Entertainment*, 44.

15. On the production politics of MGM and the Arthur Freed Unit, see Schatz, *The Genius of the System*.

16. Altman, *The American Film Musical*, 115.

17. Cohan, *Incongruous Entertainment*, 5–19.

18. Dyer, "Judy Garland."

19. Tinkcom, "'Working Like a Homosexual,'" 118.

20. Roth, "Some Warners Musicals," 47.

21. The five traits listed are the categories proposed by Dyer in "Entertainment and Utopia."

22. Ibid., 26.

23. Ibid., 28.

24. On the oneiric component in Minnelli's musicals, see Campari, *Film della memoria*, 125–129.

25. Altman, *Film/Genre*, 190; Feuer, *The Hollywood Musical*, 15.

26. Feuer, *The Hollywood Musical*, 8–9.

27. For an analysis of the cultural tradition of the western, see Nash Smith, *The Virgin Land*; and Kitses, *Horizon West*.

28. The comment is contained in the interview with the director found on the film's DVD, Turner Entertainment Co. & Warner Brothers Video, 2002.

29. Cf. http://www.harveyhouse.net (accessed January 7, 2014).

30. Schatz, *Hollywood Genres*, 34.

31. See Altman, *The American Film Musical*. I will concentrate on this aspect in the analysis of *Gentlemen Prefer Blondes* later in this chapter.

32. I do not agree with Schatz who minimizes the import of the western and considers the film a pure musical. Cf. Schatz, *Hollywood Genres*, 27.

33. The notion of a dual-focus text is again Altman's. Cf. Altman, *The American Film Musical*.

34. On this particular genre mechanism, see Feuer, *The Hollywood Musical*.

35. The film, especially thanks to Marilyn's presence, participates in the discourse of sexuality of the time and may be seen in relation to the dynamics explored in the preceding chapter. In 1953, the year of the film's release, *Playboy* appeared with Marilyn as the cover model and centerfold, and Kinsey's report on female sexuality was published as well. For an analysis of Marilyn's image in relation to the cultural panorama of the time, see Dyer, "Monroe and Sexuality."

36. See Arbuthnot and Seneca, "Pre-text and Text," with which the analysis that follows has some common elements.

37. Altman, *The American Film Musical*, 29.

38. Ibid., 28.

39. On the "progressive text," see the Introduction.

40. See Mulvey, "*Gentlemen Prefer Blondes*," 225.

41. For an interpretation of masculinity in *Red River*, see Cohan, *Masked Men*, 200–220.

42. Marilyn's reflexive acting style should be interpreted in this light. Cf. Solomon, "Reflexivity and Metaperformance."

43. Steven Cohan has shown how the film's critical appeal has produced, over the years, a whole array of interpretive strategies. See Cohan, "Case Study: Interpreting *Singin' in the Rain*."

44. On this aspect, see La Polla's in-depth analysis of the musical numbers in *Stanley Donen/Gene Kelly*, 57–95; and Wollen, *Singin' in the Rain*.

45. For example, *The Barkleys of Broadway* (Ch. Walters, 1949) and *The Band Wagon* (V. Minnelli, 1953), also written by Comden and Green for MGM. Cf. Feuer, "The Self-Reflexive Musical."

46. See Altman, *The American Film Musical*; on the relationship between cinematic genre and the music, see Feuer, *The Hollywood Musical*.

47. A final element of interest in the scene is found in the film's representation of the diegetic audience. The crowd is thronged in anxious waiting and welcomes the stars with great enthusiasm. But the public's reaction is completely artificial, its movements seem to follow the directions of an off-camera orchestra maestro. The spectators get up and shout at the exact same moment, as if they were a choir: the noisy and chaotic spontaneity typical of fans is thus completely tamed. The choice of choreographing a spontaneous collective wind seems to indicate that the theatricality of reality is not then so different from the performance of the spectacle. Thus every qualitative and neat distinction between reality and fiction collapses. We find very similar strategies in the episode in which Lorelei and Dorothy arrive at the harbor in *Gentlemen Prefer Blondes*: the reaction of the athletes, who are completely taken by the beauty of the pair, is choreographed in a similar way to that of Don and Lina's fans.

48. On this aspect, see Cohan, *Incongruous Entertainment*, 200–245.

49. Metz, "Story/Discourse."

50. On stardom and reflexivity in *Singin' in the Rain*, see also Higashi, "1952. Movies and the Paradox of Female Stardom," 69–77.

WORKS CITED

Publication dates may differ from the dates cited in the text. The latter refer to the original publications; dates herein are references to the publications from which quotes are taken.

Allen, Richard. *Projecting Illusions. Film Spectatorship and the Impression of Reality*. Cambridge: Cambridge University Press, 1995.

Alonge, Giaime, and Giulia Carluccio, eds. *Cary Grant. L'attore, il mito*. Venezia: Marsilio, 2006.

Altman, Rick, ed. *Genre: The Musical*. London: Routledge & Kegan Paul, 1981.

———. *The American Film Musical*. Bloomington: Indiana University Press, 1987.

———. "Dickens, Griffith, and Film Theory Today." *South Atlantic Quarterly* 88.2 (1989): 321–359.

———. *Film/Genre*. London: British Film Institute, 1999.

Anderson, Christopher. *HollywoodTV. The Studio System in the Fifties*. Austin: University of Texas Press, 1994.

Arbuthnot, Lucie, and Gail Seneca. "Pre-text and Text in *Gentlemen Prefer Blondes*." In *Issues in Feminist Film Criticism*. Ed. Patricia Erens. Bloomington: Indiana University Press, 1990. 112–125.

Aristotle. *Poetics*. In *The Pocket Aristotle*. New York: Washington Square Press, 1958. 342–379.

Aumont, Jacques. *Le cinéma et la mise-en-scène*. 2nd ed. Paris: Armand Colin, 2010.

Aumont, Jacques, and Michel Marie. *L'analyse des films*. Paris: Editions Nathan, 1994.

Balio, Tino. *Grand Design. Hollywood as a Modern Business Enterprise, 1930–1939*. Berkeley: University of California Press, 1993.

Barton Palmer, Robert. "The Successful Failure of Therapy in '*Now, Voyager*.'" *Wide Angle* 8.1 (1986): 29–38.

———. "The Classical Hollywood Cinema. Film Style and Mode of Production to 1960." *Post Script* 5.3 (1986): 88–91.

Basinger, Jeanine. *A Woman's View: How Hollywood Spoke to Women, 1930–1960*. London: Chatto & Windus, 1993.

Baudrillard, Jean. *Simulations*. Trans. Paul Foss et al. New York: Semiotext(e), 1983.

Baudry, Jean-Louis. "Ideological Effects of the Basic Cinematographic Apparatus." Trans. Alan Williams. *Film Quarterly* 28.2 (1974–75): 39–47.

———. "The Apparatus: Metapsychological Approaches to the Impression of Reality." Trans. Jean Andrews and Bertrand Augst. *Camera Obscura* 1 (1976): 104–126.

Bazin, André. "The Evolution of the Language of Cinema." In *What Is Cinema?* vol. 1. Ed. and trans. Hugh Gray. Berkeley: University of California Press, 1971. 23–40.

———. "The Virtues and Limitations of Montage." In *What Is Cinema?* vol. 1. Ed. and trans. Hugh Gray. Berkeley: University of California Press, 1971. 41–52.

———. "The Evolution of the Western." In *What Is Cinema?* vol. 2. Ed. and trans. Hugh Gray. Berkeley: University of California Press, 1971.

———. "William Wyler, or the Jansenist of Directing." In *Bazin at Work: Major Essays and Reviews from the 40s and 50s*. Ed. and trans. Bert Cardullo. New York: Routledge, 1997. 1–22.

———. "La Politique des auteurs." In *The French New Wave*. 2nd ed. Ed. Peter Graham with Ginette Vincendeau. London: British Film Institute, 2009. 130–147.

Bean, Jennifer, and Diane Negra, eds. *A Feminist Reader in Early Cinema*. Durham: Duke University Press, 2002.

Beauchamp, Cari. *Adventures of a Hollywood Secretary. Her Private Letters from inside the Studios of the 1920s*. Berkeley: University of California Press, 2006.

Becker, Christine. "Clark Gable: The King of Hollywood." In *Glamour in a Golden Age. Movie Stars of the 1930s*. Ed. Adrienne L. McLean. New Brunswick: Rutgers University Press, 2011. 245–266.

Bell, David, and Joanne Hollows. "Towards a History of Lifestyle." In *Historicizing Lifestyle. Mediating Taste, Consumption and Identity from the 1900s to 1970s*. Ed. David Bell and Joanne Hollows. Aldershot, Hampshire: Ashgate, 2006. 1–20.

Bellour, Raymond, ed. *Le cinéma américain*. 2 vol. Paris: Flammarion, 1980.

———. *The Analysis of Film*. Ed. Constance Penley. Bloomington: Indiana University Press, 2000.

———. "A Bit of History." In *The Analysis of Film*. Ed. Constance Penley. Bloomington: Indiana University Press, 2000. 1–20.

———. "The Obvious and the Code." In *The Analysis of Film*. Ed. Constance Penley. Bloomington: Indiana University Press, 2000. 69–76.

Belton, John. *Cinema Stylists*. Metuchen: The Scarecrow Press, Inc., 1983.

———. *Widescreen Cinema*. Cambridge: Harvard University Press, 1992.

Benjamin, Walter. "On Some Motifs in Baudelaire." In *Illuminations*. Ed. Hannah Arendt. Trans. Harry Zohn. New York: Schocken Books, 1969. 155–200.

———. "The Theory of Art in the Age of Its Technological Reproducibility." In *The Theory of Art in the Age of Its Technological Reproducibility and Other Writings on Media*. Ed. Michael J. Jennings, Brigid Doherty, and Thomas Y. Levin. Trans. Edmund Jephcott et al. Cambridge: The Belknap Press of Harvard University Press, 2008. 19–55.

Bergstrom, Janet. "Alternation, Segmentation, Hypnosis: Interview with Raymond Bellour." *Camera Obscura* 3–4 (1979): 71–103.

———. "Rereading the Work of Claire Johnston." In *Feminism and Film Theory.* Ed. Constance Penley. New York: Routledge, 1988. 80–88.

Bergstrom, Janet, and Mary Ann Doane. "The Female Spectator: Contexts and Directions." *Camera Obscura* 20–21 (1989): 5–27.

Berry, Sarah. *Screen Style. Fashion and Femininity in 1930s Hollywood.* Minneapolis: University of Minnesota Press, 2000.

Bertetto, Paolo. "L'immaginario cinematografico: forme e meccanismi." In *Enciclopedia del cinema.* vol. 1. Roma: Istituto della Enciclopedia Italiana, 2003. 62–78.

———. *Lo specchio e il simulacro. Il cinema nel mondo diventato favola.* Milano: Bompiani, 2007.

Bettetini, Gianfranco. *Produzione del senso e messa in scena.* Milano: Bompiani, 1975.

Blumemberg, Hans. "Light as a Metaphor for Truth." In *Modernity and the Hegemony of Vision.* Ed. David Michael Levin. Berkeley: University of California Press, 1993. 30–62.

Borde, Raymond, and Etienne Chaumeton. *A Panorama of American Film Noir (1941–1953).* Trans. Paul Hammond. San Francisco: City Lights Publishers, 2002.

Bordwell, David. *Narration in the Fiction Film.* Madison: The University of Wisconsin Press, 1985.

———. "The Classical Hollywood Style, 1917–1960." In David Bordwell, Janet Staiger, and Kristin Thompson, *The Classical Hollywood Cinema. Film Style and Mode of Production to 1960.* New York: Columbia University Press, 1985. 1–84.

———. "Film Style and Technology, 1930–1960." In David Bordwell, Janet Staiger, and Kristin Thompson, *The Classical Hollywood Cinema. Film Style and Mode of Production to 1960.* New York: Columbia University Press, 1985. 339–364.

———. "Contemporary Film Studies and the Vicissitudes of Grand Theory." In *Post-Theory. Reconstructing Film Studies.* Ed. David Bordwell and Noël Carroll. Madison: The University of Wisconsin Press, 1996. 3–36.

———. *On the History of Film Style.* Cambridge: Harvard University Press, 1997.

———. *The Way Hollywood Tells It. Story and Style in Modern Movies.* Berkeley: University of California Press, 2006.

Bordwell, David, and Kristin Thompson. "Technological Change and Classical Film Style." In Tino Balio, *Grand Design: Hollywood as a Modern Business Enterprise 1930–1939.* Berkeley: University of California Press, 1993. 109–141.

———. *Film Art. An Introduction.* 4th ed. New York: McGraw-Hill, Inc., 1993.

Bordwell, David, Janet Staiger, and Kristin Thompson. *The Classical Hollywood Cinema. Film Style and Mode of Production to 1960.* New York: Columbia University Press, 1985.

Bourget, Jean-Loup. "Faces of the American Melodrama: Joan Crawford." In *Imitation of Life.* Ed. Marcia Landy. Detroit: Wayne State University Press, 1991. 429–439.

Bratton, Jacky, Jim Cook, and Christine Gledhill, eds. *Melodrama. Stage, Picture, Screen.* London: British Film Institute, 1994.

Brennan, Teresa. *The Interpretation of the Flesh. Freud and Femininity*. London: Routledge, 1992.

Breuer, Josef, and Sigmund Freud. *Studies on Hysteria*. Trans. James Strachey. New York: Basic Books, 1957.

Brooks, Louise. *Lulu in Hollywood*. New York: Knopf, 1982.

Brooks, Peter. *The Melodramatic Imagination*. New York: Columbia University Press, 1985.

———. "Melodrama, Body, Revolution." In *Melodrama. Stage, Picture, Screen*. Ed. Jacky Bratton, Jim Cook, and Christine Gledhill. London: British Film Institute, 1994. 11–24.

Burke, Peter. *What Is Cultural History?* 2nd ed. Cambridge, U.K.: Polity, 2008.

Butler, Judith. *Gender Trouble*. New York: Routledge, 1989.

Cahiers du Cinéma. "John Ford's *Young Mr. Lincoln*." In *Movies and Methods*. vol. 1. Ed. Bill Nichols. Berkeley: University of California Press, 1976. 493–529.

———. "Morocco de Josef von Sternberg." *Cahiers du Cinéma* 225 (1970): 5–13.

Callahan, Vicky, ed. *Reclaiming the Archive. Feminism and Film History*. Detroit: Wayne State University Press, 2010.

Campari, Roberto. *Film della memoria. Mondi perduti, ricordati e sognati*. Venezia: Marsilio, 2005.

Carluccio, Giulia, and Linda Cena. *Otto Preminger*. Firenze: La Nuova Italia, 1990.

Casella, Donna R. "Feminism and the Female Author: The Not So Silent Career of the Woman Scenarist in Hollywood—1896–1930." *Quarterly Review of Film and Video* 23 (2006): 217–235.

Casetti, Francesco. *Eye of the Century: Film, Experience, Modernity*. Trans. Erin Larkin with Jennifer Pranolo. New York: Columbia University Press, 2008.

Cavell, Stanley. *Pursuits of Happiness: The Hollywood Comedy of Remarriage*. Cambridge: Harvard University Press, 1984.

Cleto, Fabio, ed. *Camp: Queer Aesthetics and the Performing Subject*. Ann Arbor: The University of Michigan Press, 1999.

Cohan, Steven. *Masked Men. Masculinity and the Movies in the Fifties*. Bloomington: Indiana University Press, 1997.

———. "Case Study: Interpreting *Singin' in the Rain*." In *Reinventing Film Studies*. Ed. Christine Gledhill and Linda Williams. London: Arnold, 2000. 53–75.

———. "Introduction. Musicals of the Studio Era." In *Hollywood Musicals. The Film Reader*. Ed. Steven Cohan. London: Routledge, 2002. 1–15.

———. *Incongruous Entertainment: Camp, Cultural Value, and the MGM Musical*. Durham: Duke University Press, 2005.

———, ed. *Hollywood Musicals. The Film Reader*. London: Routledge, 2002.

Comolli, Jean-Louis. "Technique and Ideology: Camera, Perspective, Depth of Field (Parts 3 and 4)." Trans. Diana Matias. In *Narrative, Apparatus, Ideology: A Film Theory Reader*. Ed. Philip Rosen. New York: Columbia University Press, 1986. 421–443.

Comolli, Jean-Louis, and Jean Narboni. "Cinema/Ideology/Criticism." Trans. Susan Bennett. In *Movies and Methods*. vol. 1. Ed. Bill Nichols. Berkeley: University of California Press, 1976. 22–30.

Cook, Pam. "Duplicity in *Mildred Pierce*." In *Women in Film Noir*. Ed. E. Ann Kaplan. London: British Film Institute, 1978. 68–82.

———. "Approaching the Work of Dorothy Arzner." In *Feminism and Film Theory*. Ed. Constance Penley. New York: Routledge, 1988. 46–56.

Copjec, Joan, ed. *Shades of Noir*. London: Verso, 1993.

Costa, Antonio. *Il cinema e le arti visive*. Torino: Einaudi, 2002.

Cott, Nancy F. *The Grounding of Modern Feminism*. New Haven: Yale University Press, 1987.

———. "The Modern Woman of the 1920s, American Style." In *A History of Women in the West*. Ed. Françoise Thébaud. Cambridge: Harvard University Press, 1994.

———. *Public Vows. A History of Marriage and the Nation*. Cambridge: Harvard University Press, 2000.

Cowie, Elizabeth. "Woman as Sign." In *The Woman in Question: m/f*. Ed. Parveen Adams and Elizabeth Cowie. Cambridge: The MIT Press, 1990. 117–133.

———. *Representing the Woman: Cinema and Psychoanalysis*. Minneapolis: University of Minnesota Press, 1997.

———. "Feminist Arguments." In *Representing the Woman: Cinema and Psychoanalysis*. Minneapolis: University of Minnesota Press, 1997. 15–35.

———. "Fantasia." In *Representing the Woman: Cinema and Psychoanalysis*. Minneapolis: University of Minnesota Press, 1997. 123–165.

Crafton, Donald. *The Talkies. American Cinema's Transition to Sound, 1926–1931*. Berkeley: University of California Press, 1997.

Crary, Jonathan. *Techniques of the Observer. On Vision and Modernity in the Nineteenth Century*. Cambridge: The MIT Press, 1992.

Dabakis, Melissa. "Gendered Labor. Norman Rockwell's *Rosie the Riveter* and the Discourse of Wartime Womanhood." In *Gender and American History since 1890*. Ed. Barbara Melosh. London: Routledge, 1993. 182–204.

Dall'Asta, Monica. *Trame spezzate. Archeologia del film seriale*. Genova: Le Mani, 2009.

Dayan, Daniel. "The Tutor-Code of Classical Cinema." *Film Quarterly* 28.1 (1974): 22–31.

de Lauretis, Teresa. *Alice Doesn't. Feminism, Semiotics, Cinema*. Bloomington: Indiana University Press, 1984.

———. "Desire in Narrative." In *Alice Doesn't. Feminism, Semiotics, Cinema*. Bloomington: Indiana University Press, 1984. 103–157.

———. *The Practice of Love. Lesbian Sexuality and Perverse Desire*. Bloomington: Indiana University Press, 1994.

Deleuze, Gilles. *Cinema 2. The Time-Image*. Trans. Hugh Tomlinson and Robert Galeta. Minneapolis: University of Minnesota Press, 1989.

———. "The Simulacrum and Ancient Philosophy." In *The Logic of Sense*. Ed. Constantin V. Boundas. Trans. Mark Lester with Charles Stivale. New York: Columbia University Press, 1990. 291–320.

———. "How Do We Recognize Structuralism?" In *Desert Islands and Other Texts 1953–1974*. Ed. David Lapoujade. Trans. Michael Taormina. New York: Semiotext(e), 2004. 170–192.

D'Emilio, John, and Estelle B. Freedman. *Intimate Matters. A History of Sexuality in America*. 2nd ed. Chicago: The University of Chicago Press, 1997.

Dickstein, Morris. *Dancing in the Dark. A Cultural History of the Great Depression*. New York: W. W. Norton & Company, 2009.

Dimendberg, Edward. *Film Noir and the Spaces of Modernity*. Cambridge: Princeton University Press, 2004.

Doane, Mary Ann. *The Desire to Desire. The Woman's Film of the '40s*. Bloomington: Indiana University Press, 1987.

———. *Femmes Fatales. Feminism, Film Theory, Psychoanalysis*. London: Routledge, 1991.

———. "Film and the Masquerade: Theorizing the Female Spectator." In *Femmes Fatales. Feminism, Film Theory, Psychoanalysis*. London: Routledge, 1991. 17–32.

———. "Aesthetics and Politics." In *Beyond the Gaze: Recent Approaches to Film Feminisms*. Ed. Kathleen McHugh and Vivian Sobchack. *Signs* (Special Issue) 30.1 (2004): 1229–1235.

———. "Vicinanza, distanza e scala." In *Otto Preminger, regista. Generi, stile, storie*. Ed. Giulia Carluccio. Torino: Kaplan edizioni, 2009. 33–51.

Doherty, Thomas. *Pre-Code Hollywood*. New York: Columbia University Press, 1999.

Dooley, Roger. *From Scarface to Scarlett: American Films in the 1930s*. New York: Harcourt Brace Jovanovich, 1981.

Doss, Erika E. "Images of American Women in the 1930s: Reginald Marsh and *Paramount Picture*." *Woman's Art Journal* 4.2 (1983–84): 1–4.

Dyer, Richard. *Heavenly Bodies: Film Stars and Society*. New York: St. Martin's Press, 1986.

———. "Monroe and Sexuality." In *Heavenly Bodies: Film Stars and Society*. New York: St. Martin's Press, 1986. 19–66.

———. "Judy Garland and Gay Men." In *Heavenly Bodies: Film Stars and Society*. New York: St. Martin's Press, 1986. 141–194.

———. *Stars*. With a supplementary chapter and bibliography by Paul McDonald. London: British Film Institute, 1998.

———. "Entertainment and Utopia." In *Hollywood Musicals. The Film Reader*. Ed. Steven Cohan. London: Routledge, 2002. 19–30.

Ehrenreich, Barbara. *The Hearts of Men*. New York: Anchor Press, 1983.

Eitzen, Dick. "Evolution, Functionalism, and the Study of American Cinema." *Velvet Light Trap* 28 (1991): 73–85.

Elsaesser, Thomas. "Film History as Social History: The Dieterle/Warner Brothers Bio-pic." *Wide Angle* 8.2 (1986): 15–31.

———. "Tales of Sound and Fury. Observations on the Family Melodrama." In *Home Is Where the Heart Is*. Ed. Christine Gledhill. London: British Film Institute, 1987. 43–69.

———. "Classical/Post-classical Narrative." In Thomas Elsaesser and Warren Buckland, *Studying Contemporary American Film*. London: Arnold, 2002. 26–43.

———. *The Persistence of Hollywood*. London: Routledge, 2011.

Elsaesser, Thomas, and Warren Buckland. *Studying Contemporary American Cinema*. London: Arnold, 2002.

Feuer, Jane. *The Hollywood Musical*. 2nd ed. Bloomington: Indiana University Press, 1993.

———. "The Self-Reflexive Musical and the Myth of Entertainment." In *Film Genre Reader II*. Ed. Barry Keith Grant. Austin: University of Texas Press, 1995. 441–455.

Fisher, Lucy. "Bette Davis: Worker and Queen." In *Glamour in a Golden Age. Movie Stars of the 1930s*. Ed. Adrienne McLean. New Brunswick: Rutgers University Press, 2011. 84–107.

Flitterman-Lewis, Sandy. "To See and Not to Be: Female Subjectivity and the Law in Alfred Hitchcock's *Notorious*." *Literature and Psychology* 33.3–4 (1987): 1–15.

Foucault, Michel. *The Archeology of Knowledge and the Discourse on Language*. Trans. A. M. Sheridan Smith. New York: Pantheon Books, 1971.

———. *Discipline and Punish: The Birth of the Prison*. Trans. Alan Sheridan. New York: Pantheon Books, 1977.

———. *The History of Sexuality. Volume 1: An Introduction*. Trans. Robert Hurley. New York: Vintage Books, 1978.

Francke, Lizzie. *Script Girls. Women Screenwriters in Hollywood*. London: BFI Publishing, 1994.

Freedman, Estelle B. "The New Woman: Changing Views of Women in the 1920s." *Journal of American History* 61.2 (1974): 372–393.

Freud, Sigmund. "The Dissolution of the Oedipus Complex." Trans. James Strachey. SE, vol. 19. London: Hogarth Press, 1956–1974. 173–179.

———. "Some Psychical Consequences of the Anatomical Distinction between the Sexes." Trans. James Strachey. SE, vol. 19. London: Hogarth Press, 1956–1974. 248–258.

———. "Analysis Terminable and Interminable." Trans. James Strachey. SE, vol. 23. London: Hogarth Press, 1956–1974. 216–253.

Fuller, Kathryn H. "'You Can Have the Strand in Your Own Town': The Struggle between Urban and Small-Town Exhibition in the Picture Palace Era." In *Moviegoing in America*. Ed. Gregory A. Waller. Malden: Blackwell Publishers, 2002. 88–98.

Gaines, Jane. "Introduction: Fabricating the Female Body." In *Fabrications. Costume and the Female Body*. Ed. Jane Gaines and Charlotte Herzog. New York: Routledge, 1990. 1–27.

Gaines, Jane, ed. *Classical Hollywood Narrative. The Paradigm Wars*. Durham: Duke University Press, 1992.

Gaines, Jane, and Charlotte Herzog, eds. *Fabrications. Costume and the Female Body*. New York: Routledge, 1990.

Gaines, Jane, Ruth Vatsal, and Monica Dall'Asta, eds. *The Women Film Pioneer Project*. http://cdrs.columbia.edu/wfppguidelines/ (accessed January 28, 2014).

Garrett Cooper, Mark. *Universal Women*. Urbana: University of Illinois Press, 2010.

Gaudreault, André. "Film, Narrative, Narration. The Cinema of the Lumière Brothers." In *Early Cinema. Space Frame Narrative*. Ed. Thomas Elsaesser. London: British Film Institute, 1990. 68–75.

Gledhill, Christine, ed. *Home Is Where the Heart Is*. London: British Film Institute, 1987.

———. "The Melodramatic Field: An Investigation." In *Home Is Where the Heart Is*. Ed. Christine Gledhill. London: British Film Institute, 1987. 5–39.

———. "Between Melodrama and Realism: Anthony Asquith's *Underground* and King Vidor's *The Crowd*." In *Classical Hollywood Narrative. The Paradigm Wars*. Ed. Jane Gaines. Durham: Duke University Press, 1992. 129–167.

Grant, Barry Keith, ed. *Film Genre Reader II*. Austin: University of Texas Press, 1995.

Greenblatt, Stephen. *Shakespearean Negotiations. The Circulation of Social Energy in Renaissance England*. Berkeley: University of California Press, 1988.

Gregg, Ron. "Cary Grant in *Who's a Fairy*. Per una storicizzazione della dimensione queer di Cary Grant." In *Cary Grant. L'attore, il mito*. Ed. Giaime Alonge and Giulia Carluccio. Venezia: Marsilio, 2006. 45–59.

Gunning, Tom. "The Classical Hollywood Cinema: Film Style and Mode of Production to 1960." *Wide Angle* 7.3 (1985): 74–77.

———. "The Cinema of Attractions. Early Film, Its Spectator and the Avant-Garde." In *Early Cinema. Space Frame Narrative*. Ed. Thomas Elsaesser. London: British Film Institute, 1990. 56–62.

———. "The Horror of Opacity." In *Melodrama. Stage, Picture, Screen*. Ed. Jacky Bratton, Jim Cook, and Christine Gledhill. London: British Film Institute, 1994. 50–61.

———. "Modernity and Cinema: A Culture of Shocks and Flows." In *Cinema and Modernity*. Ed. Murray Pomerance. New Brunswick: Rutgers University Press, 2006. 297–315.

———."An Aesthetic of Astonishment: Early Film and the (In)credulous Spectator." In *Film Theory and Criticism*. 7th ed. Ed. Leo Braudy and Marshall Cohen. New York: Oxford University Press, 2009. 736–750.

Halliday, Jon. *Sirk on Sirk*. New York: The Viking Press, 1972.

Hamad, Hannah. "Greer Garson: Gallant Ladies and British Wartime Femininity." In *What Dreams Were Made Of. Movie Stars of the 1940s*. Ed. Sean Griffin. New Brunswick: Rutgers University Press, 2011. 142–165.

Hansen, Miriam. "Pleasure, Ambivalence, Identification: Valentino and Female Spectatorship." *Cinema Journal* 25.4 (1986): 6–32.

———. "Benjamin, Cinema and Experience: The Blue Flower in the Land of Technology." *New German Critique* 40 (1987): 179–224.

———. *Babel & Babylon. Spectatorship in American Silent Film*. Cambridge: Harvard University Press, 1991.

———. "The Mass Production of the Senses: Classical Cinema as Vernacular Modernism." In *Reinventing Film Studies*. Ed. Christine Gledhill and Linda Williams. London: Arnold, 2000. 332–350.

Haskell, Molly. *From Reverence to Rape. The Treatment of Women in the Movies*. London: Penguin, 1974.

Hastie, Amelie. *Cupboards of Curiosity. Women, Recollection and Film History*. Durham: Duke University Press, 2007.

Heath, Stephen. "Film and System: Terms of Analysis Part I." *Screen* 16.1 (1975): 7–77.

———. "Film and System: Terms of Analysis Part II." *Screen* 16.2 (1975): 91–113.

———. *Questions of Cinema*. Bloomington: Indiana University Press, 1981.

———. "Narrative Space." In *Questions of Cinema*. Bloomington: Indiana University Press, 1981. 19–75.

———. "On Suture." In *Questions of Cinema*. Bloomington: Indiana University Press, 1981. 76–112.

Henderson, Brian. "La 'romantic comedy.'" In *Effetto commedia*. Ed. Claver Salizzato and Vito Zagarrio. Roma: Di Giacomo editore, 1985. 51–64.

Higashi, Sumiko. *Virgins, Vamps, and Flappers: The American Silent Movie Heroine*. Montreal: Eden Press Women's Publications, 1978.

———. "1952. Movies and the Paradox of Female Stardom." In *American Cinema of the 1950s*. Ed. Murray Pomerance. New Brunswick: Rutgers University Press, 2005. 65–88.

Hillier, Jim, and Peter Wollen, eds. *Howard Hawks American Artist*. London: British Film Institute, 1996.

Hilmes, Michele. *Radio Voices: American Broadcasting, 1922–1952*. Minneapolis: University of Minnesota Press, 1997.

Jacobs, Lea. "'Now Voyager': Some Problems of Enunciation and Sexual Difference." *Camera Obscura* 7 (1981): 89–110.

———. "The Woman's Picture and the Poetics of Melodrama." *Camera Obscura* 31 (1993): 121–147.

———. *The Wages of Sin. Censorship and the Fallen Woman Film, 1928–1942*. Berkeley: University of California Press, 1997.

Jameson, Fredric. "Postmodernism, or, the Cultural Logic of Late Capitalism." *New Left Review* 146 (1984): 59–92.

Jay, Martin. "The Camera as Memento Mori: Barthes, Metz, and the *Cahiers du Cinéma*." In *Downcast Eyes. The Denigration of Vision in Twentieth-Century French Thought*. Berkeley: University of California Press, 1994. 435–491.

———. *Downcast Eyes. The Denigration of Vision in Twentieth-Century French Thought*. Berkeley: University of California Press, 1994.

Johnston, Claire. "*Double Indemnity*." In *Women in Film Noir*. Ed. E. Ann Kaplan. London: British Film Institute, 1978. 100–111.

———. "Women's Cinema as Counter-Cinema." In *Sexual Stratagems*. Ed. Patricia Erens. New York: Horizon Press, 1979. 133–143.

———. "Dorothy Arzner: Critical Strategies." In *Feminism and Film Theory*. Ed. Constance Penley. New York: Routledge, 1988. 36–45.

Kaplan, E. Ann, ed. *Women in Film Noir*. London: British Film Institute, 1978.

———. *Women and Film. Both Sides of the Camera*. New York: Routledge, 1983.

———. "The Case of the Missing Mother: Maternal Issues in Vidor's *Stella Dallas*." *Heresies* 16 (1983): 81–86.

———. *Motherhood and Representation*. London: Routledge, 1992.

Kitses, Jim. *Horizon West*. London: Secker and Warburg/British Film Institute, 1969.

Klinger, Barbara. "'Local' Genres. The Hollywood Adult Film in the 1950s." In *Melodrama. Stage, Picture, Screen*. Ed. Jacky Bratton, Jim Cook, and Christine Gledhill. London: British Film Institute, 1994. 134–146.

———. *Melodrama and Meaning. History, Culture, and the Films of Douglas Sirk*. Bloomington: Indiana University Press, 1994.

———. "'Cinema/Ideology/Criticism' Revisited: The Progressive Genre." In *Film Genre Reader II*. Ed. Barry Keith Grant. Austin: University of Texas Press, 1995. 74–90.

Kosofsky Sedgwick, Eve. *Between Men: English Literature and Male Homosocial Desire*. New York: Columbia University Press, 1985.

Kracauer, Siegfried. "Cult of Distraction." In *The Mass Ornament: Weimar Essays*. Ed. and trans. Thomas Y. Levin. Cambridge: Harvard University Press, 1995. 323–328.

Krutnik, Frank. *In a Lonely Street: Film Noir, Genre, Masculinity*. New York: Routledge, 1991.

Kuzniar, Alice. "'It's Not Often that I Want a Man': Reading for a Queer Marlene." In *Dietrich Icon*. Ed. Gerd Gemünden and Mary R. Desjardins. Durham: Duke University Press, 2007. 239–258.

Landy, Marcia, ed. *Imitation of Life*. Detroit: Wayne State University Press, 1991.

LaPlace, Marie. "Producing and Consuming the Woman's Film. Discursive Struggle in 'Now Voyager.'" In *Home Is Where the Heart Is*. Ed. Christine Gledhill. London: British Film Institute, 1987. 138–166.

La Polla, Franco. *Stanley Donen/Gene Kelly. Cantando sotto la pioggia*. Torino: Lindau, 1997.

———. *Stili americani*. Bologna: Bononia University Press, 2003.

LaSalle, Mick. *Dangerous Men. Pre-Code Hollywood and the Birth of the Modern Man*. New York: St. Martin's Press, 2002.

Lawrence, Amy. "Constructing a Woman's Speech: Sound Film. '*Rain*' (1932)." In *Echo and Narcissus. Woman's Voices in Classical Hollywood Cinema*. Berkeley: University of California Press, 1991. 71–107.

———. "James Mason. A Star Is Born Bigger than Life." In *Larger than Life. Movie Stars of the 1950s*. Ed. R. Barton Palmer. New Brunswick: Rutgers University Press, 2010. 86–106.

Lévi-Strauss, Claude. *The Elementary Structures of Kinship*. Trans. James Harle Bell et al. Boston: Beacon Press, 1969.

Lugowski, David M. "Claudette Colbert, Ginger Rogers, and Barbara Stanwyck. American Homefront Women." In *What Dreams Were Made Of. Movie Stars of the 1940s*. Ed. Sean Griffin. New Brunswick: Rutgers University Press, 2011. 96–119.

MacCabe, Colin. "Realism and the Cinema: Notes on Some Brechtian Theses." *Screen* 15.2 (1974): 7–27.

Mahar, Karen Ward. *Women Filmmakers in Early Hollywood*. Baltimore: The Johns Hopkins University Press, 2006.

Mayne, Judith. *The Woman at the Keyhole*. Bloomington: Indiana University Press, 1990.

———."Marlene, Dolls and Fetishism." In *Beyond the Gaze: Recent Approaches to Film Feminisms*. Ed. Kathleen McHugh and Vivian Sobchack. *Signs* (special issue) 30.1 (2004): 1257–1264.

McElvaine, Robert S. *The Great Depression: America 1929–1941*. New York: Times Books, 1984.

McHugh, Kathleen, and Vivian Sobchack, eds. *Beyond the Gaze: Recent Approaches to Film Feminisms. Signs* (Special Issue) 30.1 (2004).

McLean, Adrienne L., ed. *Glamour in a Golden Age. Movie Stars of the 1930s*. New Brunswick: Rutgers University Press, 2011.

Meisel, Michael. "Scattered Chiaroscuro. Melodrama as a Matter of Seeing." In *Melodrama. Stage, Picture, Screen*. Ed. Jacky Bratton, Jim Cook, and Christine Gledhill. London: British Film Institute, 1994. 65–81.

Melosh, Barbara, ed. *Gender and American History since 1890*. London: Routledge, 1993.

Metz, Christian. *The Imaginary Signifier. Psychoanalysis and the Cinema*. Trans. Celia Britton et al. Bloomington: Indiana University Press, 1982.

———. "Story/Discourse (A Note on Two Kinds of Voyeurism)." In *The Imaginary Signifier. Psychoanalysis and the Cinema*. Trans. Celia Britton and Annwyl Williams. Bloomington: Indiana University Press, 1982. 89–98.

Milkman, Ruth. "Women's Work and the Economic Crisis." In *A Heritage of Her Own. Toward a New Social History of American Women*. Ed. Nancy F. Cott and Elizabeth H. Pleck. New York: Simon and Schuster, 1979. 507–541.

Mitchell, Juliet. *Psychoanalysis and Feminism. Freud, Reich, Laing and Women*. New York: Vintage Books, 1974.

Mizejewski, Linda. *Ziegfeld Girl: Image and Icon in Culture and Cinema*. Durham: Duke University Press, 1999.

Modleski, Tania. *The Women Who Knew Too Much. Hitchcock and Feminist Theory*. New York: Routledge, 1988.

Mordden, Ethan. *The Hollywood Studios. House Style in the Golden Age of the Movies*. New York: Simon & Schuster Inc., 1989.

Morin, Edgar. "Author's Preface to the 1978 Edition." In *The Cinema, or the Imaginary Man*. Trans. Lorraine Mortimer. Minneapolis: University of Minnesota Press, 2005. 219–228.

———. *The Cinema, or the Imaginary Man.* Trans. Lorraine Mortimer. Minneapolis: University of Minnesota Press, 2005.

Mulvey, Laura. "Notes on Sirk and Melodrama." In *Home Is Where the Heart Is.* Ed. Christine Gledhill. London: British Film Institute, 1987. 75–79.

———. *Visual and Other Pleasures.* Bloomington: Indiana University Press, 1989.

———. "Visual Pleasure and Narrative Cinema." In *Visual and Other Pleasures.* Bloomington: Indiana University Press, 1989. 14–26.

———. "Afterthoughts on 'Visual Pleasure and Narrative Cinema' Inspired by King Vidor's *Duel in the Sun* (1946)." In *Visual and Other Pleasures.* Bloomington: Indiana University Press, 1989. 29–38.

———. "'It Will Be a Magnificent Obsession.' The Melodrama's Role in the Development of Contemporary Film Theory." In *Melodrama. Stage, Picture, Screen.* Ed. Jacky Bratton, Jim Cook, and Christine Gledhill. London: British Film Institute, 1994. 121–133.

———. "*Gentlemen Prefer Blondes*: Anita Loos/Howard Hawks/Marilyn Monroe." In *Howard Hawks. American Artist.* Ed. Jim Hillier and Peter Wollen. London: British Film Institute, 1996. 214–229.

———. "Thoughts on the Young Modern Woman of the 1920s and Feminist Film Theory." In *Visual and Other Pleasures.* 2nd ed. London: Palgrave Macmillan, 2009. 213–232.

Muraro, Luisa. "Female Genealogies." In *Engaging with Irigaray.* Ed. Carolyn Burke, Naomi Schor, and Margaret Whitford. New York: Columbia University Press, 1994. 317–333.

Muscio, Giuliana. *Hollywood's New Deal.* Philadelphia: Temple University Press, 1997.

———. "Roosevelt, Arnold, and Capra, (or) the Federalist-Populist Paradox." In *Frank Capra. Authorship and the Studio System.* Ed. Robert Sklar and Vito Zagarrio. Philadelphia: Temple University Press, 1998. 164–189.

Naremore, James. *Acting in the Cinema.* Berkeley: University of California Press, 1988.

———. *The Magic World of Orson Welles.* rev. ed. Dallas: Southern Methodist University Press, 1989.

———. *More than Night. Film Noir in Its Contexts.* Berkeley: University of California Press, 1998.

———. "Hitchcock at the Margins of Noir." In *Alfred Hitchcock. Centenary Essays.* Ed. Richard Allen and S. Ishii Gonzalès. London: British Film Institute, 1999. 263–277.

———. "The Magician: Orson Welles and Film Style." In *The Wiley-Blackwell History of American Cinema.* vol. II, 1929 to 1945. Ed. Cynthia Lucia, Roy Grundmann, and Art Simon. West Sussex, U.K.: Wiley-Blackwell, 2012. 339–357.

Nash Smith, Henry. *The Virgin Land.* New York: Vintage Books, Random House, 1950.

Neale, Steve. *Cinema and Technology. Image, Sound, Color.* Bloomington: Indiana University Press, 1985.

———. "Melo Talk: On the Meaning and Use of the Term 'Melodrama' in the American Trade Press." *Velvet Light Trap* 32 (1993): 66–89.

———. *Genre and Hollywood*. London: Routledge, 2000.

Nichols, Bill, ed. *Movies and Methods*. vol. 1. Berkeley: University of California Press, 1976.

———. *Ideology and the Image*. Bloomington: Indiana University Press, 1981.

———. "*Blonde Venus*. Playing with Performance." In *Ideology and the Image*. Bloomington: Indiana University Press, 1981. 104–132.

———, ed. *Movies and Methods*. vol. 2. Berkeley: University of California Press, 1985.

———. "Form Wars: The Political Unconscious of Formalist Theory." *South Atlantic Quarterly* 88.2 (1989): 487–515.

Nowell-Smith, Geoffrey. "Minnelli and Melodrama." In *Home Is Where the Heart Is*. Ed. Christine Gledhill. London: British Film Institute, 1987. 70–74.

Orr, Christopher. "Closure and Containment: Marylee Hadley in *Written on the Wind*." In *Imitation of Life*. Ed. Marcia Landy. Detroit: Wayne State University Press, 1991. 380–387.

Oudart, Jean-Pierre. "Cinema and Suture." *Screen* 18.4 (1977–78): 35–47.

Patterson, Martha H. *The American New Woman Revisited. A Reader, 1894–1930*. New Brunswick: Rutgers University Press, 2008.

Peiss, Kathy. *Cheap Amusements. Working Women and Leisure in Turn-of-the-Century New York*. Philadelphia: Temple University Press, 1986.

Penley, Constance, ed. *Feminism and Film Theory*. New York: Routledge, 1988.

Petro, Patrice. *Aftershocks of the New. Feminism and Film History*. New Brunswick: Rutgers University Press, 2002.

———. "The Hottentot and the Blonde Venus." In *Aftershocks of the New. Feminism and Film History*. New Brunswick: Rutgers University Press, 2002. 136–156.

———. "Film Feminism and Nostalgia for the Seventies." In *Aftershocks of the New. Feminism and Film History*. New Brunswick: Rutgers University Press, 2002. 157–173.

———. "Reflections on Feminist Film Studies, Early and Late." In *Beyond the Gaze: Recent Approaches to Film Feminisms*. Ed. Kathleen McHugh and Vivian Sobchack. *Signs* (special issue) 30.1 (2004): 1272–1278.

Place, Janey. "Women in Film Noir." In *Women in Film Noir*. Ed. E. Ann Kaplan. London: British Film Institute, 1978. 35–54.

Polan, Dana. *Power and Paranoia. History, Narrative, and the American Cinema, 1940–1950*. New York: Columbia University Press, 1986.

Pomerance, Murray. "1957. Movies and the Search for Proportion." In *American Cinema of the 1950s. Themes and Variations*. Ed. Murray Pomerance. New Brunswick: Rutgers University Press, 2005. 177–200.

Pravadelli, Veronica. *Alfred Hitchcock. Notorious*. Torino: Lindau, 2003.

———. "Cinema and the Modern Woman." In *The Wiley-Blackwell History of American Cinema*. vol. II, 1929 to 1945. Ed. Cynthia Lucia, Roy Grundmann, and Art Simon. West Sussex, U.K.: Wiley-Blackwell, 2012. 247–268.

———. *Le donne del cinema. Dive, register, spettatrici*. Roma-Bari: Laterza, 2014.

Pye, Douglas. "Bordwell and Hollywood." *Movie* 33 (1989): 46–52.

Rabinovitz, Lauren. *For the Love of Pleasure. Women, Movies and Culture in Turn-of-the-Century Chicago*. New Brunswick: Rutgers University Press, 1998.

Rabinovitz, Paula. *Black & White & Noir. America's Pulp Modernism*. New York: Columbia University Press, 2002.

Ray, Robert B. *A Certain Tendency of the Hollywood Cinema, 1930–1980*. Princeton: Princeton University Press, 1985.

———. "The Bordwell Regime and the Stakes of Knowledge." In *How a Film Theory Got Lost and Other Mysteries in Cultural Studies*. Bloomington: Indiana University Press, 2001. 29–63.

Reid, David, and Jayne L. Walker. "Strange Pursuit: Cornell Woolrich and the Abandoned City of the Forties." In *Shades of Noir*. Ed. Joan Copjec. London: Verso, 1993. 57–96.

Renov, Michael. "From Identification to Ideology: The Male System of Hitchcock's *Notorious*." *Wide Angle* 4.1 (1980): 30–37.

———. *Hollywood's Wartime Women: Representation and Ideology*. Ann Arbor: UMI Research Press, 1989.

Rivette, Jacques. "The Genius of Howard Hawks." In *Cahiers du Cinéma. The 1950s: Neo-Realism, Hollywood, New Wave*. Ed. Jim Hillier. Trans. Russell Campbell and Marvin Pister. Cambridge: Harvard University Press, 1985. 126–131.

Robé, Chris. "Taking Hollywood Back: The Historical Costume Drama, the Biopic, and Popular Front U.S Film Criticism." *Cinema Journal* 48.2 (2009): 70–87.

———. *Left of Hollywood. Cinema, Modernism, and the Emergence of U.S. Radical Film Culture*. Austin: University of Texas Press, 2010.

Rodowick, David N. "Madness, Authority and Ideology. The Domestic Melodrama of the '50s." In *Home Is Where the Heart Is*. Ed. Christine Gledhill. London: British Film Institute, 1987. 268–280.

———. *The Crisis of Political Modernism. Criticism and Ideology in Contemporary Film Theory*. Urbana: University of Illinois Press, 1988.

Roosevelt, Eleanor. "Woman's Place after the War." *Click* August 7, 1944, now in http://newdeal.feri.org (accessed May 20, 2006).

Ross, Sara. "Banking the Flames of Youth: The Hollywood Flapper, 1920–1930." Diss., University of Wisconsin-Madison, 2000.

Roth, Mark. "Some Warner Musicals and the Spirit of the New Deal." In *Genre: The Musical*. Ed. Rick Altman. London: Routledge & Kegan Paul, 1981. 41–56.

Rowe, Kathleen. *The Unruly Woman. Gender and the Genre of Laughter*. Austin: University of Texas Press, 1995.

Rubin, Martin. "Busby Berkeley and the Backstage Musical." In *Hollywood Musicals. The Film Reader*. Ed. Steven Cohan. London: Routledge, 2002. 53–61.

Ryan, Mary P. "The Projection of a New Womanhood: The Movie Moderns in the 1920s." In *Our American Sisters. Women in American Life and Thought*. Ed. Jean E. Friedman and William G. Shade. Boston: Allyn and Bacon, Inc., 1976. 366–384.

Salizzato, Claver, and Vito Zagarrio, eds. *Effetto commedia.* Roma: Di Giacomo editore, 1985.

Sanders, James. *Celluloid Skyline. New York and the Movies.* New York: Alfred Knopf, 2003.

Sarris, Andrew. "Howard Hawks." In *Howard Hawks American Artist.* Ed. Jim Hillier and Peter Wollen. London: British Film Institute, 1996. 103–106.

Schatz, Thomas. *Hollywood Genres.* New York: McGraw-Hill, Inc., 1981.

———. "La 'screwball comedy' degli anni '30." In *Effetto commedia.* Ed. Claver Salizzato and Vito Zagarrio. Roma: Di Giacomo editore, 1985. 65–82.

———. *The Genius of the System.* New York: The Pantheon Books, 1988.

———. *Boom and Bust. American Cinema in the 1940s.* Berkeley: University of California Press, 1997.

Schneider, Stephen J. "1942. Movies and the March to War." In *American Cinema of the 1940s.* Ed. Wheeler Winston Dixon. Oxford: Berg, 2006. 74–93.

Scott, Joan Wallach. "Gender: A Useful Category of Historical Analysis." In *Gender and the Politics of History.* rev. ed. New York: Columbia University Press, 1999. 28–50.

Silverman, Kaja. "Historical Trauma and Male Subjectivity." In *Psychoanalysis and Cinema.* Ed. E. Ann Kaplan. London: Routledge, 1990. 110–127.

Simmel, Georg. "The Metropolis and Mental Life." In *Georg Simmel on Individuality and Social Forms.* Ed. Donald N. Levine. Trans. Edward Shils. Chicago: University of Chicago Press, 1971. 324–339.

Simmons, Christina. "Modern Sexuality and the Myth of Victorian Repression." In *Gender and American History since 1890.* Ed. Barbara Melosh. London: Routledge, 1993. 17–42.

———. *Making Marriage Modern. Women's Sexuality from the Progressive Era to World War II.* Oxford: Oxford University Press, 2009.

Singer, Ben. *Melodrama and Modernity.* New York: Columbia University Press, 2001.

Sklar, Robert. *Movie-Made America. A Cultural History of American Movies.* rev. ed. New York: Vintage Books, 1994.

Sklar, Robert, and Vito Zagarrio, eds. *Frank Capra. Authorship and the Studio System.* Philadelphia: Temple University Press, 1998.

Solomon, Matthew. "Reflexivity and Metaperformance. Marilyn Monroe, Jayne Mansfield, and Kim Novak." In *Larger than Life. Movie Stars of the 1950s.* Ed. Robert Barton Palmer. New Brunswick: Rutgers University Press, 2010. 107–129.

Stamp, Shelley. *Movie-Struck Girls. Women and Motion Picture Culture after the Nickelodeon.* Princeton: Princeton University Press, 2000.

Steinberg, Cobbett S. *Film Facts.* New York: Facts on File, Inc., 1980.

Stokes, Melvyn. "Female Audiences of the 1920s and Early 1930s." In *Identifying Hollywood Audiences.* Ed. Melvyn Stokes and Richard Maltby. London: British Film Institute, 1999. 42–60.

Strauven, Wanda, ed. *The Cinema of Attractions Reloaded.* Amsterdam: Amsterdam University Press, 2007.

Studlar, Gaylyn. *In the Realm of Pleasure. Von Sternberg, Dietrich and the Masochistic Aesthetic*. New York: Columbia University Press, 1988.

Taves, Brian. "The B Film: Hollywood's Other Half." In Tino Balio, *Grand Design: Hollywood as a Modern Business Enterprise, 1930–1939*. Berkeley: University of California Press, 1993. 313–350.

Telotte, J. P. *Voices in the Dark. The Narrative Patterns of Film Noir*. Urbana: University of Illinois Press, 1989.

Tinkcom, Matthew. "'Working Like a Homosexual.' Camp Visual Codes and the Labor of Gay Subjects in the MGM Freed Unit." In *Hollywood Musicals. The Film Reader*. Ed. Steven Cohan. London: Routledge, 2002. 115–128.

Todd Wiley, Ellen. *The 'New Woman' Revised. Painting and Gender Politics on Fourteenth Street*. Berkeley: University of California Press, 1993.

Trimberger, Ellen Kay. "Feminism, Men and Modern Love: Greenwich Village, 1900–1925." In *Powers of Desire*. Ed. Ann Snitow, Christine Stansell, and Sharon Thompson. New York: Monthly Review Press, 1983. 131–152.

Turim, Maureen. *Flashbacks in Film. Memory & History*. New York: Routledge, 1989.

Tyler May, Eileen. *Homeward Bound. American Families in the Cold War Era*. New York: BasicBooks, 1988.

Vegetti Finzi, Silvia. "Introduzione." In *Psicoanalisi al femminile*. Ed. Silvia Vegetti Finzi. Roma: Laterza, 1992. vii–xviii.

———. "Le isteriche o la parola corporea." In *Psicoanalisi al femminile*. Ed. Silvia Vegetti Finzi. Roma: Laterza, 1992. 1–50.

———, ed. *Psicoanalisi al femminile*. Roma: Laterza, 1992.

Vernet, Marc. "The Filmic Transaction: On the Openings of Film Noir." *Velvet Light Trap* 20 (1983): 2–9.

Walker, Janet. *Couching Resistance. Women, Film, and Psychoanalytic Psychiatry*. Minneapolis: University of Minnesota Press, 1993.

Weiss, Andrea. "'A Queer Feeling when I Look at You': Hollywood Stars and Lesbian Spectatorship in the 1930s." In *Multiple Voices in Feminist Film Criticism*. Ed. Diane Carson, Linda Dittmar, and Janice R. Welsh. Minneapolis: University of Minnesota Press, 1994. 330–342.

Welter, Barbara. "The Cult of True Womanhood: 1820–1860." In *The American Family in Social-Historical Perspective*. 2nd ed. Ed. Michael Gordon. New York: St. Martin's Press, 1978. 313–333.

White, Patricia. *Uninvited. Classical Hollywood Cinema and Lesbian Representability*. Bloomington: Indiana University Press, 1999.

Wiesen Cook, Blanche. *Eleanor Roosevelt, vol. 2, 1933–1938*. New York: Viking, 1999.

———. "ER's New Deal for Women." In *Eleanor Roosevelt, vol. 2, 1933–1938*. New York: Viking, 1999. 70–91.

Williams, Alan. "Narrative Patterns in 'Only Angels Have Wings.'" *Quarterly Review of Film Studies* 1.4 (1976): 357–372.

Williams, Linda. "Something Else besides a Mother: *Stella Dallas* and the Maternal Melodrama." *Cinema Journal* 24.1 (1984): 2–27.

———. "Discipline and Fun: *Psycho* and Postmodern Cinema." In *Reinventing Film Studies*. Ed. Christine Gledhill and Linda Williams. London: Arnold, 2000. 351–378.

———. *Playing the Race Card. Melodramas of Black and White from Uncle Tom to O. J. Simpson*. Princeton: Princeton University Press, 2001.

———. "Film Bodies: Gender, Genre and Excess." In *Film Theory and Criticism*. 7th ed. Ed. Leo Braudy and Marshall Cohen. New York: Oxford University Press, 2009. 602–616.

Williams, Raymond. *Marxism and Literature*. Oxford: Oxford University Press, 1977.

Willis, Nadine. "'110 Per Cent Woman': The Crotch Shot in the Hollywood Musical." *Screen* 42.2 (2001): 121–141.

Winston Dixon, Wheeler, ed. *American Cinema of the 1940s*. Oxford: Berg, 2006.

Wollen, Peter. "The Auteur Theory." In *Signs and Meanings in the Cinema*. 3rd ed. Bloomington: Indiana University Press, 1972. 74–115.

———. *Singin' in the Rain*. London: British Film Institute, 1992.

Worland, Rick. "Humphrey Bogart and Lauren Bacall: Tough Guy and Cool Dame." In *What Dreams Were Made Of. Movie Stars of the 1940s*. Ed. Sean Griffin. New Brunswick: Rutgers University Press, 2011. 70–95.

Young-Bruehl, Elizabeth, ed. *Freud and Women. A Reader*. New York: W. W. Norton & Company, Inc., 1990.

Zaretsky, Eli. *Secrets of the Soul. A Social and Cultural History of Psychoanalysis*. New York: Alfred A. Knopf, 2004.

Zeitz, Joshua. *Flapper: A Madcap Story of Sex, Celebrity, and the Women Who Made America Modern*. New York: Three Rivers Press, 2006.

INDEX

VERONICA PRAVADELLI is a professor of film studies and director of the Center for American Studies at Roma Tre University and a former visiting professor at Brown University. She is the author of several books including *Performance, Rewriting, Identity: Chantal Akerman's Postmodern Cinema*, *Alfred Hitchcock. Notorious* and *Le donne del cinema: dive, registe, spettatrici*. She has recently edited *Cinema e piacere visivo*, an anthology of essays by Laura Mulvey. The Italian edition of *Classic Hollywood* won two prizes for Best Book in Film Studies.

The University of Illinois Press
is a founding member of the
Association of American University Presses.

Composed in 10/13 Sabon
by Lisa Connery
at the University of Illinois Press
Designed by Dennis Roberts
Manufactured by Cushing-Malloy, Inc.

University of Illinois Press
1325 South Oak Street
Champaign, IL 61820-6903
www.press.uillinois.edu